*How to Create and Nurture*
*a Nature Center in Your Community*

# How to Create
# and Nurture
# A NATURE CENTER
# in Your Community

by Brent Evans & Carolyn Chipman-Evans
Drawings by Carolyn Chipman-Evans
Foreword by Robert A. Thomas

AUSTIN  UNIVERSITY OF TEXAS PRESS

*Dedicated to the Friends of the Cibolo Wilderness*

Support for this book comes from
an endowment for environmental
studies made possible by generous
contributions from Richard C. Bartlett,
Susan Aspinall Block, and the National
Endowment for the Humanities.

**Library of Congress
Cataloging-in-Publication Data**

Evans, Brent.
How to create and nurture a nature center
in your community / by Brent Evans &
Carolyn Chipman-Evans ; drawings by
Carolyn Chipman-Evans.—1st ed.
        p.    cm.
Includes bibliographical references (p.    )
and index.
ISBN  0-292-72097-1 (pbk. : alk. paper)
1. Nature centers—Planning.
I.  Chipman-Evans, Carolyn.   II. Title.
QH75.E835  1998
508—dc21                    97-38068


Design and typography by
George Lenox Design, Austin

---

**Photographic and illustration credits**
*(by page)*

Shawn Bonner  vi, vii,  8 (top), 44, 54
John Branch (cartoon) 158–159
Eleanor Crow 218
Chanda Day 160
Bettie Edmonds (drawing) 250
Greg Evans  117
Carolyn Chipman-Evans  Cover
Patrick Heath  2
Jan Wrede 46, 199
James Yaich  18

# Contents

# Foreword

I AM ONE OF THE LUCKY FEW. I was given the chance to grow a nature center from the dreams of the New Orleans community, from a dedicated board, staff, and volunteers, and from within my soul. On my first day on the job, Trustee Brucie Rafferty met me in a ten by ten square foot office on the forty-first floor of a central city building. Over coffee, she briefed me on several years of planning. Upon leaving, she stood in the doorway and said, "Build us a nature center." Within two hours, I had read through all the files—minutes and plans. I will never forget the lonely feeling of sitting at my desk, reflecting on my situation, and quietly verbalizing my thoughts: "What do I do now?"

Many of the directors of our earliest nature centers had the same experience. There were few written guidelines, so we consulted with colleagues at other nature centers and used our basic instincts. There have been glorious successes, false starts, and a few abject failures.

Though there are excellent examples of nature centers that were founded during the 1950s and earlier, the 1960s was the decade of growth. So, when does a field, such as nature-center-based education, become a mature profession? I am reminded of a seminar presented by Bob Fluchel, then director of the Fontenelle Forest Nature Center, on the topic of personnel policies. Bob presented a document that was at least fifty pages long. As a relatively new administrator, bedeviled by the many tasks that confronted me and my staff, I asked when he found the time to develop such an impressive document. His answer: "When you've been open twenty to thirty years, you'll have one, too." He was right. It takes two to three decades for a nature center to mature, and the same is true for our thirty-something-year-old profession.

Brent Evans and Carolyn Chipman-Evans's book, *How to Create and Nurture a Nature Center,* cites several early published guidelines for starting a nature center, but it is the first comprehensive approach to the hows and whys of developing a nature center in your community. Through insights that can be gained only by grassroots experience, they have compiled the steps, presented in a logical sequence, that should be taken to methodically plan, build, and operate a nature center. They have chosen to focus on small communities, but their template is perfectly applicable to urban areas.

Among the many strengths of this text is a clear sensitivity to early and continual community involvement. There is a clear message that nature centers should not only serve their community educationally and recreationally, but also provide a heartfelt, spiritual connection.

As to the professional, your time with this volume will provide you with either an excellent model or a reinforcement of lessons learned. For the community activist, it will take you on a step-by-step excursion terminating in an educational star in the crown of your hometown. For the naturalist, you will be infected with the irresistible urge to become a nature center activist!

Enjoy Carolyn and Brent's nature education passion as I have! May the proliferation of nature centers begin!

Robert A. Thomas, *Naturalist*
*Loyola University, New Orleans*

# Acknowledgments

INDIAN GRASS

THIS PROJECT has been the fruit of our lives, and of the lives of many others. Nature lovers tend to be eccentric, talented, interested people. Regardless of backgrounds, philosophies, or even politics, nature center people gather together easily. A sense of community, based on a shared passion for nature, creates a powerful coalition. This book is the outgrowth of years of activities with positive people—people determined to give something to the world, and to have fun doing it.

The cooperation of several organizations was essential to the quality of this book. The Association for Nature Center Administrators, the National Audubon Society, the National Association of Interpretation, and the Natural Science for Youth Foundation have provided vital information. We are indebted to the many nature center administrators who spoke with us, encouraged us, and shared the depth of their experience. A list of the ninety-one nature centers that supplied information is available in Appendix C, Nature Centers Surveyed.

We also had the advantage of highly experienced technical editors: Robert A. Thomas of the Audubon Institute, Founding Director of the Louisiana Nature Center and current holder of the Loyola University Chair for Environmental Communications; and Michael E. Riska, the Executive Director of the Delaware Nature Society, and Administrator of the University of Delaware's Environmental Institution Management Course and Professional Leadership Institute. The years of experience and accomplishments of these gentlemen are well known within the nature center community. We are deeply in their debt.

When we look back over the list of donors and helpers, volunteers, and supporters of the last ten years, we begin to appreciate how a community can build a nature center, and how a nature center can create community. The relationships grow like a family tree, each new branch bringing in new energy for the project. The list of donors and volunteers now reaches into the thousands. Their energy, loyalty, and timing proved instrumental in helping our family tree grow and prosper.

We dedicate this book to the Friends of the Cibolo Wilderness, a small community of nature lovers, living in a small watershed in the Texas Hill Country. They were the dreamers and doers who created the model we can now share with other communities. We also are forever indebted to the City of Boerne, whose mayor, city council, and city staff formed a coalition with volunteers, teachers, businesses, and the Chamber of Commerce to do something of visionary proportions. And we thank our children, Jonah and Laurel, for supporting and encouraging our work and for giving us so much joy along the way. They donated their enthusiasm, their ideas, their time, and even their friends.

# Introduction

*There is no quiet place in the white man's cities. No place to hear the unfurling of leaves in the spring, or the rustle of insects' wings. . . . And what is there to life, if a man cannot hear the lonely cry of the whippoorwill or the argument of the frogs around the pool at night?*

— ATTRIBUTED TO **CHIEF SEATTLE,**
*upon surrendering his tribal lands in 1856. ***

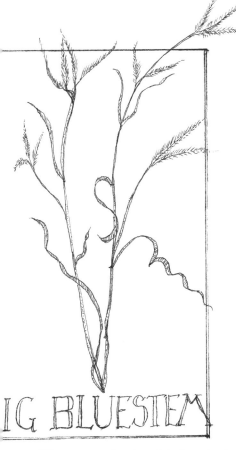

IG BLUESTEM

*\*We are aware that the original words of Chief Seattle have been retranslated and altered significantly through the years. However, we sense that our civilization is in dire need of aboriginal wisdom. So we have decided to include these words, precisely because they have served to open the door to Native thought for many in our culture, and should be honored for that reason.*

IN THE AUTUMN OF 1988, the two of us ventured onto a parcel of public land on a whim. The land had been sold out of Carolyn's family years before, but a strong connection to it persisted, through ancestral journals and childhood memories. As the creekside vegetation thickened, we pushed through tall grasses, mustang grape vines, poison ivy, and brush. Then we came into an opening, where the creek meandered through a stand of giant bald cypress, gurgling and shimmering. We couldn't believe our eyes. A natural cathedral glistened in the filtered sunlight. Birds scattered about, fish darted beneath the mossy cypress roots. It was paradise, undiscovered, unappreciated, and in need of protection. There had been rumors of developing this city property for a golf course, or perhaps a water treatment plant. We sat and watched in absolute awe. Although we didn't know it, the Cibolo Nature Center was born that day.

We had already been active in connecting people with nature. Carolyn taught classes such as "Gardening as Art" and spearheaded a tree ordinance for the City of Boerne. She was a horse person, a canoer, an artist, a swimming hole addict, and long-legged hiker. Brent, too, had an incurable nature obsession, and had been a long-time social worker, initiating nature programs for children in a psychiatric hospital, at Earth Day, at a bioregional congress, at an international ecology camp, and in therapeutic gardening programs. Both of us loved nature and found emotional and spiritual gifts in wilderness settings. We had married in the woods, and had lived there for years, without neighbors, without many modern conveniences, and had loved it. We raised our children in the woods and often vacationed in remote and fabulous wild habitats. We owed good old Mother Earth plenty. But neither of us imagined that we could actually save this piece of ground, or use it for conservation programs for our community.

Neither of us had any formal training in conservation or ecology. Would City Hall want to leave it wild? Would saving this spot of pristine beauty be considered worthwhile by the people of Boerne, Texas? At first, we envisioned a nature trail. As we began researching how to start a nature trail, we were surprised to learn that there was precious little how-to information available. Luckily, we fell upon some out-of-print Audubon publications from the early 1960s. They were tremendously useful, particularly because they talked about *nature centers.* The idea of a nature center, as a place to help people fall in love with the wild, seemed absolutely perfect. What could be more important than locally relevant environmental education? But the books were thirty years old, and it seemed that no one had written a book on the subject since. Frankly, we just learned as we went along. Little did we know that a thousand or so communities across the country had been doing the same thing.

Since those early days we have discovered a number of resources and organizations that can help the beginner as well as the seasoned nature center administrator. We also discovered the kindness and generosity of friends and strangers who came to share the dream. Our little nature center has been nurtured along to the point that we have a "Friends" organization with 436 active members, a wonderful 1898 building for our headquarters, a 1996 budget of $112,500, four paid employees, and a wide variety of programs for our community. This partnership between local government and volunteers created a useful model of grassroots community organization. We received the 1995 Governor's Award for the best example of a community-based environmental organization in the State of Texas.

THE PURPOSE of this book is to enable more communities and individuals to gain ground by creating natural sanctuaries and sharing them with their neighbors. Our book is meant to inspire, inform, and enable the reader to create a local nature center, or help an existing nature center grow and prosper. This is a resource for nature center pioneers, as well as volunteers, board members, donors, government officials, or new members who want to educate themselves about the operation and potential of a nature center in their community. The good news is that you don't need a Ph.D. in environmental science, or lots of money, or political power, or special training to nurture a nature center. The single most important qualification is catching fire with the dream.

We have reported lessons we learned personally as well as ideas from a wide spectrum of sources, and we have also directed the reader to the other publications and organizations that can provide good information, funding resources, and even expert consultation.

This is an opportune moment in history, when our communities are wanting to save these places and set them aside for appreciation, recreation, education, and tourism. Such projects conserve natural resources, provide places of quiet recreation, give students and teachers outdoor classrooms, engender a real sense of community, and promote respect for life.

So much of nature is privately owned. Most members of our society have little access to, yet feel an instinctive craving for, nature. Our parks and wilderness areas are used more than ever. Wildlife watching is the fastest-growing form of recreation in the United States. Along with public awareness of environmental concerns, there is a growing popular appreciation for green space. However, development continues to be driven by our booming population. More and more of our wonderful places are being destroyed to make way for ambitious enterprises.

We live in an age of catastrophic biological degradation. Scientists all over the world, from the National Academy of Scientists, the Royal Society, and the Union of Concerned Scientists to ninety-nine Nobel Prize winners, are warning that human beings and the natural world are on a collision course.

Their concern is that the size and activity of the current human population is not sustainable, and that the functional integrity of the biosphere could be destroyed in thirty-five years.

As Calley O'Neill points out in the April 1997 newsletter of the Hawai'i Center for Integral Healing,

> **The truth is that human beings are now the dominant species in all the world's ecosystems and the most powerful geological force on earth. From this perspective,** *we do not have environmental problems, the biosphere has a people problem.* **(Quoted from William Rees,** *Planning for Sustainable Development: A Resource Book,* **1988)**

However, although habitat destruction continues, public awareness is growing, and the movement for saving ecosystems and educating ourselves is indeed gaining ground. Only a change in the consciousness of humanity can change the technologically driven course of destruction. By educating the public, by helping people rediscover a personal connection with nature, we can move toward a healthy and sustainable relationship with our planet. We need to encourage communities around the world to develop their own centers of locally relevant environmental education. We need to save wild lands, and help people fall in love with nature. We need nature centers.

In every town and every community there are wild gardens. These are gardens planted by wind and rain, by mammals, birds, and insects—wild places where native flora and fauna are thriving. Some of these places are public, some private, some undiscovered, some abused. These gardens can be sanctuaries for the mind and heart, feasts for the senses, and food for the soul. They are, for the most part, unnoticed, until someone introduces the community to its own natural shrine.

Many civic-minded leaders are looking for ways to increase commerce while protecting natural resources for future generations. Any community or neighborhood within a community can embark on the adventure of discovering its own secret garden, protecting it, and providing its citizens and visitors with access. If your community already has a nature center, there are many ways to pitch in, add programs, extend boundaries, or even start another center in the same community. A number of communities support more than one center, since educational programs can vary significantly, even between nature centers within the same region.

Part one will tell our story and the stories of other centers, define nature centers, describe their goals, and provide examples of different facilities and program possibilities. Part Two will focus on how to develop nature centers, gather support, help existing centers, organize, fund, and plan, and will include practical considerations and advice for the novice.

We hope our book serves to encourage you, the reader. You *can* have a nature center in your community, whether you live in a city, in a town, or in the country. You can invest your energy, talent, wisdom, and wealth in community efforts to develop a local ethic of conservation. And there is help available! So, dare to dream of saving some wildness. Your life and your community will be enriched beyond your wildest dreams.

**WORD TO THE WISE**

**It is important to examine both the science and art of nature center development, so that the heart of this endeavor is not lost in the quest for facts and funds. Many a student has been bored to tears by a biology teacher who was not in love with the subject. Appreciate nature. Stay in touch with the natural world. Share your wonder at the little miracles. The magic in nature is the reason we are doing this. We must not get so zealous in the enterprise of organizational development that we end up indoors all the time. Read a section of this book, and then get outside.**

# Part One

# THE NATURE OF NATURE CENTERS

A natural cathedral glistens in the filtered sunlight.

# Chapter 1 The Cibolo Nature Center Story

*We need to preserve a few places, a few samples
of primeval country so that when the pace gets too fast
we can look at it, think about it, contemplate it,
and somehow restore equanimity to our souls.*

— SIGURD OLSON, *SEEDS OF PEACE*

TEXAS GRAMMA

## HISTORY

Like so many nature centers around the world, the Cibolo Nature Center was created by a handful of folks with some special interests and talents. In fact, all the ingredients that are required are a place, a person, and a dream. However, the well-known nature centers we initially heard of were long-established, were located near large population centers, and had huge budgets. Our concern was how to develop a nature center in a smaller community, without access to big money or large numbers of members. The same questions exist for neighborhoods within large cities. Some of our fellow citizens thought that there were just not enough nature lovers in a city of five thousand to warrant the use of eighty acres of city-owned land. We proved that assumption wrong, and also demonstrated that a small group of citizens, with full-time jobs and families to raise, could still make a nature center happen.

When we started out, we basically wanted to protect the land. So we developed a nature trail, and called our project the Cibolo Wilderness Trail (CWT). As the project gained increasing support, we were given the old Audubon books on nature centers, and fell in love with the idea of a small piece of wilderness that would promote conservation. But funding seemed to be the hurdle. How could the little town of Boerne, Texas, afford to put in trails or construct a nature center building? How could we get the community involved? The answer proved to be persistence, serendipity, and the enthusiasm that natural beauty can inspire.

Here is our story. We hope it encourages others to follow their own dream of a nature center and demonstrates that even a small community, with limited resources, can conserve natural resources and create a sanctuary and tourist attraction

**For years, people dumped refuse to fill this forgotten marsh.**

that benefits the entire community. John Javna, nationally syndicated columnist and author of *50 Simple Things You Can Do to Save the Earth,* wrote the following in his nationally syndicated newspaper column, Earthworks, in June of 1992:

> Today, many Americans are focusing on traditional values—like developing a strong sense of community. . . . As Carolyn Chipman-Evans proved in Boerne, one effective way to rebuild America's communities is through environmental action.
>
> Near Chipman-Evans's house, there was a large parcel of land that the city of Boerne had purchased for a park. One half was developed with ball fields, running tracks and swimming pools; the other half was considered useless—a thicket of woods and marsh with the Cibolo Creek running through it. . . . "I'd always been drawn to the wild spots around Cibolo Creek," she says. "And, the more I explored the creek area, the more special it became to me." After a while, she noticed the spot was becoming littered, and no one was taking care of it. So Carolyn decided to do something.
>
> She met with Boerne's land use planner and pointed out the Cibolo Creek area was a great place for a nature trail. Chipman-Evans knew that the city government was interested in drawing visitors to the town, so she suggested that such a trail could be a good tourist attraction.
>
> "I didn't approach the project with a 'you can't fight city hall' type attitude," she says. "I was positive. In most cities, staff are overloaded with criticism and complaints. They liked the trail idea because it was a project they could get rewarded for rather than criticized about."
>
> The city put up money for large-scale improvements such as clearing out the marsh and building a boardwalk. When it turned out that the city didn't have the funds for the educational/nature center portion of the project, Carolyn formed a group, the Friends of the Cibolo Wilderness, to raise money and coordinate publicity, educational programs and special projects.

Excavation for marsh restoration project begins. The project took an entire year to complete.

An 1898 vintage building is moved to City Park, to become the Cibolo Nature Center headquarters.

After crews removed fill and started building the boardwalk, we saw how much work lay ahead.

The boardwalk is completed, enabling young minds to explore.

**Lions Club volunteer Jerry Rittimann eyeballs our new roof.**

The history of our nature center is a story of *relationships*. Our early core group seemed to come together magically, the right person showing up just at the right time. Eric Lautzenheiser of the San Antonio Botanical Center was our first "angel," giving us advice and the Audubon books that inspired our interest. Chris Turk, Director of Parks and Planning for Boerne, was receptive and supportive, and gave the project its first real "Yes." Mayor Pat Heath and City Manager Ron Bowman provided continued encouragement and help along the way. Chuck Janzow, a high school environmental science teacher, required community service from his class, to promote participatory citizenship. George Plummer donated the building, and Murray and Barbee Winn donated funds to help move and restore the building. Colonel Milt Hawkins financed the new roof, and the Lions Club built it. Bill and Susan Block were our guardian angels, providing vital support at crucial times, which enabled the project to keep its head above water.

Gradually, the community started pitching in: the Optimist Club, the Chamber of Commerce, Boerne Printing, Rittimann's Plumbing, P. J. Scheutze the painter, the Brown Foundation, other businesses, the *Boerne Star*, the *Hill Country Recorder*, and various individuals. The school district also joined in, from the superintendent, Joe Doenges, to the principals, to teachers such as Barb Herbst (high school biology) and Sandy Abernathy (middle school biology). We received support from early believers like Pat and Tom Frost Jr., Roger and Dot Hemminghaus, and Juanita and Guy Chipman Jr. Volunteers showed up, and became vital links in the organiza-

## WORD TO THE WISE

**Awards don't come out of the blue. Most awards are granted to groups or individuals that *apply* for them. Public relations is the name of the game. Go after awards, and don't be shy about it. In the Texas Hill Country, the old-timers say, "It's a sorry dog that won't wag its own tail."**

tion: Colonel Lola Ball (grounds caretaker), Ellie Dillon (office mom), Vivian Rule and Gary Whiting (volunteer coordination), David Pipes (construction), Sandy Elkins (accountant), and Larry Ross (bookkeeping). Maury Maverick Jr., long-time columnist for the *San Antonio Express-News,* provided public encouragement. Friends like George Thompson and Grace Lovelace, Diane Rolfe, Chanda Day, Gary Whitford, and Mark and Jill Mason helped us define our vision.

Since those early beginnings, the list of participants has become literally hundreds of names long. Those initial relationships spawned other relationships, and the project grew, person to person. The Friends of the Cibolo Wilderness provided Boerne and Kendall County with a sanctuary to appreciate, an outdoor classroom for schools and the public, a tourist destination, and a means of bringing a diverse citizenry together. This ten-year partnership between the City of Boerne and a nonprofit citizens' organization has resulted in a model project that other communities are interested in emulating.

Publicity for the Grand Opening of the CWT in 1990 was terrific. CBS Nightly News featured visitors from the Soviet Union planting a tree for peace and the environment at the CWT on Earth Day 1990. We accepted an invitation to travel to Russia and the Ukraine to dedicate a sister park and consult with local conservationists.

Awards helped. They gave our project good publicity and validated our organization in the eyes of the public. The CWT has received local, state and national recognition, including the Chamber of Commerce Ambassador Award, Civic Organization Award, and President's Award, the Boerne Area Historical Society's Award, the Bexar Audubon Society's Scholarship Award, the Texas Forest Service's Urban Forestry Award, and the Firestone/Firehawks Award for Excellence in Environmental Education.

Carolyn was selected as 1991 Environmental Woman of Action for the State of Texas. The Trail project has been featured in *Texas Monthly Magazine* and numerous times in the major San Antonio newspapers. *Local Government Agenda,* Summer, 1990, used the Cibolo Wilderness Trail as an example for other communities, saying, "It's not just an ordinary piece of land, but a unique representation of what a city and its citizens can accomplish with a little inspiration and a lot of hard

Our recycled head-
quarters provides a
classroom, displays,
shop, office, porches,
and outdoor theater.

Boerne Mayor
Patrick Heath
helps Carolyn cut
the ribbon for our
grand opening.

work." In November 1994, Carolyn was featured in *Texas Parks and Wildlife Magazine* for her work with the CWT and creation of the Friends of the Cibolo Wilderness. The Friends of the Cibolo Wilderness won the Governor's Award for Environmental Excellence in May of 1995, over 250 other competing organizations.

The mission of the Friends of the Cibolo Wilderness is conservation of natural resources through education. Our role is to promote nature appreciation and education. The Cibolo Wilderness Trail now travels from native prairie to cypress-lined creek bed, from a restored marshland to woodland, demonstrating a broad cross section of the habitats, animal life, and flora native to the Texas Hill Country. This diversity of species is considered extremely valuable and unique by such groups as the Texas Native Prairie Society, the Texas Native Plant Society, the Texas Parks and Wildlife Department, the Texas Natural Resource Conservation Commission, the Texas Forest Service, the San Antonio Botanical Center, and local chapters of the National Audubon Society.

The Cibolo Nature Center headquarters is a renovated historic structure housing exhibits, displays, meeting room, library, and office. Surrounding the building is a Texas Wildscape Garden demonstration site, utilizing many plants that encourage butterflies, hummingbirds, and other wildlife. An arboretum of native trees has been started. A rain-harvesting system is in the works.

Our community appreciates the Cibolo Wilderness Trail and Nature Center in City Park as a vital part of the neighborhood. The project has been excellent public relations for the city, being mentioned in major tourism articles written about our area. The Cibolo Nature Center logs eleven thousand annual visitors, and twenty-five hundred schoolchildren attend the outdoor classroom each year. Educational programs include a conservation curriculum for local students, science projects, workshops on local wildlife management, xeriscaping, recycling, composting, watershed management, scout and youth activities, wildflower workshops, bird-watching programs, ecological awareness projects, tree planting, and good old nature appreciation.

Three hundred thirty-six citizens pay an annual membership fee to support the Cibolo Nature Center and its programs. Our newsletter reaches two thousand households. Last year, volunteers logged over three thousand hours of service. The Cibolo Kids Club has seventy-five members, and the teen-agers club, the "Trailblazers," has forty-five members.

Our annual budget is about $112,000, including $10,000 of funding from the City of Boerne hotel/motel taxes. All other funds are *privately* raised. Our Partners in Education Program for local schools received a $33,000 matching grant, which was duplicated by contributions from local businesses, enabling continued field trips and discovery learning. The Center is now open to the public every day of the week. The Nature Center building is at the completion of phase two construction, which provides us with finished wrap-around porches and outdoor stage, maximizing use of outdoor space. An interpretive guidebook for the woodland and creek trails has been developed. A beautiful mural has been painted on the interior wall of a pavilion, depicting wildlife at the park.

The Cibolo Nature Center currently provides nature appreciation and educational programs to reach the growing numbers of schools needing outdoor classrooms and hands-

**Multiuse space is vital for the many varied activities of nature centers.**

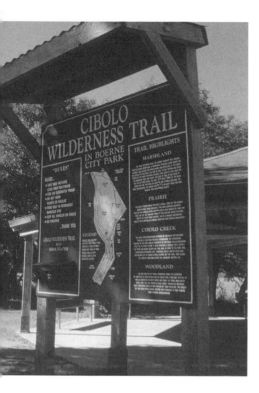

on experiences for their students. As an interpretive center for environmental education, we offer programs for the region's schoolchildren, teacher and docent training, and visitor awareness. Interpretive centers educate the public, encourage responsible visitor behavior, and introduce visitors to a world they have never seen. Interpretation at nature centers heightens awareness and understanding of the natural environment, inspiring visitors and adding perspective to their lives. (See Appendix B: Publications, *The Interpretive Guidebook: Techniques for Programs and Presentations,* by Regnier, Gross, and Zimmerman.) The staff and volunteers use on-site displays, hands-on exhibits, touching areas, brochures, reference materials, audiovisuals, and curriculum specifically developed for the Cibolo Nature Center. They work to teach appreciation and better understanding of natural areas and their related ecosystems. Summer day camp provides a scholarship program enabling needy children to experience the fun and wonder of our natural heritage.

Today, Nature Center headquarters includes the following:

- Displays of Kendall County minerals, native plants, fossils, geology and archeological artifacts, soils, and native ecosystems.

- Touching areas with animal and plant items (feathers, bones, leaves, etc.). Aquariums and terrariums containing selected plants and animals also serve to enhance the learning experience.

- A limited reference library supplied with field books, guides, and associated periodicals.

- Dioramas and displays of the marsh environs, upland woods, river bottom, and prairie. Plant and animal communities in displays give visitors more complete understanding of the relationships of natural communities.

- Other "nitty gritty" items, like chairs, tables, shelving, storage facilities, and equipment for educational programs, such as research equipment, microscopes, nets, projector, VCR/TV, field guides, water test kits, weather station, specimen boxes, environmental curriculum materials, and so forth.

- An outdoor stage/theater for presentations to large groups.

ALL THE EXHIBITS, facilities, and tools we have came from our generous community of donors, volunteers, and friends.

*Friends of the Cibolo Wilderness News*
January 1993

The Cibolo Nature Center is coming to life. The autumn months found us renovating the old house we had moved to the park: We have been busy rehanging windows, insulating and wiring behind the walls, patching floors, caulking, renewing plumbing, and doing the myriad of other essential repairs that an old house demands. At last, though, with the good help of our dedicated crew, David Pipes, Doug Manion, Jose Colon, and Murray Winn, we have been able to start on the more rewarding and visible projects. The new bathroom is built, the hall has terrific closets that will hold a world of educational experiences, the office has shelves and a window to the main room, and the wood stove is warm. Paul Schuetze has started our paint job and the true colors of the Center can now be seen.

Large porches now wrap around the old house. The handicap ramp is functional, leading up to the wide porch overlooking the prairie. We have come a long way since last summer, when the old ramshackle house with one wall missing rolled down the streets of Boerne.

Now the task at hand is to take this empty shell and give it life. With the new year just starting, we are optimistic. With your help we can bloom by spring. Our goal is to be open for school field trips and special events by late March. BUT we can't do it alone. We need your involvement. Look over the needs list and see if there is an area where you can help celebrate the wonder of our beautiful Hill Country by helping the Cibolo Wilderness Trail and Nature Center.

—Carolyn Chipman-Evans

**THE WISH LIST**

**Construction Materials**
- Pressed tin skirting
- V-Crimp tin roofing (10' x 14')
- Old, but good condition 1 x 12s (shelving)
- Cedar railing
- 2 x 4 porch rafters (10' x 14')
- 1 x 4 porch sheathing

**Educational Materials**
- Large-screen TV
- Video camera
- Cassette player
- Water test kits
- Binoculars
- Compound microscope
- Heavy-duty wheeled carts
- Slide synchronization machine
- Large projector screen
- Weather station

**Other Essentials**
- Folding metal chairs
- Pruners, rakes, shovels, etc.
- Locking file cabinets
- Folding tables
- Fire extinguishers

## LESSONS LEARNED

A partnership is always a challenge, be it a marriage, a business, or a citizens/city enterprise. The challenge is to approach the inevitable conflicts with mutual respect, and a good sense of humor. The advantages of a partnership with the city were obvious: They owned land, they had heavy equipment, they had manpower, they had money. Beautiful natural settings are usually very expensive, while city-, county-, or state-owned property often has wells, septic systems, electricity, and roads already in place, or easily provided.

The disadvantages were not immediately apparent, but gradually became obvious: We did not have control of our project. We sometimes had little say in decisions over traffic management, land management, or planning. However, these were minor disagreements, and our city government was willing to work out compromises every time. We eventually developed a Master Plan and Lease Agreement in cooperation with the city. We learned that frequent communication is essential in such a partnership. We have been lucky.

Some partnerships between citizens' groups and government entities have experienced serious breakdowns, compared with the minor difficulties we have had. In more serious partnership breakdowns, egos get involved, communication falls apart, and individuals become more interested in winning than developing common ground that can support a vibrant nature center in the future. Many a community project in this country has collapsed because individuals got fed up with other individuals.

So, if you can develop your nature center as a totally private enterprise, great. Our advice is to restrain yourself from the temptations of government involvement, if you have the resources to do it without their help. On the other hand, if it is public land that you are trying to save and use as a nature center, then go into your partnership with your eyes wide open, with consensus building as your fundamental approach, and attempt to get a master plan agreed upon as soon as possible in the relationship.

Although it is preferable to have a clear master plan all along, the local government may want to observe your group in practice over an extended period of time to develop trust, or to just maintain control. If this is the case, then frequent communication and informal relationships will be the most important tools in developing a true partnership.

A community-based nature center is, after all, a reflection of the community. The Cibolo Nature Center has been a compromise between many points of view, and does not totally conform to our original vision. This is usually the case in grassroots conservation projects. If you need to be in control, stay private. But if you can't beg or buy a piece of land, and if you believe in community, a partnership with local government may be your best bet. Democracy has worked for us.

We have also been told of instances where local civil servants, rather than elected officials, became the greatest helpers or hindrances. In our case, it has been city staff that really made our partnership with local government possible. The day-to-day operation of city government is in the hands of the employees, and your personal relationship with them becomes the key to a successful partnership. Better and more frequent communication usually results in more functional relationships, where most conflicts are prevented or readily worked through. Most nature lovers would rather saunter through the wild than sit in a meeting, but a community-based nature center can only thrive in a *communicating* community.

Our project has grown in unexpected jumps and starts. As new volunteers joined, new ideas emerged. Certainly, every community will have its own unique growth pattern. With all the limitations that a partnership can have, we still feel that a small group of activists can join with local government, create a nature center, and make the world more livable. Local talent, including Audubon organizations, herb groups, and plant enthusiasts, were extremely helpful. We were all very busy people, and we didn't know what we were doing. If we have been able to do it, you can too. When you find that wild place that speaks to you, the journey has already begun.

**WORD TO THE WISE**

**It should be noted that going private does not guarantee a conflict-free enterprise at all. A non-profit organization is governed by a board of trustees, which changes over time. We spoke with one founding director who was in extreme conflict with the board. Choose your first board members with care, and nurture the relationships like a marriage. The board needs to be intimately knowledgeable with the nature center mission and operations, to ensure that their decisions are not of the ivory tower variety.**

# Chapter 2 More Nature Center Stories

*Everybody can be great, because anybody can serve.*

— DR. MARTIN LUTHER KING JR.

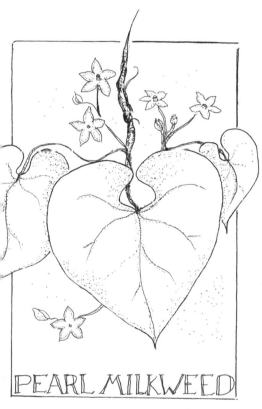

PEARL MILKWEED

ONE OF THE GREATEST JOYS we have experienced is visiting other nature centers and their administrators. Finding like-minded people who are activists in their communities provides a combination of camaraderie and information exchange that is invaluable. Visit as many as you can. Nature centers vary considerably by mission, size, funding, community involvement, and structure, as well as by ecological features. In developing your vision, it helps to know what other communities have discovered, so that you don't have to reinvent the wheel.

The Natural Science for Youth Foundation published the sixth edition of the *Directory of Natural Science Centers* (see Appendix B) in 1990, listing 1,261 entries from the United States and Canada. Nature centers, museums, environmental education centers, some state parks, botanical centers, zoos, and aquariums around the country are listed, along with mission, site and program features, and access information. In addition the directory provides thorough information about the nature center big picture across the country:

- 19% are located on 5 acres or less, and 31.4% are over 500 acres.
- 80% provide day programs only, whereas 20% provide residential programs.
- 63% use volunteers.
- 61.9% employ between one and five full-time staff members.
- Two-thirds serve more than 10,000 people annually, and 35.6% serve more than 50,000 annually.

Nature center stories vary considerably. Fontenelle Forest was established in 1913. Most nature centers came into being in the sixties and seventies, thanks in large part to the instrumental roles of the National Audubon Society and John Ripley Forbes of the Natural Science for Youth Foundation. We surveyed about one hundred nature centers that were members of the Association of Nature Center Administrators (ANCA), and a few that were not members, requesting information about history, funding, mission, membership, budget, facilities, services, programs, and favorite fund-raising tactics. We want to thank the centers that provided information for this book (see Appendix C, Nature Centers Surveyed).

**Jamestown Audubon Nature Center, New York.**

We have included stories of successful centers throughout the country, many of which have grown significantly since their humble beginnings, so do not be intimidated by the size of some of these nature centers. Many of the founders never dreamed the centers would experience such growth. Communities tend to support nature centers as quality programs start reaching the citizenry. The following profiles of a few nature centers will provide more detailed glimpses of various types of facilities and their beginnings.

The **Anita Purves Nature Center** in Urbana, Illinois, is a 59-acre private preserve with a public nature center. In 1963 Catherine Klassen, whose family had long owned this parcel of the original Big Grove Timber land, decided to offer the land for development as an industrial park. In anticipation of this, much of the low-lying woods was filled with brick and rubble, the remains of which can be seen in the woods today. Mrs. Klassen may not have initially realized what "Busey Woods" meant to the community, but when many letters appeared in the newspapers protesting the destruction of Busey Woods, she offered the land for sale to the public. The Committee for the Preservation of Busey Woods was formed and actively sought ways to designate the woods as a nature preserve.

In 1971 Mrs. Klassen and her sister, Miss Tawney, donated Busey Woods to the University of Illinois Foundation for use as a research area. By late 1974 the Urbana Park District had secured a twenty-year lease from the University of Illinois for Busey Woods and had developed a master plan for the woods' management as a nature study area.

As the environmental movement of the early 1970s swept across the nation, a small group of local citizens organized themselves and began taking schoolchildren on nature awareness walks. The Natural Areas Study Group developed trails in Busey Woods and trained volunteers to lead school tours. In 1973 the group convinced the Urbana Park District to take over the school tour program and assisted the district in establishing the Environmental Awareness Center.

One of the Natural Area Study Group's active members was Anita Parker Purves. In addition to her involvement with this group, Anita was a charter member of the Urbana Park District Advisory Committee, taught nature study in the local school enrichment program, and was instrumental in the formation and development of the Thornburn Environmental Awareness Center. She died of cancer in 1975, and at her request a memorial fund was established to help secure funds for the construction of the nature center. This dream was realized in 1979 when the Urbana Park District opened and dedicated the Anita Purves Nature Center with these words: "This (building) is but a small tribute to a spirited young woman who inspired both children and adult members of the community to share her enthusiasm for the kinship of all living things."

The Anita Purves Nature Center is at the northern end of Crystal Lake Park, and is an environmental education facility open to the public. The nature center provides four multipurpose rooms, an exhibit hall, an observation room, an Audubon nature gift shop, and an educator resource room. Other facilities include Busey Woods, the 60-acre Meadowbrook Prairie, and even an all-terrain wheelchair. An extensive array of nature programs are available to the public and to schools. The current annual budget is $225,000. Their favorite fund-raising tactic is described as "begging."

The **Aullwood Audubon Center and Farm** in Dayton, Ohio, opened its 70 acres to the public in 1957. Marie Aull had approached Hon H. Baker, then president of the National Audubon Society, with the idea of creating the first nature center in the Midwest. She envisioned a nature sanctuary where teachers and children could learn about plants, animals, and ecological concepts. Her gift of land, funds to build the center, and an endowment to the National Audubon Society created a center that would eventually total 350 acres and come to be considered one of the country's premier nature centers.

In 1962 the 120-acre Antrim farm adjacent to Aullwood Audubon Center was placed on the market, which endangered the freshwater springs that fed Aullwood Brook. Mrs. Aull purchased the farm and gave a portion of it to the National Audubon Society. Here she dreamed of a children's farm with livestock that children could see, touch, and hear, and fields where they could watch crops grow. This facility operated independently from the center until 1978, when the operations and staffs were combined. In 1979 the Friends of Aullwood was incorporated to generate greater community and financial support. In 1986 the National Audubon Society agreed to extend primary responsibility for funding and operation of the center to the Friends of Aullwood. In 1989 the farm was transferred to the Dayton Foundation, with the management retained by the Friends of Aullwood.

With a membership of 1,700 and an annual budget of $670,000, Aullwood's facilities include a nature center with interpretive exhibits, an organic educational farm with an interpretive center, a century-old barn, a sheep barn, chicken and rabbit coops, a sugar house, a spring house, a tractor barn, and a 140-acre reclaimed tall-grass prairie. Nearly twenty different guided and self-guided programs are provided for school and youth groups. Many workshops and classes are offered for teachers and youth leaders. Special classes are provided for youth during the summer and winter months. Workshops are offered for adults on a variety of topics. Weekend, weekday morning, and evening walks/programs are offered for the general public. Special events include the Wildlife Festival, the Apple Fest, the Enchanted Forest, Happy Bird-Day, Amish Quilt Auction, Holiday Open House, Earth Rhythms, and a variety of special exhibits.

The **Battle Creek Cypress Swamp Nature Center** is a 100-acre facility including three separate parks, and an annual budget of $225,000. It began with two local employees of the U.S. Geological Survey in Washington D.C. who identified the Battle Creek Cypress Swamp as an unusual phenomenon in Maryland. They approached the Nature Conservancy to purchase the swamp with funds raised by the Federated Garden Clubs of Maryland in 1957. Local Calvert County officials recognized the potential of this significant natural site and convinced the Calvert County government to lease the sanctuary from the Nature Conservancy, to manage the property, and to make appropriate improvements. In 1977 Calvert County purchased twenty-seven adjacent acres, hired the first manager of the site, and funded the construction of the nature center and boardwalk trail. Funding is provided by Calvert County, with annual supplements of approximately $25,000 from a "Friends" organization. Currently the Calvert County Natural Resources Division operates three public access parks for the purpose of environmental education, employing six full-time and ten seasonal and part-time staff.

The **Blackacre State Nature Preserve** of Kentucky is a 179-acre nature preserve with forest, fields, ponds, and streams. Facilities include trails, an Appalachian double-crib-style barn, a passive solar-heated demonstration building, a recycling center, composting restrooms, a rainwater collection system, gardens, livestock, and a historic homestead. Judge Macauley Smith donated Blackacre to the Kentucky State Nature Preserves Commission in 1979 as Kentucky's first nature preserve. It is administered through a three-way agreement between the Blackacre Foundation, Inc., the Jefferson County Public Schools, and the Nature Preserves Commission, each organization having a role in protection, stewardship, and maintenance. An extensive environmental education program is now in place, servicing Louisville and surrounding areas.

Judge Smith's wife, Emilie, observed, "It was not to save the houses that our gift is primarily designed. Houses are not sacred. Fire or tornado can too easily destroy them. It is the land that is sacred. The land can never be restored after bulldozers and blacktop. I can well imagine in fifty years what urban people will need most to see is not what our museums hold, but what did farm land look like? There will be very little to be seen."

The 12-acre **Children's Schoolhouse Nature Park,** formerly known as Riverside School #2 in the Kirtland Township School District of Ohio, originally opened its door to students in 1894. Its owners donated the facility to Lake Metroparks, a public county park district, in 1988, to teach children about the natural world through environmental education. The historic schoolhouse has been renovated into two classrooms. The attached residence has been remodeled into an exhibit area, wildlife observation room, and hands-on Discovery Room.

Facilities at Children's Schoolhouse Nature Park include the following:

- a half-mile trail traversing 12 acres of meadow, forest, stream, and wetland;
- the Bateman room, featuring an invertebrate zoo, butterfly rearing cages, and seasonal nature display (this also houses two stream tables, used to teach students about stream erosion);
- the Nest story room, featuring a fabric story wall and a wildlife observation room;

- a wildlife feeding area outside the Nest complete with an outdoor microphone and audio system to bring bird songs into the room;
- a Discovery room, where "Please touch!" is the rule and students learn about nature by exploring the discovery boxes, looking through a microscope, or observing a box turtle, salamander, snake, or fish; and
- a deck used as a teaching space.

The Children's Schoolhouse Nature Park has won several awards for excellence in curricula and exhibits. One unique fund-raising approach is the presentation of a family concert, including sales of albums with songs specifically written about the facility and its programs.

**Effie Yeaw, remembered for her gentle manner and concern for all living things.**

The 77-acre **Effie Yeaw Nature Center** in Carmichael, California, constitutes a highly successful institution that evolved out of the efforts of a crusading conservationist. Being an elementary school teacher who loved the outdoors, Effie Yeaw took her classes on nature excursions throughout the fifties. She pioneered the American River Parkway, promoted the designation of fifty nature study areas in Sacramento County, founded the Save the American River Association, pushed for a county tree ordinance, and was tireless in efforts to educate the public about their natural environment. When she died in 1970, public support for an Effie Yeaw nature center swelled. In 1976 the Effie Yeaw Interpretive Center was formally dedicated near the woods that she so often used for excursions with her children.

The Effie Yeaw Center is funded by the Sacramento County Parks Department, with an annual budget of $432,000. It has a 2.5-mile trail system, a 2-acre landscaped picnic area, a 1.2-acre replica of a Maidu village, and a 5,160-square-foot nature center headquarters with exhibits, live animals, a gift shop, and an outdoor amphitheater. The nonprofit supporting organization, the American River Natural History Association, has a membership of eight hundred.

**Effie Yeaw Nature Center in Carmichael, California.**

**Flat Rock Brook Nature Center** is a 150-acre preserve and environmental education center situated on the western slope of the Palisades in Englewood, New Jersey. Its story begins with a naturalist and nature photographer, Campbell Norsgaard, in the early 1960s. He became increasingly concerned about the fate of undeveloped land adjacent to his property, which contained nearly the last remains of the primeval Palisades forest, including 180-million-year-old volcanic bedrock formations, wetlands, ponds, a cascading stream, meadows, and a stone quarry. Development of this land would have eliminated a unique resource for the people of the area. He enlisted the help of the League of Women Voters, formed a group called "Green Lands for Englewood," and set in motion a long chain of events, campaigns, and battles. This ultimately culminated in a publicly owned environmental education center serving over twenty-five hundred students from

*"Nature centers have a unique opportunity and urgent responsibility to impact not only individuals but entire communities through education."*
—Bo Townsend,
Ijams Nature Center

over twenty different schools and seventeen towns. The Flat Rock Brook Nature Association annual appeal will attempt to raise $50,000 for 1997 programs, about one-third of the annual budget.

The **Ijams Nature Center** is an 80-acre city park and community nature center in Knoxville, Tennessee. In 1910 Harry P. and Alice Yoe Ijams built their family home along the banks of the Tennessee River. They spent the next five decades tending the land, maintaining a greenhouse for propagating small native plants and shrubs, which were later transported to the grounds; growing wildflowers and ferns; and developing ponds with marine life. H. P. died in 1954; Alice died ten years later. Following their deaths, civic-minded residents of the city and county sought to buy the Ijams property for use as the ideal nature park for the Knoxville community. Under the leadership of Mrs. Hobart Dunlap of the Knoxville Garden Club, and with the cooperation of the Knox County Council of Garden Clubs and the City of Knoxville, the park was established as a memorial to the Ijams couple. City funds and a federal open-spaces grant allowed the purchase of property— 20 acres of mature woods and meadow bordered on one side by the Tennessee river—from the Harry Ijams family.

A board of trustees was established in 1976 under a loose arrangement with the City of Knoxville. In 1989 the partnership was formalized, with private management under the board's direction and partial operating subsidies from the city. Other principal sources of funding each year include Knox County, memberships, special events, donations, and grants. In 1990 Ijams used city and state moneys to purchase 60 acres adjacent to the original property, thus allowing for expansion of trail systems and construction of a new headquarters building to replace the center's current piecemeal arrangement of business and educational offices. The picturesque but cramped original Ijams family homestead had been serving as an education building, and a small house was used for administrative offices. In 1992 a master plan was completed that incorporated the entire 80 acres into one facility, including three miles of trails and a new education and administrative building with exhibit hall utilizing "green" architecture.

The **Louisiana Nature Center** is an 86-acre facility on city-owned land that was founded in 1974; it has a current annual budget of $600,000 and a membership of 6,000. Its founding director, Robert Thomas, wrote us the following note on the center's history:

> At the beginning of LNC [1978], we had a cautious relationship with the city, which owned our land and which we used as a conduit to get an Economic Development Administration grant to build our first building. We reported to the Parks and Parkways Commission. Of the 86 acres, we had a 2-acre construction

**Louisiana Nature Center, in New Orleans, a premier U.S. nature center.**

zone (full use, needing no permission from the city), an 8-acre buffer zone (if either LNC or the city wanted to do anything on these 8 acres, they had to get the other's permission), and we had use of the other 76 acres. It was designated for use by the LNC, but there were constant threats from "ideas" to use a portion for parking, a nine-hole golf course, model planes, and so forth. We could charge admission to the buildings, but not to the land. In 1981 (3 years later), when I had an opportunity to get a $100,000 grant to build a board-walk on the 76 acres, I convinced them that no donor would give money if there were no controls. I was not greedy, and suggested that the 8-acre buffer be ex-tended to 84 acres. They would still have a veto, and we would be guaranteed that no one would run wild on our land. They agreed. As we proved that we are good citizens and serve the public well, we went back to the Parks and Parkways Commission and petitioned to close in the entire site for security reasons, and to charge admission to the grounds in general. They supported our request and considered it reasonable. Obviously, this would never have happened at the beginning when no one really knew that we would be an honorable group seeking the best use of publicly owned land.

Director Bob Marye commented further:

The Nature Center has carried out the bulk of its work through funds that it has generated through admissions, program fees, gift shop sales, and member-ships, or funds raised from private gifts and corporate grants. Public money has played a relatively small role in the Nature Center's financial history, especially over the last few years. One part of the Nature Center's success has been its ability to recruit, train, and retain a large cadre of dedicated volunteers. Volunteer service to the Nature Center has an average of over twenty thousand hours per year for at least the last five years.

The center has developed state-of-the-art exhibits through skillful fundraising and community support. The educational facilities were completed at a cost of $2,500,000, including a seventy-seat indoor amphitheater for programs and audiovisual presentations, an upstairs Discovery Loft, a gift shop, a volunteer room, animal care facilities, a changing exhibit space of about 1,800 square feet, and storage and support areas. Original exhibits on crabs, mosquitoes, and animal architecture, costing $175,000, were designed and produced out of house in 1979. They were followed by the following exhibits: "The Mississippi River Delta," @ $90,000; "Whales," @ $10,000; "To Fly Like a Bird," @ $12,000; "Our Coastal Wetlands," @ $30,000; "The Gulf of Mexico," @ $30,000; "The Paleontology Lab," @ $10,000; "The Tchefuncte People," @ $40,000; and "The Herpetology Lab," @ $10,000. In 1994 the Louisiana Nature and Science Center was merged into the Audubon Institute. The scale of achievement at this center has been tremendous, owing to the ambitious activities of its board of trustees, staff, and membership.

**Manitoga, Inc.,** in Garrison, New York, includes the home of Russel Wright, an ecologically designed landscape and education center. This 79-acre showplace was purchased by Russel Wright in 1942, having been damaged by a century and a half of quarrying and logging. From the 1930s through the 1950s the words "designed by Russel Wright" elicited an instant response. He was one of the best-known designers of home furnishings in the United States and an outspoken proponent of an American aesthetic. He was known for his love of natural, organic shapes, and his home, Dragon Rock, was his masterpiece of aesthetic harmony with nature. For thirty years he restored the land and designed a living theater in which all who came would experience "an innate kinship with the land."

Wright named this land Manitoga, which in Algonquin means Place of the Great Spirit, because he shared with Native Americans a respect for the earth. Though the landscape appears natural, it is actually a carefully designed backdrop of native trees, ferns, mosses, and wildflowers.

In 1975, one year before his death, Wright opened his land to the public. In continuing Wright's mission, Manitoga offers programs throughout the year for children and adults that emphasize ecology, science, art, and design. These programs are supported by Manitoga's membership of 550. The annual budget is $165,000.

**Adrienne Forbes,
Oxbow Interpreter,
with young
nature lover.**

The **Oxbow Nature Study Area** in Reno, Nevada, grew out of unusual circumstances. In 1961 the Nevada Fish and Game Commission received a U.S. land patent, at the total cost of $50, to 5.91 acres of land on the Truckee River known as "Doyle Island," for recreation and wildlife habitat. This Sierran river flows down from Lake Tahoe, through Reno, into the desert and empties into the mystical Pyramid Lake. The small preserve remained landlocked for approximately twenty-one years. In 1979 the director of Reno Parks and Recreation requested that the Wildlife Commission transfer the property, on a long-term lease agreement, for fisherman access and nature interpretation purposes. The Wildlife Commission approved a ninety-nine-year lease with the city of Reno in 1981. The city also purchased a contiguous 1.8 acres of land including a portion of right-of-way to a public road. In 1986 the Board of Wildlife Commissioners approved the development plan for the Oxbow Nature Study Area, including construction of an observation tower, a boardwalk trail, handicapped fishing decks, interpretive signs, and an environmental education building/center. The total estimated cost of the project was $563,000.

On January 1, 1997, the Truckee River crested at 14.91 feet as it raged through the Oxbow Nature Study Area. The torrential flood waters eliminated the existing trail system and scoured a new path through the lush riparian habitat. New land features such as river front beaches and sand dunes are now part of this river corridor. Nevertheless, the Truckee has reclaimed an original path and flowing waters ripple through the oxbows, while rainbow trout, migratory birds, muskrats, mink, cottontail rabbits, and mule deer flourish in this teeming 17-acre habitat.

Some twenty thousand students and other visitors come to the park annually. The park has now grown from eight to 30 acres; it is managed by the Oxbow Interpreter, an employee of the Nevada Division of Wildlife, and is maintained by the City of Reno Parks Division.

The **Pine Jog Environmental Education Center** was established by Mr. and Mrs. Alfred G. Kay as a wildlife sanctuary on 150 acres of wilderness, surrounded by West Palm Beach in Florida. The Kays purchased the property in 1946 for the purpose of growing flowers, fruits, and vegetables. The

Kays were involved in many philanthropic community projects, and in 1960 created Pine Jog to educate young students about their natural environment and to instill in them a feeling of stewardship toward their environment. In 1970 Pine Jog established a formal relationship with Florida Atlantic University, creating a unique public/private sector partnership.

Pine Jog is now a self-supporting unit within the College of Education of Florida Atlantic University. With an annual budget of $600,000, it has seven full-time staff, fifteen part-time staff, and an annual visitation of 29,000. Recently two donors gave endowments and gifts of over $13,000,000 to ensure the continuation of the dream. Pine Jog is a prime example of an educational facility that has received such wide community approval and support that it has steadily become one of the finest and most successful nature centers in the nation.

The **Riverside Nature Center** in Kerrville, Texas, had its beginnings around the same time ours did, and we have been able to observe their progress at close hand. It is an excellent example of determination and community involvement. The following is their story, written by Founding Executive Director Susan Sander:

**Pine Jog
Environmental
Education Center
in West Palm
Beach, Florida.**

An idea sprouted in March 1987, while I was photographing a hillside of wildflowers, purple storks-bills, and bluebonnets, and again a month later when it turned golden with green thread and Indian blankets. I was working as a newspaper photographer, and was relatively new to Texas and armed with a brand-new master's degree in environmental land-use planning. I started to ask questions: Who owned the land, and what were they going to do with it?

A Houston investment group had purchased the land in 1983 for commercial development, and it was for sale. But it was also full of history. The nine-acre plot was located in Kerrville's historic district along the Guadalupe River. On a thirty-foot bluff sat the original home of Captain Whitfield Scott, a Civil War veteran who had built the Victorian-styled house in 1897 and called it Riverside. In essence, the unworked landscape represented the natural heritage of Kerrville before it was settled. Since the vegetation was 90 percent native, it seemed a waste to lose it to commercial development.

After I had carried around photographs of the changing hillside wildflowers for two years, talking to everyone I could about the possibility of a nature center, a small group met in March of 1989 and by September had taken the steps toward being a nonprofit educational organization. By the end of our charter year we had 125 members.

The hitch was that the owners were asking $1.6 million. Then fate intervened. On November 12, 1991, the old Victorian house, the oldest wooden home in Kerrville, went up in smoke. And so did a lot of our dreams. Time to reassess. What I had really wanted to do with the land was use it for educating the general public and schoolchildren about the natural resources that are part of our everyday lives. I was already conducting programs with the Kerrville Parks Department as well as school and adult education out of the back of my car. And although our membership continued to grow, $1 million requires lots of fundraising. We decided to look elsewhere.

On July 8, 1992, the group, by then formally established as the Riverside Nature Center, bought a smaller former farm upstream, still in downtown Kerrville, but at the confluence of Town Creek and the Guadalupe River. Hardly native, the 3.5 acres had a forest of bamboo, lots of chinaberries, ligustrums, and thistles, plus several buildings unsafe for public use.

In retrospect, it has proven to be the better choice. Our center being located on a well-trafficked street, the community has been watching our slow but steady progress. We cleared bamboo, recycled old buildings, planted an arboretum of more than one hundred different species of Texas trees, and created and planted berms with native shrubs and wildflowers.

Now, four years later, we have more than four hundred members. Our land is paid for, our two-year-old arboretum is filling out. Our programs have expanded. Daily visitation increases. Our support has come entirely from our community, through memberships, corporate donations, and community trust grants; it has enabled us to restore a neighborhood grocery store for our visitor's center and office, construct an open pavilion for programs and special events, and pay a half-time director.

The **Riverside Urban Environmental Center** in Milwaukee, Wisconsin, is a 12-acre county park that has been recently transformed into a nature center. In 1890 the Riverside Park opened, amid industrial and residential development, becoming a major recreational gathering point for boating, swimming, strolling, and winter carnivals. As heavy industry moved in from 1890 to 1920, the Milwaukee River was polluted and beaches were closed. As the Great Depression developed, public funding declined, resulting in declining park maintenance. And between 1940 and 1960 industries on the site closed or burned down. Then, in 1976 the Milwaukee public school system leased some of the park land for a new athletic facility. A ravine and tunnel running through the park were filled in, and the park continued to revert to its natural state as maintenance declined. When the North Avenue Dam opened in 1990, renewed plant growth occurred over the mudflats.

In 1991 the Friends of Riverside Urban Environmental Center founded the facility, using the very limited personal funds of an environmental scientist, a poet, a landscape architect, and a neighborhood organizer. With an annual budget of $45,000 and a membership of 250, the current facility has a classroom trailer with two rooms, and offers school programs for 2,500 students per year. The facility also offers community programs, internships for college students, apprenticeships for high school students, workshops for teachers, and a variety of other programs.

The **Rye Nature Center** is a 47-acre natural area located in southern Westchester County, New York. The Parsons family home, built in 1905, mysteriously burned down in 1942. In 1945 the City of Rye acquired 35 acres of the Parsons estate, and in 1956 the tract was set aside as a natural area, at the persuasion of a group of concerned citizens led by Mrs. Bayard Read. In 1959 the Parsons barn and garage and 2 acres were purchased by the City of Rye. In 1964 the local conservation commission saw a need for an organization that would continuously encourage the development, use, and protection of this nature center. The Rye Conservation Society was formed, and 10 acres of adjacent property, threatened by development, was purchased. From 1981 through 1983 the Nature Center Building Fund Drive was implemented for expansion and renovation of the interpretive building.

The Rye Nature Center facilities now include a museum, a multipurpose room, a library resource room, a passive solar greenhouse, a laboratory, a bird-feeding station, a workshop, kitchen facilities, and facilities for the handicapped. Programs involve public interpretive activities, group programs and tours, outreach programs, school programs, preschool nature programs, research projects and internships, naturalist training workshops, after-school programs, special events, and summer ecology programs. The annual budget is $260,000, with a membership of 750.

The **Waterman Conservation Education Center** is a private facility in Appalachin, New York, with an annual budget of $157,000. Nestled on a wooded hilltop overlooking the Susquehanna River, this nature center opened in 1975 with

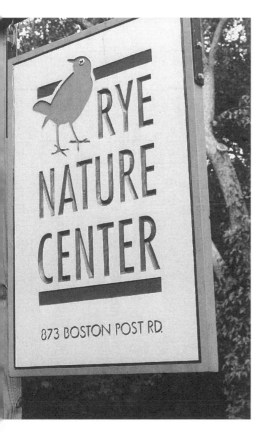

**Rye Nature Center in Westchester County, New York.**

the donation of 90 acres of farmland by Lolita C. Waterman. The subsequent purchase of a former church building on the adjacent property allowed for expansion. After much work, this building took shape as an interpretive facility which now houses a natural history museum, an auditorium, classrooms, a reference library, a nature gift shop, offices, a kitchen, and restrooms.

Waterman is actually made up of four separate properties. The main interpretive facility offers 94 acres of mature woods, fields, and gardens. Five miles of trails visit a stream gorge, a waterfall, a cornfield, and a bluebird area. Visitors can enjoy programs in an outdoor amphitheater, observe wildlife at one of the feeding areas, or picnic under a covered pavilion. A backyard wildlife habitat area demonstrates how landowners can attract wildlife. The Waterman Center also owns 24 acres of urban wetlands with wildlife observation blinds. Waterman also manages Appalachian Marsh, a 40-acre state-owned wildlife sanctuary, and Hiawatha Island, a 112-acre sanctuary, environmental study site, and outdoor recreation area. As a private, nonprofit nature center, all operating expenses come from the twelve hundred memberships, program fees, donations, fund-raising events, sales in the Nature Shop, and special program-related grants.

The **Wilderness Center,** in Wilmot, Ohio, has a history demonstrating persistence and faith. In the early spring of 1964, the fledgling Canton Audubon Society announced an open meeting concerning the possible establishment of an outdoor education center. Several interested citizens responded. A subcommittee exploring potential sites soon highly recommended the Sigrist Estate (251 acres) near Wilmot. It was quickly discovered that heirs of the estate were anxious to realize the moneys from the sale of the property, and if the land was to be saved for an educational center, positive action would be necessary.

An ad hoc committee of National Audubon Society members and other interested citizens agreed that an independent nonprofit corporation should be formed. That accomplished, the group contracted with the Nature Centers Division of the National Audubon Society for a field team evaluation of the site, which cost $850. On the date of incorporation, an option to purchase the Sigrist Estate for $50,000 was signed,

**The Interpretive Building of the Wilderness Center, in Wilmot, Ohio.**

with a deposit of $1,000 to be forfeited if the additional $49,000 was not paid by the end of a six-month period (December 19, 1964). This $1,000 was available through the faith donations (i.e., contributions made in the hope that others will follow, to achieve the goals of the donor) of Mrs. Bernice MacKenzie Frease and Dr. Thomas Soehnlen ($500 each).

In the meantime plans were developing for a community fund drive that would redeem the faith endeavors and bring to fruition the dream of an outdoor education center. By December 2, 1964, a $44,000 loan had been obtained from the Canton National Bank. This, with a $5,000 donation from the Canton Garden Center, was used for the purchase of the 251-acre Sigrist Estate, fifteen days prior to the stated deadline. On

January, 21, 1965, the Stark County Foundation announced a gift of $30,000, which was followed on January 26, 1965, by the announcement of a $67,000 donation from the Timken Foundation. The faith of many had now been rewarded as these foundations had invested in the dream. These contributions, along with corporate and private gifts, provided the necessary moneys for the dream to materialize.

The 68-acre contiguous Warstler property, with an imposing hillside and a six-room house, was deemed essential to the development of the center. On September 12, 1964, for a consideration of $300 against the total purchase price of $17,500, an option to purchase was signed. Continuing development of the Wilderness Center has taken place over the years, including hiring staff, further land acquisition, a new interpretive building, Pioneer Farm, Wilderness Lake, Kiwanis Tower, picnic shelters, and trails. With an annual budget of $426,000, nine full-time staff, two part-time staff, and an annual visitation of 100,000, the Wilderness Center continues to build community while the surrounding communities continue expanding the center.

THE PRECEDING STORIES illustrate only some of the many avenues to nature center development. Whether your community currently has no center, has a center that needs to grow, or has need of an additional center, there is a way. The next time that you are driving about in your community, let your imagination wander. Where are there remaining wild places? Where do wildlife still abound? Wouldn't there be students and educators who would love an outdoor classroom? Isn't there a current feeling in your community that something is being lost with all the progress of our times, and that conservation is a wise and wonderful endeavor? Shouldn't we try?

*Chapter* **3** **Why a Nature Center?**

> *A man's heart away from nature becomes hard. . . .*
> *Lack of respect for growing, living things*
> *soon leads to lack of respect for humans too.*
>
> —**LAKOTA BELIEF,** *TOUCH THE EARTH*

LOVEGRASS

HUMANS ARE ENCHANTED by natural beauty, by the sound of gurgling streams and pounding surf, by the sight of ancient trees, or by the smile of a flower. We are drawn to these scenes all over the world, across lines of politics and religion, culture, and generation. Recreation often takes the form of reconnecting with "creation," in forests and parks, rivers and lakes, mountains and deserts, or in our own backyards. We put windows in our walls, and adorn our homes with pictures of nature. We garden. We have pets. Our most cherished childhood memories often hearken back to places of natural wonder. Now, with 75 percent of humanity living in urban environments, and with many rural areas being developed, there is a global craving for parks and greenspaces. And because our planet did not come with instructions, we need a place that can teach us about this world that we have such an appetite for.

A nature center protects a piece of ground that can both inspire and teach. A nature center is a sample of the native environment of a community—wild land preserved and interpreted for the enjoyment and education of the public. It is an area of undeveloped land near or within a city or town. It can provide interpretive services such as outdoor programs in natural sciences, nature study and appreciation, and conservation. Some nature centers leave most of the "development" to Mother Nature, while others involve landscape architecture, extensive planting programs, or habitat restoration. Some may have no buildings or structures of any kind, while others include museums or elaborate indoor facilities. The possibilities are limited only by imagination (and fund-raising).

A nature center provides local communities with a sanctuary to appreciate, an outdoor classroom for schools and the public, and a tourist destination, and it actually helps create a sense of community. Local citizens find their skills as volunteer trailblazers, hosts, interpretive guides, teachers, and entertainers, producing programs that can touch every segment of the population. Examples include conservation curriculum for local students, science projects, workshops on local wildlife management, xeriscaping (dry landscaping), recycling, composting, watershed management, scout and youth activities, wildflower workshops, bird-watching programs, fishing and hunting information, ecological awareness projects, tree planting, story telling, outdoor concerts, living histories, and good old nature appreciation.

*Friends of the Cibolo Wilderness News*
May 1993

When the sun shines low in the sky, dappling through new leaves of cypress and dogwood, I am taken back. There was a time when few footsteps touched the paths along the Cibolo, when squirrel and titmouse owned the woods and all was theirs. Now when I walk these paths, I realize that I am a guest. It is a privilege to be able to share this exquisite beauty, this lush paradise, with those who have lived here long before man ever set foot along the Cibolo. It is the right thing to protect the ancestral land of squirrel and titmouse, of dogwood and cypress. One can tell what is right when a walk is rewarded by a soaring heart and a peaceful mind.

—Carolyn Chipman-Evans

A wild sanctuary can take on many forms. A "nature preserve" protects habitat and restricts public access. A "green space" is a preserved piece of undeveloped public land open to recreational activities. "Green corridors" or "greenways" permit activities such as hiking, biking, horseback riding, or picnicking along stretches of public land or easements through private properties. A "nature center" gains ground on several levels. It conserves and protects the native flora and fauna, and it educates the public through interpretive programs, naturalist activities, and events that promote the conservation ethic. "A nature center provides leadership in bettering man's awareness and reverence for life, and helps create a sense of individual responsibility for the care and wise use of natural resources" (*Armand Bayou Park and Nature Center Field Survey and Guidelines for Development,* 1974).

The Association of Nature Center Administrators defines a nature center as follows:

> A nature center brings environments and people together under the guidance of trained professionals to experience and develop relationships with nature. . . . A nature center consists of:
>
> • a natural site or home base to conduct educational programs;
>
> • a separate legal entity with a precise mission statement managed by a governing body;
>
> • a paid professional staff;
>
> • an established education program.

The reasons for establishing nature centers usually center around three major goals: education, conservation, and recreation. Having a clear set of goals is crucial, so that the project can evolve in an intentional and focused way.

**EDUCATION**

Education was considered the primary goal of most of the administrators we surveyed. The public can learn how and why to conserve water, protect their environment, adopt lifestyle habits that promote a healthy environment, and much more. Experiential learning is always the most powerful. Many

**Hands-on programs inspire curiosity. Lucas Miller conducts a "Schoolhouse Safari" with the aid of a friend.**

residents will want to learn about local flora and fauna. You will find popular interest in programs on wildflowers, trees, grasses, birds, butterflies, wildlife, weather, water, soil, and just about every area of natural science you can imagine.

The first public outdoor education programs in the United States began in children's museums in the early 1800s. A century ago, John Muir began his campaign of public education; he founded the Sierra Club in 1892, saying, "The great wilds of our country once held to be boundless and inexhaustible are being rapidly invaded and overrun in every direction, and everything destructible in them is being destroyed. Every landscape low and high seems doomed to be trampled and buried." He eventually helped inspire Teddy Roosevelt to develop the national park system.

In that same period, a group of citizens banded together to stop the slaughter of herons and egrets, whose feathers were being used to adorn ladies' hats. Engaging in public education and advocacy for the passage of new protective laws, the group grew into the National Audubon Society. A few nature centers, like Fontenelle Forest, also began early in the twentieth century.

In the 1950s, John Ripley Forbes began funding and inspiring the development of nature centers, and later established the Natural Science for Youth Foundation. In the 1960s and 1970s, awareness began to grow. The National Audubon Society led the growing nature center movement and helped finance or inspire the creation of hundreds of nature centers around the country. Environmental education began to flourish. The World Wildlife Fund was created. The Sierra Club conducted its first Inner City Outing for Urban Youth Program. Donald and Jo Ann Rees pioneered the Yosemite Institute and went on to develop the Headlands Institute and the Squaw Valley Institute. Earth Day in 1970 sparked international activity.

Today the National Audubon Society(NAS) has 550,000 members, 525 chapters, 15 field offices, and more than 250 national and local wildlife sanctuaries.

> "We dedicate ourselves to the pleasant task of opening the eyes of young and old that all may come to enjoy the beauty of the outdoor world, and to share in conserving its wonders forever."
> —Statement of Audubon philosophy,
> Robert S. Lemmon, 1956.

To approach its goal of creating a "culture of conservation," the National Audubon Society is now emphasizing the importance of a community-based education system. "Common to all of these centers will be a focus on experiential learning, personal and community-based stewardship, and local action."—David Heil, who is executive director of this generation of Audubon centers. The NAS plans pilot projects at Audubon sanctuaries, at local nature centers, in community storefronts, and at kiosks in national and state parks—even shopping malls. Audubon centers will be linked through the "Virtual Audubon Center," an electronic meeting place that can be visited by anyone through computer access. New or existing nature centers may find advantages in associating with local Audubon chapters or the NAS under this new initiative.

The dream of many nature centers throughout the country is one that should be nurtured. As the population expands, and the public desire for contact and education continues to grow, more and more nature centers can be established.

There is a great deal of debate among educators as to philosophy, goals, and methods. Some programs are basically scientific, teaching names and functions of different species. Some emphasize relationships within ecosystems, while others focus on the impact of humanity. Some programs seek to fundamentally change life-styles toward more environmentally sound practices. These are not small differences of opinion, but fundamental questions in the nature center field today. Are we teaching about nature, or about how to best interact with nature?

> "I sincerely believe that for the child, and for the parent seeking to guide him, it is not half so important to *know* as to *feel*. . . . Once emotions have been aroused—a sense of the beautiful, the excitement of the new and the unknown, a feeling of sympathy, pity, admiration or love—then we wish for knowledge about the object of our emotional response. Once found, it has lasting meaning. It is more important to pave the way for the child to want to know than to put him on a diet of facts he is not ready to assimilate."
>
> —Rachel Carson, *A Sense of Wonder,* 1965

The tone of a nature center will be created by its leaders, their values, and their resources. It is vital that the educational goals be clear. For example, appreciation of nature and respect for natural places are essential qualities of an informed citizenry. Keeping these goals in mind can help staff and volunteers have a clear focus on their mission and prevent the common practice of merely asking students to memorize

## WORD TO THE WISE

**What about politics? Advocacy for good stewardship of the land is a goal of some nature center educational programs. We have decided to focus on the positive aspects of conservation. By being inclusive with your community, you will reach a wide range of people. If your community contains people who want to save forests and people who make a living from forests, your nature center can bring them together for dialogue and learning, or drive them apart by taking sides. And there is room for legitimate debate among people of good will. However, there are times when your organization may choose to enter a political debate. If you choose to take a public position on a local environmental issue, do your homework, have the support of your board of directors, bring all interests together to share information, have a reasoned approach, work to find solutions, and provide good leadership. In so doing, a nature center can advocate for conservation and remain a source of information and inspiration, rather than a source of division and conflict.**

names of species, with facts and figures. In this regard, read *Earth Education,* by Steve Van Matre.

The education program can begin as a small series of talks by local experts and grow in several directions. The nature center can work with local schools to develop curricula, and provide informative programs for the public. Areas of public interest or concern can be addressed by local and visiting naturalists. A public awareness program can seek to instill the conservation ethic in the community.

Once teachers learn of a nearby nature center, you will meet the innovative and energetic ones. Many nature centers collaborate with local schools to develop an "outdoor classroom" concept. This is not "desks outside." Outdoor classrooms are programs of inquiry, designed to place students in natural areas with learning challenges. While children are learning poetry writing or math skills, they can also be developing a deep appreciation and understanding of nature. Teachers report that their students are more exuberant and interested in outdoor settings, and tend to seek more innovative and creative solutions to problems. There are a number of educational curricula in existence, such as *Project Wild, Project Learning Tree, Green Box, Ranger Rick, Project Adventure, Audubon Adventures,* and Steve Van Matre's innovative programs, including *Earthkeepers* and *Sunship Earth.* Joseph Cornell has developed a series of excellent books on introducing children and adults to the joy of nature. (See Appendix B: Publications.)

Probably the wisest approach to an educational curriculum for local students is to start small, with a few interested teachers designing field trips for their classes. As interest builds, you can collaborate with the teachers and administration to develop a plan that suits your particular bioregion and cultural community. Eventually teachers can be paid for time spent in helping to develop a curriculum to be used at the nature center that also accomplishes some of their primary objectives. Their personal investment in the curriculum will result in more enthusiastic teaching. Field trips need to be more than a walk in the park if they are to truly educate. Some nature centers have large budgets that provide staff and materials for fabulous educational programming. Other centers have little or no funds for such activities, and rely on the creativity and energy of volunteers and local educators.

Some teachers will want to use your outdoor classroom for their own curriculum ideas. Be sure that these activities are discussed thoroughly with your nature center staff. Well-meaning teachers may not realize how their activities might impact the environment or other visitors. Having all activities cleared through the nature center is essential. At one facility, an "experienced outdoor educator" used fluorescent orange spray paint on rocks and trees for temporary trail markers for his group on a one-day excursion. Be familiar with visiting educators, know what their plans are, or at least have a trusted volunteer along for the day.

**Environmental science students from Marshall High School in San Antonio use a plant key to identify shrubs at the Cibolo Nature Center.**

Students will want to do their science projects at your facility. Groups like the National Audubon Society, the Sierra Club, hikers associations, scout troops, home schoolers, and many others may want to conduct programs at your nature center. Good communication and coordination is vital. We recommend written rules and suggestions for visitors, along with a strong volunteer trail-guide or docent program.

"Environthons" involve competition between student teams, testing their environmental and conservation knowledge with hands-on inquiry learning. In 1979 three counties in Pennsylvania began a regional environthon, and in 1996 there has been participation by teams from 33 states, 4 Canadian provinces, 2 Mexican states, and Japan. Contact the Hashawha Environmental Appreciation Center for more information.

There is a large body of resource material for environmental educators: The National Association for Environmental Educators produces publications and conferences (see Appendix A: Organizations). Outdoor Biological Instructional Strategies (OBIS) is a program for fifth and sixth graders in ecology (see Appendix B: Publications). The National Association for Interpretation provides information, including the *Journal of Interpretation,* for naturalists, historians, park rangers, educators, museum technicians, curators, administrators, recreation specialists, authors, volunteers, and nature center staff (see Appendix A: Organizations).

The College of Natural Resources at the University of Wisconsin has created an excellent series available for helping your nature center develop interpretive programs. Interpretive programs are intended to provoke a response in the visitor, to inspire as well as educate. The basic book on interpretation is *The Interpretive Guide Book: Techniques for Programs and Presentations.* This book details how to give talks and various kinds of interpretive programs, with valuable tips, checklists, and resources (see Appendix B).

Also see the following organizations in Appendix A:

- Institute for Earth Education
- National Wildlife Federation
- North American Association for Environmental Education
- The National Consortium for Environmental Education and Training

Bob Marye, of the Louisiana Nature Center in New Orleans, reports that their center provides services, over a wide geographic area, that include educating large numbers of citi-

"The Cibolo River, one of the most charming mountain streams in the whole state, pure running  water over a gravel bed, as clear as a crystal. . . . there are pools 5 to 6 ft. deep in which grown people can enjoy a bath and between the pools the water is so shallow that the merest little toddler may be allowed to go in with perfect safety. No harm comes from bathing here, our boys often go in five or six times a day and nearly every night and no bad results."
–Boerne  Campers Association, printed in the Boerne Advance, April 4, 1890.

zens of southeast Louisiana on a broad range of environmental topics.

> On the level of housing, the Nature Center as part of its overall mission has communicated information on improving home energy efficiency, home recycling, and environmental gardening. . . . The Nature Center is not simply dry education. Most of our programs have a strong recreational and entertainment component. Linking fun, family-oriented elements to the messages we communicate makes the message more effective.

Tim Merriman, the executive director of the National Association of Interpreters, has spoken of "edutainment," a hybrid approach that combines education and entertainment to ensure that education is fun. As any teacher knows, if you bring your subject to life, your students will learn. If your programs are entertaining, people will come.

Steve Van Matre has been a prolific writer about environmental education issues (see Appendix B, *Earth Education: a New Beginning*). He has also been an outspoken critic of many nature centers. He sees the nature center as a place to help visitors appreciate natural systems and communities directly, and learn environmentally sound life-styles.

You will take your own stand on these issues by the actions you choose to take. Many passions find expression in this area of the nature center experience. Keep your sense of humor. Good luck!

## CONSERVATION

Many nature centers have been born out of a community's desire to preserve a piece of natural beauty forever. Helping a bit of wilderness stay wild may seem fairly easy to the novice, but there is much more to nurturing wilderness than just leaving it alone. What constitutes wildness? Should invasive plant species be allowed to flourish, or should they be eradicated, and how? Which species are "native," and which are "naturalized?" Should the public be permitted in all areas, no matter how fragile? How should motorized and foot traffic be controlled? Could this public natural setting be literally "loved to death?"

You will eventually need to answer these questions with a land management plan, which will also evolve through time with changes and revisions. At the earliest stages of development, cleanup projects are great motivators and good public relations. However, when you start thinking about where to build trails, or what to plant, or what to "weed out," seek professional advice. Your project will require a clearly stated master plan, so that it can serve your community on a long-term basis. Lack of foresight can result in the needless destruction of your original vision. (See Chapter 11, Managing Land Without Managing to Ruin It.)

It is also important to understand that a nature center is not a nature preserve, although it can include one. Beyond preserving habitat, a nature center addresses public education. Unless public attitudes and behavior are changed, more habitats will be unappreciated and destroyed. A nature center protects the habitat as far as possible, and welcomes visitors in a way that promotes appreciation and conservation. A local nature center "thinks globally and acts locally." Most researchers agree that we have the resources to address our most serious environmental problems, but not the political will. A serious conservation effort involves community outreach. Educate the public and the leaders will follow.

BRINGING IN VISITORS will inevitably stress the land. The stress can be minimized by limiting access to fragile areas and using farsighted techniques in designing your traffic flow. For example, access roads to your park can attract persons who are not interested in nature appreciation and are more likely to vandalize. Therefore, having a limited number of entrances that are clearly designed for nature interpretation will encourage use by interested parties, rather than potential vandals. The balancing act of protecting the land while bringing in visitors is an age-old issue for parks and preserves. Some excellent resources in considering conservation issues are *Helping Nature Heal: An Introduction to Environmental Restoration, Restoration and Management Notes, Wilderness Magazine,* and *Natural Areas Journal.*

BLUE-EYED GRASS

*Friends of the Cibolo Wilderness News*
May 1992

Scissor-tailed flycatchers darting over the wide prairie, red-shouldered hawk dodging pointed attacks from mad mockingbirds, foxglove and blue-eyed grass claiming ground—these are a few of my personal favorites . . . this season. Time spent at the Cibolo Wilderness Trail opens windows to new experience; offers a deeper understanding, secrets revealed, and appreciation unbounded.

Progress need not always be hard on nature; in fact, the restoration of nature is a true sign of progress in the nineties. Boerne now has the reputation of a forward-thinking community that cares about the quality of life, a place where wilderness thrives and people work hard to preserve the rare and precious.

But we must strive to do more than we ever have before. There is no time to waste. Our environment, our earth, our children need us to care and to make positive changes. We all need to look at our lives and take action. There is so much we can do.

The Friends of the Cibolo Wilderness feel that developing appreciation and understanding of our natural world is a critical goal. Simply put, people take care of things they love. Future generations will be better equipped to protect the environment if they have had learning experiences in nature. That is exactly what they are getting at the Cibolo Wilderness Trail (CWT). Trained guides give tours to children from Boerne and surrounding area schools, taking these children out of the world of books, into the realm of first-hand experience. The children who come to the CWT leave with more than a fun memory; they have tools for the future.

—Carolyn Chipman-Evans

## RECREATION

The primary reason people venture into a natural setting is because it is fun: a quiet saunter down a woodland trail, a vigil at the marsh, a stroll into the prairie, a trek up the mountain, a dunking in the swimming hole, a doze in the shade of a kind old tree, a race with the kids down the hill, a chance to spy on animals in the wild. Some like the physical exercise, while others claim that a stroll through nature provides a mental health break.

When people enter nature, tension seems to diminish, and a general sense of well-being is aroused. There is an inborn craving for contact with the wild. Hunters and anglers often admit that their sport has more do with getting out in nature than anything else. Outdoor recreation need not be organized or structured. Quiet recreation is sought after, and often quite hard to find. A nature center can meet the needs mentioned here, as long as the artifacts of humanity are minimized, and nature has a chance to thrive.

Accommodating families means remembering the needs of various ages. Children need physical activity, while parents need a break, and grandparents need benches. Some centers provide points of interest that include activities for children, providing welcome relief for weary elders. A climbing apparatus near a picnic area may prevent a lot of broken tree limbs and trampled vegetation. A visitors' guide can suggest a variety of appropriate recreational activities for visitors of all ages.

Recreation is indeed a major purpose of a nature center. Recreational programs help build community, which in turn builds and supports your center. Hiking, canoeing, backpacking, camping, spelunking, rock climbing, music and story telling, art classes and photography lessons, bird-watching, walking-club outings, quilting clubs, folk crafts, songfests, poetry workshops, and even cross-country races can all generate visitors, appreciation, and goodwill.

People in the United States spend between 85 percent and 95 percent of their lives *indoors.* Affluent families live in air-conditioned spaces, traveling in sealed vehicles, having only marginal contact with a distorted and manipulated landscape. The poor live in marginal housing in crowded, devastated neighborhoods. The middle class is sequestered in their

**The Japanese have a kind of garden gate called the** *torii,* **a post and lintel construction with delicately curved lines, through which the garden's visitors pass and become transformed. When entering the garden, one must leave all worldly concerns behind, and enter with the a mind open to poctic inspiration It is that gate that a nature center can provide—the gate to relaxation and wonder, the gate that all of us have passed through at one time or another.**

**Family Bonding Activity**

**Try this. Take your family, a blanket, a picnic, and a song in your heart, and go to a pretty spot in nature. When everyone has eaten, take turns thanking each other for as many things as you can think of—family bonding in nature's arms.**

**Wildlife watchers spend even more tourist dollars than hunters or anglers. Nature centers are good for local economies.**

homes, cars, and offices most of the time. The divorce from nature has been so complete, in such a short space of time, that the consequences have been profound.

We have reacted precisely the way animals do when they are put in zoos, experiencing aggression, hoarding, neglect and abuse of young, depression, and susceptibility to disease. Should we be surprised that these problems thrive in the population centers of humanity? Fascination with violence and the accumulation of material wealth abound. Perhaps the worldwide rise in war, crime, and mental health problems are a direct outgrowth of the same phenomenon: separation from nature and overcrowding. Perhaps the development of nature centers can help "ground" people, re-create a sense of connectedness to nature, and generate healthy communities.

*Friends of the Cibolo Wilderness News*
Winter 1993, Field Notes

Today I feel I am in the depths of winter, a heavy, gray blanket covers from horizon to horizon. Snowflakes are drifting lightly down and birds are flocked at the feeders. Tonight should be a truly cold one.

It was only last week that a warm spring rain came to the Trail and filled our drying marsh and greened the early spring grass. It felt too warm too early and, frankly, I am relieved to know we will have a few more days of cold to set things right.

The stark beauty of winter never fails to astound me. The sight of trees, undressed and silhouetted against a cold and rosy sky, makes time stand still. Empty nests, filled with promise, cling in the stark limbs. Flocks of cedar waxwing and robin light on outstretched limbs like paper ornaments.

This winter a world has opened to me. With a new pair of binoculars, I have suddenly become a ruthless spy into the world of birds. To see their lives unfold, without the slightest concern over me, is a great joy. The unconscious actions, preening a feather, gathering a twig, splashing in the birdbath, are simply mysterious. My binoculars are small and in some magical way let in enough light to make the birds seem even more brilliant than they look from afar. I feel as if I had opened a door into a world I never knew existed.

This experience is not new; nature continually opens doors and allows us to see deeper into the world and into ourselves. Myself, I plan on taking more walks, looking open-eyed and open-hearted for the wonder before me.

— Carolyn Chipman-Evans

# Chapter 4 Facility Options

*Each town should have a park or rather
        a primitive forest of five hundred acres,
where a stick should never be cut for fuel.*
— HENRY DAVID THOREAU, *WALDEN*

BRINGING PEOPLE into a wild area involves compromise. Their visits will impact on an area from a number of sources: their vehicles, their foot traffic, their noise, their children, their curiosity, and the occasional lack of good judgment, or even vandalism. The methods you chose to provide access, direct traffic, offer programs, and reach your audience will alter the landscape you have come to love. But in the process, if you do it right, you will enable others to fall in love with nature, too. Involve your community in the decision-making process. What kinds of facilities does the community want? Ask! Talk to as wide a range of potential users as possible, including some experts. The locale itself will suggest some possibilities, considering the lay of the land, for example:

- environmentally fragile areas (easily damaged);
- areas that lend themselves to high-impact activities, such as building, parking, picnicking, restrooms, exhibits, points of interest, water access, camping, hiking, and interpretive trails; and
- high-interest areas, such as waterfalls, ponds, wildflower meadows, wildlife-viewing areas, etc.

Nature center facilities vary considerably. Fontenelle Forest and Neale Woods Nature Center in Nebraska have 1,311 acres and 554 acres, respectively, while Riverside Nature Center in Kerrville, Texas, is a 3.5-acre facility. Some centers serve many thousands of visitors every year, whereas some serve much smaller communities. For educational programs, the size of the acreage is less significant than the creativity of the staff and the design of the experience for the visitor. There is a substantial range in budgets. The Delaware Nature Society has a budget of $1,500,000, while Ansonia Nature and Recreation Center in Connecticut operates on $50,000 a year. Also, many communities can support more than one nature center, where different programs and ecosystems can appeal to the broad spectrum of the public. Minneapolis has some twenty-seven nature centers, which perform different functions in order to avoid competition. There is room for many more nature centers of great diversity to be born. Small nature centers often have certain advantages over large operations: lower operational budgets, fewer land management challenges, and greater sense of ownership by the membership. Dream on!

**Signage helps at the National Wildflower Research Center in Austin, Texas.**

**Construction at a nature center should complement the surrounding landscape; an exemplary  nature center is the Bay Beach Wildlife Sanctuary in Green Bay, Wisconsin.**

Careful planning from the onset can ensure a top-quality center and prevent the land from being abused and degraded. The Natural Science for Youth Foundation's *1990 Directory of Natural Science Centers* contains a matrix presentation of centers and their particular facilities (see Appendix B: Publications).

The following list of considerations that go into determining facility options is prioritized from the most basic requirements to the most extravagant options:

## PARKING

Unimproved parking areas become muddy, and teenagers love to play with their vehicles there. Unless drivers are clearly directed to acceptable parking places, they are likely to just pull off the road and abandon their vehicles anywhere. Placing large rocks or logs to designate where to park, and where vehicular traffic should stop, is an important first step. High-impact areas will inevitably develop near vehicles. Some people like to play their radios and picnic near their cars. Vandals don't usually walk a long way to do their dirty work. Keep your fragile areas well separated from parking zones.

## RESTROOMS

Unless there are public restrooms nearby, visitors will answer nature's call in the bushes, streams, or right in the middle of a trail. Since most visitors are not trained in low-impact hiking, you will find used toilet paper and disposable diapers decorating your lovely little paradise. Until you can afford a flush toilet or composting toilet system, a portable toilet can be rented, or (better yet) donated. If a port-o-let is used, it should be camouflaged so that it is not an eyesore. Some nature centers report that composting toilets have been problematic in high-traffic parks, so research your options carefully to avoid a pile of trouble later!

## LITTER BARRELS

Visitors do use litter barrels. You get to figure out how to purchase them, who is going to service them, and if they need to be secured. If your volunteers routinely pick up litter, your trails suffer less abuse. As time goes by, regular hikers will become your trail's best friends by picking up litter and caring for the park. Some parks are going to a "carry in–carry out" policy, which promotes education and personal responsibility.

---

Science Project
by Our Fourteen-Year-Old Daughter, Laurel

Decoy litter was placed in a picnic area on three alternating weekends, and the area was left litter-free on three alternating weekends. At the end of each weekend, the litter was counted and results were tallied. The results confirmed the hypothesis that people are much more likely to litter an area that is already littered than an area that is litter-free. An average of eleven times more litter was found on decoy weekends than on litter-free weekends. Possible explanations for the findings:

1. People feel uncomfortable littering areas that are pristine.

2. People feel as if "one more piece won't count" in an area that is already littered.

3. People tend to copy behavior of others—they tend to be messy in messy areas, and clean in clean areas.

---

**TRAIL CONSTRUCTION**

Trailblazing is a great early activity with volunteers. Plan a clear goal with visible results and publicize the need for help. Most nature trails develop in stages. Initially, even on relatively unspoiled land, there are animal trails and spontaneously developed foot trails that may or may not be in the right places. Trails create erosion, becoming little rivers during rainstorms. As traffic increases, some areas, like steep grades or sharp turns, can become difficult or even hazardous. Before getting out your machete and shovel, get some professional advice on trail building, or even a botanical survey. *It is easy to cut a trail in the woods, but extremely time-consuming to repair a damaged area.* Just a short walk with an experienced trailblazer can help develop a rudimentary plan that will prevent future problems. (See "Trail Building," in Chapter 11: Managing Land Without Managing to Ruin It.)

### SIGNS

The public will need to know that they have arrived, where the trails are, and what is special about this area. More importantly, signs should carry the unified theme of your project, your interpretive message.

**The soul of a nature center can be expressed in its sign. Visitors at Aullwood are struck by the dedication and vision of its staff, who feel that any time you visit nature is a good time.**

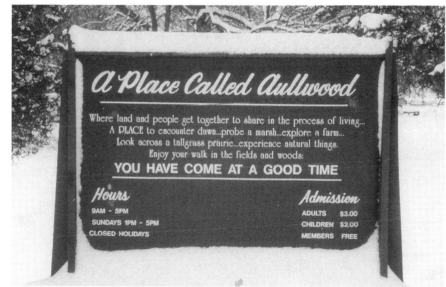

In the beginning, you may only be able to afford a handmade sign displaying the name of the trail. But keep in mind that signage creates your public image. A professionally produced sign that is very aesthetically pleasing will communicate your concern for the land and your seriousness about the project. The best source that we found for learning how to plan and produce top-quality signs is *Signs, Trails, and Wayside Exhibits: Connecting People and Places.* Sign makers will often volunteer their services for publicity. Eventually grant moneys can be obtained for signage.

## DRINKING WATER

It is not essential that you provide drinking water, although visitors will feel more accommodated and comfortable if it is available. If your area is in a hot and dry climate, this issue becomes more pressing.

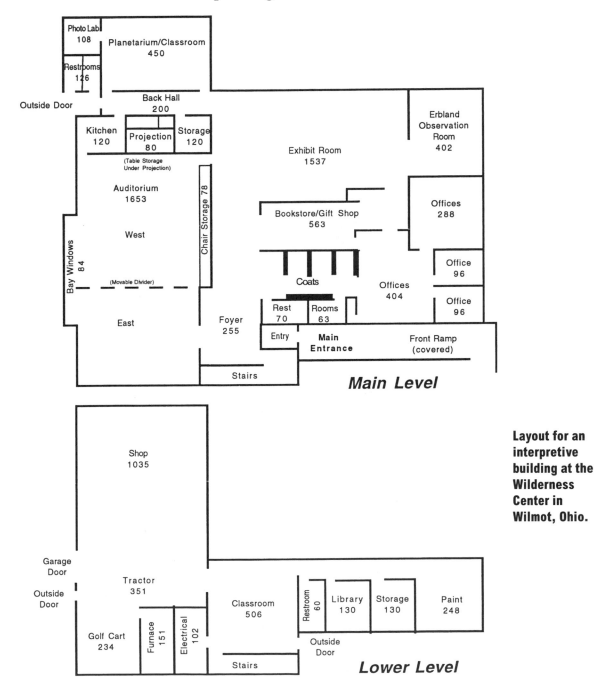

Layout for an interpretive building at the Wilderness Center in Wilmot, Ohio.

## HEADQUARTERS BUILDING

Having your administrative activities located at your site enables people to find you, and enables you to keep an eye on your project. Many nature centers begin without such a luxury, setting up shop at the home of the founding director or some cheerful volunteer. This arrangement may be needed for some while, during which time funds can be developed to renovate an existing structure, build a new one, or move a building onto the land. We contend that you don't need a headquarters before you have the land, an organization, a paid director, and a functioning newsletter.

In planning your headquarters, the size of your budget will definitely limit the accommodations. Here is a list of

**Discovery boxes are experiential!**

**Observation hives are fascinating but require frequent care.**

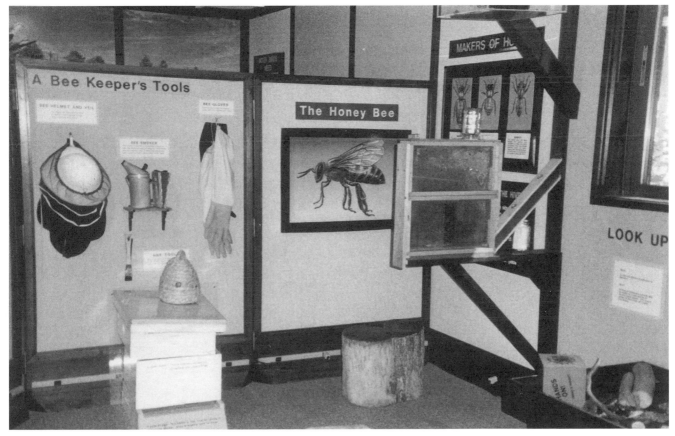

optional functions that different nature centers plan into their headquarters buildings:

- Administrative office—the nerve center, phone, message machine, computer, copier, FAX, mail, records.
- Classrooms—how many groups do you want to accommodate at one time?
- Laboratory—will you really need one?
- Computer terminals, electronic highway, etc.
- Discovery rooms—experiential learning areas—discovery boxes (Aullwood Nature Center and Farm has published a how-to booklet on constructing discovery rooms—see Appendix C).
- Indoor exhibits, dioramas, multimedia presentations.
- Live animal exhibits and aquariums.
- Library—collecting information about local flora and fauna.
- Bookstore or shop—can be a source of income, but will require serious bookkeeping and volunteer training.
- Public phone.
- Restrooms and drinking fountain.
- Indoor or outdoor theater.
- Storage, storage, storage.

**Museum-quality specimens provide visitors a close encounter with native species at Bear Creek Nature Center in Colorado Springs, Colorado.**

**Be careful not to overbuild. Remember to start small and grow with the needs of your community. Also, remember that it takes staff to run a center. Don't create a building without a staff to operate it.**

Some nature center headquarters buildings are showplaces, with museum-quality interpretive displays and state-of-the-art "green architecture," like the new Ijams Nature Center, with a $4 million construction budget. Others, such as the Randall Davey Audubon Center in Santa Fe, New Mexico, are more modest, having a small administrative office and nature shop. Remember, a nature center can grow for hundreds of years, so start small and grow at a sustainable pace.

Costs often dictate the availability of facilities, but the creativity of the local community should never be underestimated. In our community, a local druggist named George

---

A Description of the Cibolo Nature Center

The Cibolo Nature Center is an 1898 house that was moved to the Cibolo Wilderness Trail in Boerne City Park and renovated, little by little. The 1,200-square-foot building has one large room, one small office, one large walk-in closet, a big attic, a restroom, three large covered porches that wrap around the building, and an outdoor theater. It has some permanent displays and aquariums and a newly opened gift shop. The most wonderful thing about the Center is its flexibility. We can make it camp headquarters with forty children sitting on the floor. We can decorate and have an elegant dinner party for our Benefactors' Club. We can seat fifty people inside for a slideshow or seat hundreds outdoors for a concert or puppet show. The Center is always evolving to meet our needs.

The closet stores our educational equipment, nets, microscopes, television, and so forth; tools and maintenance equipment; extra inventory for the gift shop; and chairs and tables and displays. It seems there is never enough storage, although we have begun to look closely at what gifts we accept. Sometimes that extra display case just won't fit!

Plummer needed to move an old structure off his property, to make way for a parking lot. He donated the structure to the city when he heard that the new nature center needed a building, and our Friends organization joined with the City of Boerne to finance the move. Moving an old building can be incredibly less expensive than building a new one, and the character and charm of old structures can usually be salvaged. House movers often know of such deals. Look in the yellow pages or want ads of the nearest city under "houses to be wrecked and moved" or "house movers." If a building is donated, we recommend having a no-strings-attached policy, to prevent unforeseen complications.

Another good tactic is an old-fashioned barn raising that brings together local builders, service groups, and volunteers. Portable buildings have served as headquarters for many young nature centers. Hay bale construction, underground housing, or other environmentally innovative techniques can be employed. The Riverside Urban Environmental Center in Milwaukee utilizes a trailer that provides two classrooms for its visiting students.

Foundations and large charitable organizations are more likely to fund construction of physical structures rather than operations and staffing. In Dayton, Ohio, the Dayton–Montgomery County Park District has constructed a million-dollar underground nature center, near Germantown. Successful fund-raising for a significant structure may take from months to years. Therefore, some groups, like the Riverview Nature Center in Kerrville, Texas, gathered enough support from local citizens to actually borrow money and fund their own building. As your group gathers momentum, you never know what kind of opportunities will emerge.

**WORD TO THE WISE**

**Bird seed that is permitted to become wet and moldy can make birds sick. The acid from black oil sunflower seed remnants can kill grass and lawn areas. Animal feeding can also upset the natural balance in certain areas in dramatic ways, so consult with experts regarding placement, food choices, and consequences to the environment as you plan such facilities. (See Appendix A: Organizations, National Bird Feeding Society, National Audubon Society, and the American Birding Association.)**

## OUTDOOR EXHIBITS

Interpretive signs, tangible cultural artifacts, agricultural or reclamation demonstrations, audio exhibits, viewing blinds for observing wildlife, kiosks with words and pictures—all can help orient and sensitize visitors to their environment. Bird and animal feeding stations can be of tremendous popular appeal but must be planned with knowledge.

Other outdoor exhibits include xeriscape gardens, wildscape or backyard habitat demonstration areas, pay-for-view binoculars, overlook or vista viewing stations, board-walks, wetland overlooks, viewing towers, and prairie dog town interpretive areas. Remember that the outdoor exhibit should not detract from the natural beauty of the area.

**Right: Pine Jog Executive Director Pat Welch uses an outdoor informational kiosk for visitor orientation. Below: Observation post for a "harvester" ant colony.**

**A tree stump imported from a local construction site that designates local historical mileposts on growth rings, along with global population statistics.**

## OUTDOOR STAGES, THEATERS, AND INTERPRETIVE CIRCLES

A great variety of facilities have been designed for public presentations. From a circle of large landscaping boulders or tree stumps to log benches or expensive outdoor stadium seating—the public needs to be relatively comfortable. Folding chairs can work.

The more versatile your facility is, the greater the variety of programs you can offer: naturalist presentations, slide shows, concerts, puppet shows, plays, community meetings, and demonstrations with plants, animals, tools, or ideas.

## RECYCLING AND/OR COMPOSTING CENTERS

Some centers provide recycling facilities for the public. However, this is a large commitment of time, space, and resources. Recycling can be introduced to a community by a nature center, but the large scope of a community-wide program is best addressed by local government. Composting organic materials can provide needed rich soil additives, and demonstrate to home owners some ecologically sound methods of dealing with lawn and garden refuse.

**An outdoor interpretive circle makes the visitor comfortable, so that the interpretive message can be delivered.**

## LIVE ANIMAL ENCLOSURES

Keeping wild animals requires top-quality accommodations, permits, expertise, and an ongoing budget for feed, staff, veterinary care, and upkeep. Check with state and local authorities regarding ordinances and permits required. Also, understand that a large number of nature lovers have problems with captured and incarcerated wild animals. A wild animal may have more trouble adjusting to captivity than humans would. However, wild-animal rehabilitators do come across animals that cannot be returned to the wild, such as declawed cougars or "tamed" animals that no longer fear humans. These animals may be candidates for assuming the role of "ambassadors of goodwill" for their species by enabling the public to have close contact, engendering sympathetic understanding of the plight of wild animals. Domesticated animals often can adapt to captivity more easily and provide a more friendly reaction to visitors. Turtle enclosures that permit touching, gerbil habitats that enable the animals to burrow, rabbit hutches with "runs," small aquariums with local species, reptile habitats, and pigeons at large—all can be simple, inexpensive, and very popular.

Observation beehives are great attractions, demonstrating the miraculous ingenuity of bees and the fascinating activity of the colony (see Appendix A: Organizations, Drapers Super Bee Apiaries, Inc.).

**"Archie," the archangel pigeon, provided the wonder of an up-close visit.**

## WILDLIFE REHABILITATION FACILITIES

Check around for a wild-animal rehabilitator. A partnership would benefit both the nature center and the rehabilitator. Your organization may be able to provide facilities that rehabilitators need, and your nature center could benefit from the public's attraction to live animals. However, this can be a huge commitment of time and energy, and rehab centers can be overwhelmed by public demand for assistance (see Appendix A: Organizations, National Wildlife Rehabilitation Association).

## GREENHOUSES AND GARDENS

Your facility can help connect people with the plant world with hands-on gardening experiences, or you may wish to demonstrate how to propagate native species. Community gardens provide gardening space to your neighbors and can nourish participants in a number of ways. (See Appendix B: Publications, *Community Greening Review* or *Creating Community Gardens.*) Organizations such as the American Horticultural Society, American Horticultural Therapy Association, and the National Council of State Garden Clubs can provide valuable information on gardening projects.

## FARMERS MARKETS

By providing local farmers a parking lot in which they can sell fresh fruits and vegetables on a Saturday morning, you encourage sustainable agriculture and promote public understanding. There is growing public awareness of health issues and our food supply, and locally grown organic produce is now in high demand. To succeed, the facility would need to be located in an area with enough public traffic to make it worthwhile for the farmers. This is a community-building activity not traditionally associated with nature centers, but it is certainly an option worth considering.

## WILDSCAPES OR BACKYARD HABITATS

More and more communities are recognizing the need to conserve water, plant native plants, and encourage wildlife around their dwellings. Such projects educate and can also be used to rehabilitate a disturbed area at the same time. The National Wildlife Federation has a well-developed Backyard Habitat program (see Appendix A).

## ALTERNATIVE ENERGY AND BUILDING SYSTEMS

By demonstrating solar panels, solar hot-water systems and cookers, wind-powered generators, composting toilets, cisterns, and other alternative energy systems, a facility can educate the public about conservation through technology. The small Ansonia Nature Center in Connecticut is planning a new facility that will demonstrate geothermal heating, photovoltaic generation of electricity, and solar hot-water heaters. The Riveredge Nature Center's 11,000-square-foot physical plant contains a geothermal heating system. The Ijams Nature Center in Knoxville, Tennessee, demonstrates the high-tech approach to "green architecture," using modern simplified building systems and minimal materials, while maximizing natural light, air quality, and energy conservation. This $4 million facility utilized oriented strand board and beaded polystyrene board for insulated structural panels, homasote wall board, cellulose insulation, insulated windows, metal stud construction, metal roof, low-VOC (volatile organic compound) waterborne paints and stains, recycled ceramic wall tile, a well-water heat pump, ceiling fans, an ambient lighting control system, and other energy-saving systems.

## FACILITIES FOR SPECIAL NEEDS POPULATIONS

Special needs populations seek contact with nature. With the passage of the Americans with Disabilities Act in July of 1990, nature centers are moving toward meeting the needs of persons with disabilities by removing architectural barriers and introducing interpretive programs designed to accommodate the physically or mentally challenged. Having at least a portion of an interpretive trail that is universally accessible is important. A variety of features can be used to enhance the experience of special needs groups, such as exhibits designed for mobility-impaired, hearing-impaired, or vision-impaired visitors. Contact local social service agencies to obtain information about the needs of these populations and the resources that can be helpful. Examples of helpful facilities include wheelchair-accessible bridges and boardwalks, barrier-free headquarters and restroom facilities, Braille signs, tactile animal models and relief maps, recorded interpretive programs that can be played on hand-held tape players, and sign language interpreters.

The best resource we have found for special needs groups is *Universal Access to Outdoor Recreation: A Design Guide* (see Appendix B). Expanding on the requirements of the Americans with Disabilities Act, this design guide provides a framework for determining the appropriate level of accessibility in a range of outdoor recreation settings and presents detailed guidelines for ensuring accessible paths, signs, restrooms, drinking fountains, picnic tables, tent pads, and much more (see Appendix A, The U.S. Access Board and The National Center on Accessibility).

The Brazos Bend State Park has developed a state-of-the-art accessible trail, the Creekfield Nature Trail (see Appendix A). Amanda Hughes of the Texas Parks and Wildlife Department recommends consulting with your community of special needs people *before* designing facilities. Meeting with local citizens who are wheelchair-bound, blind, hearing-impaired, mentally retarded, or elderly can provide crucial insight into how your facility can meet their actual needs, rather than relying on your own assumptions.

### OVERNIGHT LODGING

Some facilities provide the luxury of overnight lodging, making camping programs, adult retreats, seminars, and workshops possible. Some states require licensing for overnight camps, so check with local authorities.

Overnight lodging enables some nature centers to have residential programs of one to several weeks. This greatly expands the possibilities for programming experiences for visitors. The Great Smoky Mountains Institute at Tremont is a year-round environmental education center, established over twenty-five years ago as one of the first environmental education centers located inside a national park. Facilities include a large dormitory, an activity center with full-service dining hall, and large and small meeting rooms. Write GSMIT, 9275 Tremont Rd., Townsend, TN 37882. Other residential centers include Cayuga Nature Center in Ithaca, New York; Glen Helen Ecology Institute in Yellow Springs, Ohio; Goodwin Conservation Center in North Windham, Connecticut; Yosemite Institute in Yosemite National Park; Hunt Hill Nature Center and Audubon Sanctuary; Joy Outdoor Education Center in Clarksville, Ohio; the National Wildlife Federation's

**WORD TO THE WISE**

Some facilities are simple and inexpensive, like a homemade kiosk or an interpretive sign. Others can be quite extensive, like the five-thousand-volume natural history library at the Delaware Nature Society Ashland Nature Center in Hockessin, Delaware. As community involvement grows, your facilities will expand. The primary issue to remember is that people come to experience nature. Therefore the quest for more and better facilities should not overshadow the natural grandeur of your piece of wilderness. You can have too much "center" and not enough nature. Facilities created with an eye on aesthetics as well as education will enhance the experience for the visitor. Don't let visitors or facilities overpower an area. Let your facility options evolve as you learn about your community's interests, and the carrying capacity of your property. "When in doubt, leave it out."

*"By far the greatest damage we do to the Earth, and thus by far the greatest threat to our survival, comes from agriculture."*
—James Lovelock

Laurel Ridge Conservation Education Center; Treehaven in Tomahawk, Wisconsin; and Long Lake Conservation Center in Palisade, Minnesota.

## DEMONSTRATION FARMS

Working farms can demonstrate historical farming, or various modern alternative methods of agriculture. Teaching how people interact with nature to get food is a worthy goal for any nature center, particularly when emphasis is placed on sustainable agriculture. The Aullwood Audubon Nature Center and Farm is open throughout the year, and has developed extensive educational programming for its farm (see Appendix C: Nature Centers Surveyed).

## AQUARIUMS & UNDERWATER VIEWING AREAS

Visitors are always intrigued by a usually hidden view of nature. By viewing life in a pond, lake, river, or ocean from a window, visitors get a fish-eye-view, a popular though expensive attraction. The Energy and Marine Center in Port Richey, Florida, has eight specimen tanks and four floating docks to augment three classrooms and a natural history museum. The Balmorhea State Park in West Texas produced a subterranean viewing station for a restored marsh.

## ASTRONOMICAL OBSERVATORIES

Check with the nearest university or astronomical society—there is one in every major city. Local astronomers can give talks at your facility and perhaps even help you develop an observatory, if your atmospheric and financial conditions are favorable. The Fernbank Science Center is set in a 65-acre hardwood forest and includes botanical gardens, an electron microscope laboratory, a computer laboratory, a five-hundred-seat planetarium, and a 36-inch research telescope.

*"Teachers who return year after year indicate they are able to accomplish more with some students with one week in the mountains than they can the rest of the year."*
—Ken Voorhis,
Great Smoky Mountains Institute at Tremont

## CULTURAL HERITAGE CENTERS

Sometimes public support for a nature center project increases dramatically if it is linked with cultural heritage. An example is the Norskedalen Nature and Heritage Center in Coon Valley, Wisconsin. It has a combined mission of preserving and interpreting the natural history and cultural heritage of the area (see Appendix C: Nature Centers Surveyed).

## BOTANICAL CENTERS AND ARBORETA

A botanical garden captures and maintains living diversity, arranging plants according to habitat and scientific classification. Most cultivate plants from many different habitats, although native botanical gardens also exist. Arboreta are facilities that propagate and maintain trees of various species. Some nature centers have found that state parks and wildlife departments and forest services are interested in funding native arboreta at local nature centers, to encourage the public to plant and maintain native tree species. (See Appendix A, American Association of Botanical Gardens and Arboreta).

The Norskedalen Nature and Heritage Center, Inc., in Coon Valley, Wisconsin, recreates a local farm at the turn of the century.

# Chapter 5  Program Possibilities

*If you are thinking one year ahead, you plant rice.*
*If you are thinking 20 years ahead, you plant trees.*
*If you are thinking 100 years ahead, you educate people.*

— CHINESE PROVERB

THE PROGRAMS YOU DESIGN can generate life and excitement at your center. As citizens discover the natural world, and come to love and understand it, the future looks brighter. When a community comes together to work for the common good, reaching for resources to create a place of beauty and pride, it enriches itself. Learning about nature is fun, practical, and important. An educated community can make good decisions about managing its environment. The tourism dollars are also of real value, but the relationships and good times with neighbors create the *experience* of community—finding common ground with neighbors of all backgrounds and persuasions. This is where your creativity can shine, and become contagious.

There are precious few community activities that can appeal to all ages, all religious perspectives, all political points of view, and all income levels. A native plant sale, an animal appreciation demonstration, a wildflower workshop, a composting class, astronomy programs, a xeriscape conference—all cut across the usual boundaries and enable strangers to meet with a common purpose: the appreciation of nature.

## INTERPRETIVE STRATEGIES

Factual information is important, but the overall philosophy of a nature center will determine what information is presented and why. An interpretive strategy is an educational approach designed to further the mission of the nature

**Fun creates the passion to learn. David McKelvey, local naturalist, works his magic with his audience.**

center. If the mission is to instill in visitors an ethic of conservation, then the interpretive strategy will attempt to evoke an intellectual and emotional response in the visitor that will foster conservationism. Exhibits and programs should have at their core a common thread of *attitude.* In this way each nature center develops its uniqueness. For example, we have developed a buffalo interpretive display at our nature center. Local names and land features are used to arouse interest. It is an example of an interpretive exhibit designed for our specific audience in our particular community.

This buffalo theme can be continued through sales at our gift shop of buffalo puppets, buffalo stuffed toys, T-shirts, and books that tell the buffalo's story. We give thank-you wooden buffalo nickels to donors and volunteers. For us, the buffalo represents our interpretive message, that we CAN do something to conserve our natural resources.

The real fun of nature center development is in the creation of programs that connect people and nature. The most valuable resource we have found for interpretive strategies is *The Interpreter's Guidebook: Techniques for Programs and Presentations.* Entries include planning, interpretive talks, slide shows, creative techniques, trail techniques, spontaneous interpretation, interpretation for children, and gaining feedback. Being one of several publications in the University of Wisconsin's *Interpreter's Handbook Series,* the book is rich with illustrations and helpful details.

# Cibolo Means Buffalo

Cibolo is a Native American word for Buffalo, a great beast that once roamed these hills and drank from the waters of the Cibolo Creek. The buffalo, or American Bison, was the primary food source for the Tonkawas, the natives of this area.

No animal is more symbolic of the plight of nature at the hands of humanity than the American Bison. In 1800, about 30 million still thundered over the western plains. Native Americans hunted buffalo for food, clothing, shelter, and tools, and celebrated its spirit. In the Lakota tradition the lesson of the Buffalo is that *abundance* is present when all relations are honored as sacred, and when gratitude is expressed to every living part of creation. By 1889 abundance was gone. Only 551 buffalo could be found alive in North America, owing to the wasteful slaughter by settlers.

As the buffalo declined, so did habitat for wildlife all over the country. Our local landscape suffered the same fate. In the 1830s settlers reported seeing buffalo near the Cibolo by the hundreds. Settlers had to wait for three days at one river crossing while a giant herd of buffalo rested and crossed. By 1849 they were gone, and other species were fast disappearing. In 1849 Judge English, of Bonham, boasted that he had killed sixty panthers in one season. In 1854 it was reported that "there was still, at a spot near Currie's Creek [in present Kendall County], a man who made his livelihood by hunting. He kept a pack of trained hounds, and had killed 60 bears in the course of two years." By 1875, there were almost no cypress trees left on the Guadalupe River, due to logging. Grazing and farming took the vast majority of the natural habitats of Texas, while the human population exploded in the cities and towns.

In spite of all the devastation that the buffalo has come to represent, it is also a symbol of hope. Through the heroic efforts of William Temple Hornady and other early conservationists, game laws and protective measures were created to enable the surviving bison to live and multiply, rather than face extinction. The first modern breeding herd was started by Walking Coyote, a young Pend d'Oreille Native American, in 1872. (See *The Buffalo,* by Francis Haines.) By 1950, conservation efforts had helped the population of bison recover to 25,000. Today, there are over 200,000 in North America.

Conservationists have enabled the buffalo to thrive once more. The buffalo reminds us that individual effort can make a difference, and that a small group of people can do monumental conservation work. And, if you would like to learn how you could help nature on a local level, talk to one of our staff or volunteers at the Cibolo Nature Center.

## INTERPRETIVE STRATEGIES

- Trail walks and encounters
- Outdoor signs and exhibits
- Indoor exhibits, discovery rooms, discovery boxes
- Talks and demonstrations by naturalists, historians, and docents
- Slide shows, movies, multimedia events
- Theatrical presentations, puppet shows, concerts
- School curricula
- Live animal demonstrations
- Animal rehabilitation programs
- Tree-planting ceremonies, native plant workshops
- Gardening programs and projects
- Xeriscaping programs
- Storytelling programs
- Experiential events
- Service projects

## CREATIVE PROGRAMS AROUND THE COUNTRY

In surveying nature centers around the country, we were struck by the variety of programs available, and the creativity of local groups. This section will outline a variety of programs being offered, and the activities that help vitalize local communities. Included are the fees charged (when available). We will also explore the current possibilities regarding electronic networking, web sites, and "natural paths" on the information highway. We hope to demonstrate the invigorating quality of such programs, and facilitate communication between nature centers. Our survey focused on members of the Association of Nature Center Administrators and a few other selected centers.

A wide breadth of programs is being presented throughout the country. There are programs for preschoolers, families, teenagers, adults, seniors, special interest groups, special needs populations, and schools. School programs can be highly developed sequences designed in collaboration with local school districts. School programs range from one or several hours in duration, to over-nighters or weekend retreats. Outreach programs travel to the schools, and teacher workshops provide instructors with in-service training. Study units have been developed and presented as Environmental Education Contract Programs in many nature centers, such as the Chattahoochee Nature Center in Roswell, Georgia. The Delaware Nature Society alone has over three hundred titles in its repertoire.

Several programs stood out as examples of creativity and resourcefulness. The following descriptions of these outstanding programs are derived from the promotional materials of the sponsoring centers. For more information from specific nature centers, see Appendix C: Nature Centers Surveyed.

### Birthday Parties

Theodore Roosevelt Sanctuary: We offer educational and fun birthday parties with live animals and a walk here at the sanctuary or at your home. The party programs are forty-five minutes long, and you can use the sanctuary for another forty-five minutes. Birthday parties cost $100 for families of members of TRS. Programs can be held at your home with an hour of the sanctuary for an additional $25 fee.

### Burn School

Indian Creek Nature Center: Learn why and how to safely burn grasslands and woodlands to destroy invasive non-native plants, enhance oak reproduction, and establish prairie. Weather permitting, participants will help conduct a prescribed burn in the grassland and woodland. Fee is $3 for members and $5 for nonmembers.

### Celebrate Trees!

Fontenelle Forest Nature Center: This unique auditorium presentation, brought by the Fontenelle Forest Association to your school, focuses on the importance of trees, from wood products to the oxygen they produce. This 45-minute program is offered to schools between January and March. Then, in the spring, an oak tree will be provided free to students to plant at your school in celebration of Earth Day. Cost: $50. The tree is provided through a grant from the "Celebrate Trees" program, sponsored by the Papio-Missouri River Natural Resources District and KETV.

## Close Encounter of the Science Kind

Nature Discovery Center: Students from area schools incorporate the scientific method and a hands-on exploration of indoor Discovery Rooms. They develop a hypothesis, go into the park and observe wildlife, record their observations, and make a conclusion. Fee: $2 per person.

## Eco-Explorers

Stevens Nature Center: Hands-on workshops allow kids the chance to explore various aspects of natural history of the past and present through games, projects, and field activities. Parents drop off their children at the nature center for "Botany Basics," "Rock-o-Hemlock," "Recycling Revue," "Water Wonders," and other programs.

## Enchanted Forest Halloween Party

Aullwood Audubon Center and Farm: Meet animal characters who have exciting stories to tell. The animals are friendly and express concern that the visitors to their special enchanted woods understand that they have important roles to play in their ecosystems. After the walk, participants can hold their Halloween party at the center's farm. Popcorn and cider are provided. A $4 fee for adults and children is required.

Flat Rock Brook Nature Center: Environmental Study in Your Classroom—"It's a wild life for wildlife!" Environmental topics are brought into local school classrooms, introducing students to live examples of wildlife—snakes, a tree frog, tortoises, and a hawk—and the physical and behavioral adaptations which help these animals survive in the wild. Basic ecological principles and local environmental concerns are addressed. Cost: $75 per class.

## Flights of Fancy

Stoney Kill Environmental Education Center: The theme of the Eighteenth Annual Harvest Festival at Stoney Kill Farm in Wappingers Falls, New York. Regular features include: live animals, open barn, hayrides, live music, and performances. Living history at the Washington house, candle dipping, food, pumpkin and face painting, raffles, and more. Admission: $3/adult—children 12 and under free (Stony Kill Foundation members $2/adult).

### Forest/River Ecology

Chattahoochee Nature Center: Guided Walk, Grade Level: Third–Eighth. A study of the ecology of the forest or the river will be the focus of this program. Students will explore these communities and learn of the human impact on these areas. Students $3, Adults $2.

### Habitat, Habitat, Have to Have a Habitat

Bear Creek Nature Center: Vital requirements for animals and plants are presented. Indoor activities include a puppet show and sing-along. Then students take to the trails as "Habitat Detectives" and investigate the variety of habitats at the nature center. The program includes a teachers packet with pre and post activities for students in a classroom setting.

### Honey Harvest Festival

Oregon Ridge Nature Center: The Fifteenth Annual Maryland Honey Harvest Festival features beehive demos, re-enactments of the "honey hunter," honey extraction, candle dipping, mead making (honey wine), and for children, a live bee beard demonstration, puppet shows, face painting, and hay wagon rides. Live music, food, and honey items for sale.

### Kids Can Compost

Ijams Nature Center: By analyzing a traveling trash can, students discover that up to 25 percent of our waste can be turned into "black gold." Students learn the five basic requirements of composting by building their very own wire compost bin. Fee: $3 per student, $30 minimum per group for a two-hour program, or $6 per student for a four-hour program.

### Life in the Underworld

Anita Purves Nature Center: Discover life in the underworld—under rocks, logs, and leaf litter! Children use magnifying lenses to meet the critters of the forest floor with the help of fingerplays, dramatics, and songs. Fee: $1.25, with a minimum of $15 per group.

### Maple Sugaring

Teastown Lake Reservation: Rent a bucket! Sap-collecting buckets are tagged with visitors' names, and locations are mapped for easy retrieval. During sugaring season visitors can watch the sap make its journey from the bucket to the sugar house, becoming delicious maple syrup. At the end of the season, they receive an 8-oz. bottle of grade A maple syrup and two tickets to the annual pancake brunch. Fee is $30.

### Mother Nature, Mom & Me; and Babes in the Woods

Piney Run and Bear Branch Nature Center: Programs for 4 to 5 year olds and 2 ½ to 3 year olds, respectively. Children and parents discover nature through a variety of hands-on activities and outdoor fun. Classes meet once a month for three months. Fee: $8 for member child, and $19 for nonmember child.

### Native American Life-styles Workshop

Weinburg Nature Center: "Interested in learning about our local heritage? How the native people lived? How they hunted, gathered, and stored food? Their mode of transportation, their life-styles in day-to-day living before European contact? Our group will meet once a week and learn about Native culture and life-styles of the Northeast Woodland Native Americans. Be part of the construction of the components of a Native American village from wigwam building to dugout canoes; from stretch racks to flintknapping stone tools and spear points." Limited to 12–18 participants, fourth-grade students through adults. Fee: free; program supported by a grant from the Irving Sloan Foundation through the Liz Claiborne and Arthur Ortenberg Foundation.

### Ojibwe Storyteller, Anne Dunn

Deep Portage Conservation Reserve: Ojibwe grandmother Anne Dunn has walked many paths. Her mother, father, and grandmother were all storytellers. She enjoys telling stories with unexpected heroes to people of all ages. She often speaks of children and small animals who perform heroic deeds. Part of the Indian Culture Saturday Program.

### Schoolyard Discovery Walk

Jamestown Audubon Nature Center: Audubon staff help teachers develop the ability to do discovery walks at their school sites. Fee: determined on an individual basis.

### A Sense of Place

Glen Helen Nature Preserve: Many people feel a profound sense of place when considering Glen Helen Nature Preserve. The Glen offers a sense of peace and realization that cannot be found elsewhere. This fall the Glen Helen Thursday Evening Programs will explore "A Sense of Place," which will include the historical, the cultural, the geographical, and the ecological. It touches the heart, not just the head. It is about relationships, security, and peacefulness. This fall's programs will look at these connections, to understand our place, to explore how having a better sense of place can affect our lives. It will include the practical and maybe a little philosophical to help explore the spiritual connections between us and the earth—the place we ultimately share. The series will include local people providing their own thoughts and feelings on a sense of place, a tour of other local treasures that can aid in acquiring a sense of place, practical ideas for your own backyard, and a children's presentation.

### Sensing Nature

Norskedalen Nature and Heritage Center: Discover and explore the natural world and how each of us uses our five wondrous senses, and how various animals of the wild use their senses similarly. Smell the pine needles, feel the sunshine (or the drizzle), touch the moss on a rock, hear the call of a red-tailed hawk or the song of a male cardinal, see the blue of the sky or the hue of the fall trees in full color. A blindfold hike enhances the use of the other four senses, and shows how much we depend on the one sense of sight. This is combined with a scavenger hunt, a wildlife puppet show, and a presentation with a live screech owl! Fee: $2 for children, $2.50 for adults (see page 68).

### "Strive to Survive" Senior Naturalist Summer Ecology Camp

Rye Nature Center: Students from fourth to sixth grade attend a week-long session from 10 AM–2 PM daily. "Imagine being stuck in the woods alone with no food and no one to help you. What do you do? How do you get home? By the time you finish this session you will be an expert trailblazer! Survival tactics are not only important, but are a blast to learn about when you're in RNC camp. The final challenge is a hike through the Nature Center at night." Fee: $110 for members, and $125 for nonmembers.

### That Doesn't Scare Me!

Austin Nature Center: Five- to eight-year-olds spend the morning investigating animals that have a reputation of being "creepy, yucky, or scary." Some of the animals they learn about are owls, bats, snakes, insects, toads, and mice. They will visit some of these animals up close. In the afternoon, they travel to a cavern to see what it is like inside a cave.

### Traditional Plant Knowledge

Rio Grande Nature Center: This series of classes will cover some of the knowledge and uses of wild plants from traditional Native American, Hispanic, and Northern European lore. Classes focus on plants grown and gathered for food, beverages, and seasonings, for dyes, and for art and household items, such as baskets and soap. A field trip to learn plant ecology in life zones from the river to the pines is included.

**Beauty finds its way into the heart of a beholder.**

### Walking Meditation Through Nature

Cincinnati Nature Center: Dianne Lobes, psychologist and licensed professional clinical counselor, will lead a short course on the art and science of meditation while walking on the trails. Wear comfortable loose clothing and bring a pillow or floor mat. Fee: $7 for members and $10 for nonmembers.

### Weeds in the Wilderness

Riverside Urban Environmental Center: Children learn about the plants that don't belong in the park. Participants explore how the strange plants got there, why they're a problem, and how to get rid of them. Through plant identification and hands-on stewardship practices (weeding), participants will help the nature center retain native plant species and do something positive for the environment. Fee: $1.50 per student, $30 group minimum.

### Whoo Gives a Hoot?

Friends of Beaver Creek Reserve: Owls are often referred to as the tigers of the bird world. A Beaver Creek Reserve naturalist shares some of the unique adaptations of these nighttime hunters. Shakespeare, the Reserve's resident barred owl, will also be present. If weather permits, a hooting session follows the discussion. Fee: $1.50 for members, and $2 for nonmembers.

### Wildlife Rehabilitation Seminar

Greenburgh Nature Center: For adults eighteen years and over interested in becoming licensed wildlife rehabilitators and caring for injured wildlife in their homes. Fee $10.

### The Wily Coyote

Greenway and Nature Center of Pueblo: Investigation into the behavior of this canid will provide children with greater appreciation of the predator roles of coyotes, wolves, and their own pet dogs. The class explores the ecology of coyotes and the myths and realities of their existence through slides and hands-on props. They will also learn how to understand coyote communication through recorded howls (warning, play, etc.) and body language. Children will leave, "howling" with greater appreciation for the world of canids. Fee: $35 per presentation to a maximum thirty-person group.

### TIPS FOR PUBLIC PRESENTATIONS

It is crucial that public presentations, as well as school programs, be top-quality, responding to the interests of the audience. Knowing your audience will create effective presentations. Children have entirely different needs and interests than adolescents or adults. Scout troops, nursing home residents, ladies' auxiliaries, garden clubs, home schoolers—all will have their unique characteristics. With a mixed group of many ages and interests, having something for everyone is the best way to go.

Although there are many fine resources for enhancing your presentations (such as *The Interpreter's Guidebook* mentioned earlier), trial and error is the way most of us learn. You are bound to "bomb" once in a while. Experiential learning molds good teachers. The experience of inadequate preparation or poor choice of materials is quite instructive. Some guest lecturers will be wonderful, and some will help you realize that you ought to screen presenters first.

Dr. Melissa Hill, of Last Chance Forever, a raptor rehabilitation organization, develops public awareness through thrilling programs.

Working with children presents a challenge. Children respond best to presentations that are interactive and fun. Children like to touch and move and laugh. Puppets and live animals are always hits. Discovery activities and games work. Lectures do not work. Children tire of anything, especially words. Working with children requires keeping a close eye on their energy level and knowing when to move on to the next activity. We recommend that you always have extra tricks up your sleeve, like magnifying glasses and aquatic nets.

You will also find that some parents may want to use your program for baby-sitting, and want to simply drop off their children. Be clear about your policies regarding the presence of parents. If you want to take charge of children on a nature walk for an afternoon, do you have emergency phone numbers or health forms? Do you want to take on children you do not know? Some children will be hyperactive or have behavior problems. These kids can have fun, too, and actually be at their best in nature. However, you will need at least one other adult with you if a problem arises and a child needs individual attention. Children who are too rambunctious to pay attention can often become your assistants with a puppet show or live animal demonstration. When children are acting up, a humorous hint to parents may help set the limits, or

Items of curiosity can be collected, identified, and then returned to their resting places.

**Joel Handley, puppeteer, uses puppets to deliver an interpretive message in a fun and memorable fashion.**

you may have to ask more directly for cooperation. If you are unfamiliar with child supervision, invite a few veteran teachers or youth workers to present a few programs and watch how they do it. Training can be offered for staff and volunteers. There is an art to capturing the imagination and cooperation of kids, and it is learnable.

We urge you to invent your own programs. Encourage your members and acquaintances to develop experimental programs. Find out what works. Make mistakes. And while we suggest that you seek out what works at other centers, remember that your community is unique, with its own particular sensitivities.

Let your community know about your programs, make posters, use public service announcements, describe events in your newsletter, and spread the word. Good presenters prepare for these events, and they deserve a good turnout.

## SPECIAL INTEREST CLUBS

There are many groups who would love the opportunity to meet and have programs at a nature center. The Wilderness Center of Wilmont, Ohio, provides services for many groups including those focused on astronomy, backpacking, birding, fly fishing, photography, and more.

Gordon Maupin, director of the Wilderness Center recommends saying yes to any group who expresses interest as long as their goals have a relationship with the nature center's mission. He recommends providing clubs with a space, including them in publicity, and helping them in any way possible. In return the clubs provide the center with good volunteers, good programs, activity, and oftentimes help with fundraising.

**Jan Wrede, education director, at the crawdad hole.**

### The Cibolo Nature Center School Education Program

When we started the Cibolo Wilderness Trail, we decided to focus on educating the children of our community. Children are eager to help nature when given half an ounce of encouragement. They have a huge influence on their parents, and they are the ones who will grow into teenagers who will either trash and vandalize your nature center or will become your faithful guardians.

In the beginning teachers expressed interest in field trips and in helping develop them. At first the field trips consisted of one or two classes and a teacher, with Carolyn leading the students through the trails. Our only goal was to develop appreciation and caring for nature. This was a good start, but it soon became too popular to manage. So we asked volunteers to help lead groups through the trails. We had science teachers, naturalists, biologists, wildlife specialists, educators, and more. But we realized that our program needed a director. And one showed up. Jan Wrede first volunteered to lead tours. Soon we realized Jan had great talent not only in leading groups, but also in seeing the greater picture of an "outdoor classroom." With a science degree, years of teaching experience, and tireless energy, she became our volunteer education director.

Meanwhile, Carolyn found a grant possibility for the education program. It offered $11,000 and would pay for curriculum development for the Outdoor Classroom. We got it, and Jan was hired by the Friends of the Cibolo Wilderness.

Jan went right to work. Her first task was to find out what the schools and teachers wanted. So she started having meetings. She soon discovered what the "essential elements" were, what goals individual teachers had, and what overall theme might work for each grade level. With this information she began developing activities for each grade. We borrowed

**The Trailblazer Club, with an entire pick-up load of trash from a river clean-up. A camp-out is next!**

from existing curricula, and changed and altered some approaches as needed. However, lessons for outdoor education must be reviewed and tried. An activity in a book can sound delightful and enlightening to you, but may completely bore the children.

With each field trip, we learned something new, and with each class we struggled to make the curriculum more complete. Trial and error, talking to other outdoor educators, and always looking for new ideas created a curriculum that works. After five years, we are still improving it.

In working with schools, we have found that "environmental education" is not necessarily what they are looking for. Most schools are put under great stress to meet certain state standards (essential elements) and test scores. Student competencies are being stressed. Fortunately, all disciplines can be addressed in the outdoor setting.

For example, visiting sixth graders experience different activities in different locations. They learn how foresters measure trees (math), they write poetry at the creek (language arts), and they do a team challenge exercise about working together to get their team across a "poison river," so that they

**Hands-on field biology teaches students to ask their own questions and seek their own answers.**

**Trail guide teaches the gentle art of butterfly netting for a monarch count.**

**Creative writing lesson.**

can get to "City Hall," symbolizing the need for teamwork to solve community problems (social studies). The message of conservation is always expressed for visiting students, but the activities are based on the visiting school's needs.

When a busload of children arrives, we gather to discuss the nature center, its purpose, and how to care for it. Then they divide into small groups and are off to their different stations. Trail guides take the groups through the planned activities.

Trail guides are volunteers, trained by the education director. A new guide has to learn how to present only one activity. He or she will present it five times to five groups who are rotating through the Trail. We have our training sessions at the beginning of each semester. Each guide learns about the mission of the Cibolo Nature Center and our teaching philosophy. Basically we try to teach respect for life, love of nature, and a caring attitude. Trail guides receive the lesson plan they will be presenting with information about each activity. There are also suggestions for dealing with the children. We cover rules, boundaries of behavior, having a sense of humor, dealing with fears, how to encourage questions, and a few tricks of the trade.

Our program started off small, but has grown very rapidly. We have won national awards and are on the cutting edge of educational thinking. The work is tiring but very rewarding. Many talented people from our community have come to the nature center in order to share their love of nature with children.

**The Senior Activity for the Good Earth (SAGE) Program provides outreach to nursing home residents. Cherry tomato harvest is a time to celebrate at any age.**

### The SAGE Program

Many nursing home residents and elderly persons feel isolated and unneeded, yet in reality have a great deal to offer in wisdom and experience. SAGE (Senior Activity for the Good Earth) provides meaningful recreation for interested nursing home residents and retired persons in a small-group setting, through gardening activities, visits to the Cibolo Nature Center, and the opportunity for the elderly to provide schoolchildren with plants and seedlings. The program is designed and facilitated by a social worker with experience in horticultural therapy for special needs populations. The Cibolo Nature Center provides volunteers. Meaningful work and the nurturing of life invigorates and stimulates health while inspiring youth to become active with the elderly community and environmental stewardship.

**WORDS TO THE WISE**

- **Don't be afraid to just jump in and create programs. You don't have to have all the information before you start; simply share your joy and enthusiasm.**

- **Get publicity. Take pictures and keep thank-you notes from adoring and grateful children.**

- **As you grow, find help and money.**

- **Don't try to entertain every group that comes looking for a tour. You can burn out and you can have too many visitors. Pace yourself according to the time and energy of your group.**

- **Charge a little something for tours. $2.00–$3.00 per child is common practice.**

- **Nurture your volunteers. Send them thank-you notes, have lunch together, involve them in the design of the curriculum.**

- **Borrow, borrow, and borrow. There is a mountain of good information available on education in the outdoors; use it.**

- **Hire a school education director. Don't expect anyone to work this hard—and be consistently unpaid—for very long. This person schedules tours, designs curriculum, meets with school administrators and teachers, trains and schedules guides, gathers materials, creates policy, and much, much more.**

- **Don't expect outdoor education to match with clock time. Give plenty of leeway between activities and be flexible. It all works out in the end, but if everyone is expecting clockwork precision, they will get stressed.**

*Friends of the Cibolo Wilderness News*
January 1996

Mrs. Helen Marquart is 93. She was born and raised in Bergheim, Texas, where her father founded the town, built the cotton gin and general store, and gave it the name that means "home in the hills." When she was a girl, a thirty-mile trip to San Antonio took three days, one to get there, one to get supplies, and one to ride back in the wagon.

Now Mrs. Marquart is a resident of a local nursing home, across the road from the Cibolo Wilderness Trail. She is a participant in the SAGE Program (Senior Activity for the Good Earth), and visits the Cibolo Nature Center regularly. Her stories and lively remembrances inspire us and broaden our horizons. She understands change and the importance of taking care of what we have. When she plants a burr oak acorn, she is reaching to the future and offering a gift of stewardship and example.

A seedling burr oak given to a classroom of children by Mrs. Marquart and the other ladies and gentlemen involved in the program may seem like a small deed in a world with so many problems. However, the message here is much greater than the deed. Each of us has something to offer, all of us can be of service to a better future:

> Dear SAGE:
> Thank you for the wonderful trees. I'll watch them grow forever.
> > Matt

> Dear SAGE:
> Thank you for the small trees. They're pretty dead right now, but I think
> > they'll be green soon. Thank you.
> > > Byron

When we started the SAGE program we thought we were giving something to the elderly; as it turns out, they have given much more to us. The Cibolo Nature Center is building community. We are a place where almost anyone can find a niche and feel needed. Children, individuals, families, and the elderly are coming together to dream of a good life, now and tomorrow. The volunteers, staff, and supporters are building bridges and finding the secret of true joy.

—Carolyn Chipman-Evans

### The SEED Program

The SEED Program was originated for adolescent patients at Charter Real Psychiatric Hospital in San Antonio. "Self-Esteem Through Ecological Dynamics" is a four-step process repeated throughout the year: (1) going to an inspirational place in nature, (2) planning a service project, (3) carrying out the project, and then (4) receiving recognition for it. Recognition takes the form of photographs for personal scrapbooks, ceremonies, and certificates.

Nature is the perfect place for young people who are having a hard time fitting into society. When children are neglected or abused, they often doubt their own ability to contribute to the world—to be worthwhile people. Those who do not excel in academics or sports often become the depressed or angry youth that cause great heartache in our communities. However, these same young people can find a meaningful place for themselves, regardless of age, diagnosis, intelligence, or special needs. Through environmental service activities more youngsters can assume a positive, nurturing role that builds self-esteem and good citizenship.

WE HAVE PROVIDED a number of sample programs to encourage you to research, borrow, and create. The program is your means of expressing your message. This is the way you bring people in touch with nature, help them learn, and foster more curiosity. Every program is an experiment, and you will be refining and changing programs as long as you care about your nature center.

### Tell us what you think!

Name of program: _____

Presenter: _____ Date: _____

How you heard about it: _____

_____

What did you get from this experience?

_____

_____

_____

How could the program be improved?

_____

_____

What kinds of programs would you like to attend in the future? _____

_____

_____

_____

Other comments: _____

_____

_____

_____

Name: _____

Address: _____

_____

Would you like membership or program information? _____

# Part Two

## HOW TO CREATE AND MAINTAIN A NATURE CENTER

**Many programs can be offered through local volunteer talent.**

# Chapter 6  Getting Started

*Never doubt that a small group of thoughtful committed citizens can change the world. Indeed, it's the only thing that ever has.*

— MARGARET MEAD

THE BEGINNING OF A NATURE CENTER is always in the heart of a visionary. Soon that vision spreads, and interest builds. The following chapter will discuss basic practical considerations for development of fledgling nature centers, as well as suggestions for joining an existing project. Don't get intimidated by our lists of suggestions. The journey is yours, and you can take it in your own way, at your own pace.

## EDUCATING YOURSELF

The most viable group for aiding fledgling nature centers with information today is the Association for Nature Center Administrators (ANCA), which was formed in 1988. This is a nonprofit organization dedicated to promoting leadership and quality management for the nature center profession. Their newsletter, as well as their Peer Consults, which are full-range consulting services for nature centers and other environmental education organizations, can prove invaluable. ANCA is a professional support, training, and networking group that is made up of approximately 100–125 nature center directors and other senior staff. Although private nonprofit nature centers are a particular focus of ANCA, the membership includes all categories of environmental learning centers: day-use, residential, government-operated, university affiliated, nationally affiliated, and so forth (see Appendix A: Organizations).

Tracy Kay, director of the Rye Nature Center, was instrumental in the creation of ANCA. He describes the creation of ANCA as a response to the desires of most professional administrators in the field: "ANCA was formed on the recommendation of an overwhelming majority of respondents to a nationwide market survey of over 800 nature center administrators."

*Directions,* ANCA's quarterly publication, provides members with information on administrative trends and provides a forum for exchanging ideas, sharing successes, and discussing problems and concerns. The organization conducts regional workshops and an annual summit meeting for its members. In addition, ANCA provides Peer Consults, using ANCA members from around the country. Through consultations ANCA also can provide assistance with long-range planning, mission statements, facility planning, land-use planning, board training, education programs, exhibits and interpretive trails, fundraising and fiscal management, and starting a nature center.

Corky McReynolds, associate professor of resource management at the College of Natural Resources at the University of Wisconsin, and director of the Treehaven field Station in Tomahawk, Wisconsin, has conducted considerable research in the area of leadership among environmental education administrators. He has written a number of articles in ANCA's *Directions* and has been developing resources for professional development, strategic planning, and facilitation of teams. A *Leadership Development Series* has been designed to enhance the skills and attributes of leaders in the natural resource/environmental education field, including courses in team building, facilitation skills, and leadership skills (see Appendix C: Nature Centers Surveyed, Treehaven field Station).

When the Cibolo Nature Center was being established, we did not know any experts, nor did we know about the existence of ANCA, so a lot of our efforts came down to reinventing the wheel. We had to gain our knowledge through trial and lots of error. We urge interested parties to contact ANCA, or nature centers near you, and *pick their brains.* Having attended an ANCA "Summit," we can say it is the friendliest group of fascinating, creative, and motivated professionals that we've ever met. Here are folks with imagination *and* organization, and a sense of purpose. ANCA board members and participants are deeply dedicated to their calling. Anyone

*"Leaders don't get followed, they get chased."*
—Corky McReynolds

serious about starting or running a nature center will have instant and generous access to consultation of the highest quality.

The University of Delaware's environmental institution management classes have been offered by the Delaware Nature Society for thirteen years, accepting a dozen or so students each year and focusing on the practical aspects of starting up and running an environmental center. For beginners, or professionals who can spare the time, the four-week Environmental Institution Management Course is a six-credit graduate course in which students learn about goal definition and long-range planning, conservation and preservation roles, programming, fund-raising, financial management and budgeting, staff and personnel policies, coordination of volunteers, publicity and marketing, publications, and legal considerations. Scholarships and low-cost housing are available. For busy professionals who are already operating institutions, the Professional Leadership Institute is a week-long course providing directors and administrators with insight and expertise in the key components of operating an environmental institution (see Appendix A: Organizations, Delaware Nature Society).

The most complete listing of nature centers is the *Directory of Natural Science Centers,* published by the Natural Science for Youth Foundation, with over twelve hundred entries (see Appendix B: Publications). Look up the centers nearest you and visit, asking lots of questions or even volunteering as an apprentice for a while.

### INTERNET RESOURCES

Search the electronic community for information. Surfing the internet and scanning for information can greatly reduce the number of mistakes you have to make in your own learning process. At the time of our survey, only a handful of nature centers listed e-mail addresses, but many were planning to hook up (see Appendix C: Nature Centers Surveyed). We expect that in short order, most large centers and many small ones will be accessible by electronic mail.

Because the world of computers and electronic information exchange are evolving so rapidly, all we can do at the time of publication is indicate the kinds of services we are aware of now. Asking for volunteer help in this area from an already outfitted acquaintance can often result in the ability to access a wide range of information without having to spend money.

### Activity Finder

A computerized system of natural resource activities cataloged from well-known national programs such as Project WILD and NatureScopes. Over 4,400 environmental and nature-related activities have been classified into corresponding categories. It uses an IBM or compatible computer with at least 3 MB of memory. $30 plus shipping.

*Contact:* Angela Higgs, Nature & Environmental Education Teacher, (804) 261-5984 or e-mail: ahiggsneet@aol.com.

### The EarthWeb Project

Provides hypertext-based link between environmental group memberships, students, researchers, government agencies, scientists, and engineers with environmental databases, statistics, projects, programs, and information from around the world. Users access EarthWeb completely free, but must be on the Internet. Through EarthWeb, users can access the EnviroLink Network, the largest environmental information provider in the world. Over 450,000 users in ninety-five countries make use of EnviroFreenet, EnviroGopher, and Enviro-Lists services.

*Contact:* Dan Hinckley, Executive Director, The EarthWeb Project, 204 Divide View Dr., Golden, CO 80403; voice/fax: (303) 642-7330; Internet: hinckley@netcom.com.

### EcoNet

An international, computer-based communication system committed to serving organizations and individuals who are working for environmental preservation and sustainability. The intent of EcoNet is information and collaboration, enhancing the effectiveness of all environmentally oriented programs. As of September 1996, EcoNet listed 141 organizations as members with materials available. The *Meta-Index of Non-profit Organizations* includes the *Philanthropy Related Links,* listing individual foundations and nonprofits on the Internet.

*Contact:* EcoNet, 18 De Boom Street, San Francisco, CA

94107; EcoNet@igc; http://www.econet.apc.org/econet/en.orgs.html.

### EnviroLink Library

Offers the following entries: Actions You Can Take, Education, Events, General Information, Government, Opinions, Organizations, and Publications.

*Contact:* http://envirolink.org/elib

### EcoLinking: Everyone's Guide to Online Environmental Information

By Don Ritter, Peachpit Press, Inc., 1992. A thorough listing of environmental forums and databases available on EcoNet, Fidonet, Bitnet, Usenet, Internet, America OnLine, CompuServe, Genie, the WELL, and commercial online research databases. Also explains basics of buying and installing a modem, and connecting with online services.

### The Institute of Museum Services

Source of information on deadlines, descriptions, and eligibility requirements for certain federal grant applications.

*Contact:* Institute of Museum Services, e-mail: imsinfo@ims.fed.us; World Wide Web: http://www.ims.fed.us.

### The Sierra Club Green Guide

By Andrew J. Feldman, Sierra Club Books, 1996. Includes over 12,000 "essential resources," including internet sites, bulletin board systems, and electronic databases.

### Web Sites

A search for environmental web sites using the Yahoo search engine (http://www.yahoo.com) yielded the "Amazing Environmental Organization WebDirectory" (http://www.web-directory.com), a page with links to areas of interest such as agriculture, animals, education, news and events, recycling, and science, to list only a few.

In addition, the World Wide Web is a wonderful tool to investigate resources for nonprofit organizations such as the American Fundraising Institute, Empower Web, HR Boardroom, the Internet Nonprofit Center, the Nonprofit Resources Catalog, and the Support Center for Nonprofit Management.

A nature center is a small business, although few have been started by people trained in business management. Most nature center administrators start out as naturalists and must learn about business on the job. Any training or experience in business would come in handy.

It should be noted that most people who have started nature centers have not been trained how to do it. They just did it. Most board members of highly successful centers have not had previous experience with nature centers. If you can afford the luxury of a University of Delaware Environmental Institution Management course, take it! If not, this book will at least provide the basics, and warn of the pitfalls that we have learned about.

## HOW TO JOIN AN EXISTING NATURE CENTER

If you already have a nature center in your vicinity, and are interested in helping it grow, then join its community and learn about its history. Talk to volunteers and board members. Scan the scrapbook. Ask to see the mission statement and master plan. Attend events or meetings. "How can I become a member?" will be music to the ears of staff or volunteers. Understand that most nature centers eagerly welcome new energy and ideas, and will want your involvement. For a small membership fee you have access to meetings, the newsletter, the events schedule, and the people that make the center go.

If you are interested in donating funds to help a nature center, there are numerous avenues. (See The Large Gift and the Four Rs of Fundraising in Chapter 10). Giving is what nature centers are all about, from volunteer efforts to community support and donations. The joy of nature center giving is truly powerful, because you can see the results of your giving in the landscape, in the busy lives of the wildlife, and in the eyes of visitors, young and old. Whatever the size of the donation, it is a lasting gift that sends a legacy of respect for the natural world into the future. Discuss your ideas with the director, board members, and volunteers, so that your dreams can meld with theirs in a way that furthers the mission of the organization.

What kind of involvement do nature centers want? It varies, but most centers have an ongoing need for new volunteers, new educational programs, new physical facilities, new funding sources, new board members, and new ideas. Talk to the director, or look at the wish list and volunteer sign-up sheet to learn what areas are of particular need. Here are some examples:

- Trail building
- Trail guide
- Education committee
- Kids' club
- Phone committee
- Membership and outreach
- Workday help/coordination
- Grant writing
- Publicity
- Administrative help
- Fund-raising
- Gift shop coordinator
- Nature center host
- Program presentation
- Maintenance

However, it is even more important to explore your own inventory of dreams and wishes, so that your contribution is truly an expression of you. For example, you may find yourself approaching your community's nature center with a concept never considered, such as adding a sustainable agriculture component to the nature center through acquiring an adjacent farm. You may have rehabilitated animals that can provide children with inspiring contact. You may have expertise in solar energy or native plant propagation. You may have property that you are considering as a donation to the nature center. (See Appendix B: Publications: *Preserving Family Lands: Essential Tax Strategies for the Landowner.*) Whatever notion strikes you, trust your intuition and follow through with dialogue. Whether the nature center is newly formed or decades old, the influx of new ideas and personalities provides the kind of momentum that keeps a nature center viable.

If you are interested in getting something new under way, avoid the pitfall of approaching your nature center with big ideas for *them* to carry out. Most nature centers are understaffed, with plenty of ideas and projects they are committed to. Coming with projects that *you* would like to execute will be more readily received. As your relationship with the organization grows, your ideas may indeed find additional support from the membership, and eventually from the board. Most funding for nature centers is budgeted well in advance, so do not expect the organization to have immediate funding available to help with your dream project, no matter how wonderful it may be.

As an example, imagine that you would like to see a solar hot water heater at your local nature center. Most likely your local nature center membership would agree with you. If you do not have the resources to fund such a project, you could still be instrumental in helping the idea bear fruit. Research solar hot water heaters, find local resources, locate examples of such projects at other nature centers or environmental education programs, and construct a proposal. If the proposal includes a realistic budget and an explanation of the benefits of such a project, the nature center may well adopt this proposal as part of its wish list, or part of a larger proposal for funds from a major donor. If you have expertise in installing solar systems, so much the better. A donor would appreciate the advantage of the in-kind contribution you could offer.

If you are joining a nature center project, appreciate the complexity of the organization, its programs, membership, personnel, stage of development, policies, and procedures. With such understanding, your involvement will build on the contributions that have gone before, rather than run into conflict. By being sensitive to the feelings of other volunteers, and what their contributions have been, you will avoid territorial problems. Members who have been working on a xeriscape garden for three years may not appreciate the lovely tree you want to plant, which will eventually shade out an area they have sown with wildflowers. The director or volunteer coordinator will know who should be consulted about your ideas.

If you are in the position of providing a financial contribution to a nature center, you should expect the organization to respond in a professional manner. A nonprofit organization will provide a letter of receipt that can be used for documenting the contribution for the IRS. If you would like additional tracking, such as a copy of the annual financial report, or a detailed accounting of how the moneys were spent, this can be arranged. If you want your funds earmarked for specific purposes, this can be accomplished with a letter of intent that accompanies your contribution. Funds can be given for capital improvements, such as new construction, or for operations of the center and its programs. You can also request recognition in whatever form might be helpful to you. Your participation will further the cause of conservation and provide you with good friends, good times, and good work.

**STARTING FROM SCRATCH: HOW TO SELECT A SITE**

If you want to start a nature center, the first question that is usually asked is "Where?" Your community may or may not be blessed with abundant sites for potential use as a nature center or greenbelt. The land should be as undeveloped as possible, with ample native flora and fauna. According to National Audubon's now out-of-print nature center manual (Joseph J. Shomon, *A Nature Center for Your Community*, National Audubon Society, 1969),

> the ideal nature center, then, is a representative sample of the natural landscape of a community, whatever the local environment may be, such as forest, prairie, tidelands, hill country—a part of wild America set aside and interpreted for the enjoyment and the edification of the people of a community. (p. 11)

Depending on your locale, a nature center will represent a habitat: rocky coast, native woodland, fields, hills, meadows, prairie, mountains, canyons, forest, hot springs, marshland, streams, rivers, swamps, ponds, lakes, or seashore. In the desert, rain and runoff go somewhere, and these arroyos are often quite suitable, since flora and fauna are rather abundant. Unspoiled arid land can also be beautiful. Some magical spots may have been abused and damaged, but they are there, wild and waiting. Disturbed land can be "reclaimed," and such projects are tremendously fulfilling to volunteers and communities.

Anyone can study a local watershed and civic plan to discover a location for a nature center. Note which areas are near creeks and ponds or other natural attractions. Lakes, sand dunes, bogs, hilltops, woods, marshes—choose a landscape that appeals to you personally.

The land you are attracted to will be owned by someone. It may be privately owned, in which case the local tax assessor can help you locate the owner. The land may belong to the city, the county, the state, or the federal government.

Each entity poses a different kind of hurdle to the grassroots pioneer. Obviously, many possible sites will not be available, or will be encumbered by restrictions or rules.

Land can be acquired or accessed through various conservation approaches, including land trusts, conservation easements, and many more. See *Private Options: Tools and Concepts for Land Conservation,* edited by Barbara Rusmone, and *Preserving Family Lands (Essential Tax Strategies for the Landowner),* by Stephen J. Small (listed in Appendix B).

The Federal Emergency Management Agency (FEMA) helps flood disaster victims by funding buyouts of floodplain land through state or local governments (a 75%–25% matching grant). All buildings and infrastructure are removed, and the deed is restricted so that the land is not used for human habitation but can be used for greenspace, parkland, or possibly a nature center. If you live in an area that has had flooding problems, you can research this option with local authorities.

Using your own property for a nature center can be an intriguing idea for the altruistic landowner. The idea of preserving personally owned land and providing educational programs there can be appealing. This can be done on a private basis, without losing any ownership of the property. However, private enterprises are not usually eligible for grants or public funding, or for tax exemptions. Your land can be deeded to a nonprofit organization, the board of directors being the decision-making body. The frequency of programs for the public would be up to your organization. As long as you are clearly providing a public service, and not just maintaining a tax shelter, you can do yourself and your community a favor.

Our experience has been that city and county land is locally controlled, and therefore more accessible to the grassroots activist. State and federal lands typically involve regulation by remote entities, but some nature centers have been created on these lands. Don't rule out private property. Many nature centers have been created with donated or purchased local property. Never underestimate the power of the dream of wild sanctuary!

Ask local naturalists, biology teachers, farmers, or ranchers. They often know instinctively where the wild places are. Scout leaders and youth group leaders often use such areas

*Friends of the Cibolo Wilderness Trail News*

January 1992

This is the year that our prairie grass was as high as a horse's eye. This is history relived . . . tales remembered from our ancestors, told of prairies, seas of shimmering grass, of the graceful switch grass brushing against the saddle . . . children hiding in the curtains of the prairie, deer vanishing before your very eyes. Nothing before could prepare the pioneers for this experience. This was the year we were able to travel back to a day when we were innocent and nature was free.

Today, we preserve a bit of this freedom; we allow nature to show us the way. And we are rewarded. Gifts of towering prairie grass, flocks of robins returning, monarchs finding safe haven on their journey—these show us we are indeed doing the right thing.

This is the season for patience. Like gardeners planting seeds in the garden, we have been planning, planting and waiting too. As you know, we have our nature center building donated and ready to go. We have been very fortunate to have much community support and we are ready to move, but our grant from Texas Parks and Wildlife will require some delay for a site survey.

Meanwhile we will walk, we will dream, and continue to plant seeds of hope and caring and preservation. These seeds will grow, and we will once again see the rewards of our efforts.

—Carolyn Chipman-Evans

Often local children are aware of wonderful spots that may be prospective greenbelts or nature center sites.

Precious friendships often have their beginnings as community members gather to protect a natural sanctuary.

already. Talk to junior high school boys and girls about where they like to go. When they go "play in the ditch," or explore the woods, or go fishing along the creek, they may actually be blazing the trail for the whole community. Some existing park may need a "Friends" organization to help it develop into a nature center.

Your site may have all the beauty and magic in the world but have complications, such as safety hazards, problems of regulation of use, ecological disturbances, noise pollution, visual disturbances, conflicting use issues, legal problems, poorly drained areas, maintenance problems, access difficulties, parking problems, or other conditions to give you pause. So, by all means, *Pause!* Your first site consideration may have spawned the dream, but it may not need to be the final spot you choose. It needs to be right. It needs to work. Seek local consultation.

## BUILDING YOUR CORE GROUP

Once you are interested in saving a piece of ground, the dream of a nature center becomes contagious. Friends and acquaintances start hearing you talk about it. You will need to show them what you're talking about. The photographs in this book and many sources mentioned in Appendix A can help inspire potential collaborators. Understand that you cannot do this thing alone, although you may be the long-term driving force behind it. You will need help—all kinds of help. The greatest support you will need will be that small, steady group of like-minded folks who share the dream and are willing to throw some of their energy into the ring.

Support can be built through volunteer work parties, creek cleanups, bird house projects, trail construction, and other good deeds. Getting groups involved in outdoor physical activity is a primary way to develop interest, help individuals bond, and gather momentum for the dream. Fun is the vital component in attracting and maintaining supporters and volunteers.

The inspiration for a nature center can seemingly come out of the blue. In August of 1967, Olivia Dodge invited neighbors on a tractor-wagon ride through some Minnesota acreage she had fallen in love with and purchased. One of the riders, Carver County naturalist Edith Herman, suggested a nature center. The Thomas Irvine Dodge Foundation was incorpo-

**WORD TO THE WISE**

**Start a scrapbook in the early stages of your project, with photos of places and activities, newspaper articles, newsletters—anything that helps document your progress. This scrapbook is an invaluable tool in recruiting new volunteers, inspiring donors, and uniting your group. Bring your camera to all events and take pictures of people in nature, or people working as your project develops.**

rated by September. The Thomas Irvine Dodge Nature Center now encompasses three hundred acres, serves 34,500 children annually, and operates on an annual budget of $700,000.

You may be the catalyst, but the core group is the primordial soup of the project. You need to trust these people. You do not want impulsive or antagonistic individuals to alienate the community before you even get started. Remember to turn no one away, but be extremely careful about who you grant permission to represent the group. When someone comes up with a great idea, sleep on it. Your group needs to talk, share dreams, and investigate possibilities for a while, before you are ready to approach authorities and start making plans. If you are joining an organization at this point, check out your ideas with the rest of the group, so you can work in unison.

As your trusted core group grows, add some experts—folks who are naturalists and seem to be like-minded. It's great if you have access to a few people with special skills, such as a teacher, an accountant, an attorney, a builder, a landscape architect, or a gardener. Be willing to take your support where you can find it.

You may want to attract a few community leaders, but be careful. In any community, some leaders may have powerful adversaries from past political battles. If you are not intimately familiar with local politics, wait a while before including local politicians. Keep your sense of humor, and enter into such relationships with the long-term view. Whatever your attitude is about politicians, understand that most local leaders are paid little for their efforts and are often unappreciated and criticized. When they disagree, stay friendly. Leaders learn that it is safest to say no first, then wait and see. Your steadfast commitment to the cause will impress them eventually. Politicians tend to pay more attention to voters from their districts, so make sure that your group includes some of their constituents.

**WORD TO THE WISE**

A sign-in book, with space for name, address, and phone number, can be an invaluable tool for taking full advantage of the support you generate. You can use it at meetings or service activities to keep a record of who showed up and how to contact them. This documents public interest and becomes a database for your newsletter and membership drive. When you finally have a piece of ground or a facility to work with, the sign-in book is your record of usage. Statistics gathered from these sign-ins are used to justify funding levels and new projects. Shout out: "Everyone, please sign in! It helps us keep our programs going!"

# Chapter 7  Gathering Support

*We need the tonic of wildness . . .*

— HENRY DAVID THOREAU, *WALDEN*

HOW CAN YOU SELL THE IDEA of a nature center to a community? Answer: one person at a time. While everyone can benefit from a nature center, not everyone realizes it. Everyone is also a potential benefactor of the nature center, in terms of volunteer time, donations, or wisdom. Some persons may not see the need for conservation or environmental education but are interested in recreational facilities for their community. Some may simply like the idea of preserving a beautiful area. Understanding the interests of local citizens will help you shape your "sales pitch." Some folks will want to know, "What's in it for me?" It depends on *their* point of view.

## LOCAL RESIDENTS

People like nature. Citizens appreciate a peaceful place to walk. To judge from a 1995 survey of real estate agents, public safety officers, and home buyers, "trails are [seen as] an amenity to the neighborhoods around them; . . . increase the desirability of property; and provide [recreational] space for young children and adults of all ages." (See Appendix B: Publications, *The Effect of Greenways on Property Values and Public Safety.*) Just about everyone can find fascination and peace on a walk in the wild.

Taxpayers appreciate the economy of nature centers, which can be the most inexpensive recreational projects a community can develop. Compared with the costs of swimming pools, tennis courts, golf courses, and ball fields, nature centers are economical and low-maintenance, and yet they can appeal to every segment of the population. Land that makes for a good nature center is often not even appropriate for development. Watersheds, such as creek areas, wetlands, and marshes, are often susceptible to flooding. These areas are often regarded with little interest by developers, may be good candidates for nature centers, and may be donated by those developers for tax and public relations benefits.

---

*M*oment for a Working Person

Imagine . . . Your day has become difficult, hectic, and unyielding. You feel like you need a vacation. So you take one. Not a week, or even a weekend. Just an escape to the nature trail that's five or ten minutes away. Just a few minutes of fresh air, trees, and wildness. You begin to feel rejuvenated, as you take in the natural wonder of this small oasis, this secret garden planted and nurtured by Mother Nature herself. You watch local birds busily attending to their chores, while lizards soak up solar energy. As you leave your sanctuary, you vow to "do this more often."

---

**Nature center activities plant memories for families.**

### FAMILIES

As modern life separates families more and more, with fewer moments of beauty and connectedness, a saunter together through nature can do more than a dozen family therapy sessions. Let your child lead you on a walk through nature one day, and you will see life through new eyes.

Families go to parks and open spaces so that their children can be children again. Children are at their best outdoors. Without the confusion of commercialism, and the bombardment of electronic stimulation, children can get in touch with the simple joys of life, and so can parents. Thoreau had it right: "We should escape to the wild as often as possible, to save ourselves from civilization."

## Moments in the Lives of Two Fourth-Grade Students

*When I went to the Cibolo wilderness trail I herd birds singing in the forest and the creek racing against the trees. In the prairy was the beuteful prairy grass tall and thin and higher than your head. at the marsh the water was cold and calm. no crashing no splashing, no noise of the water. just like a feather planted in the mud with no wind to blow it or make it fall.*

*It was fun way to learn about the Trail. The trees were shadow-like near the mist. The pure water glided across my finger. The clay was shimmery and very slick. The high grass grew to tickle my knees. The birds sang like a flute, high and sharp. The mud stayed on my shoe until we got to the school. Like a breath, it was over so quickly.*

oment for a Family

In a culture that is seeking clarification in distinguishing the real from the unreal—a nature center, our nature center:

- puts our hands to work tending our environment,
- connects our family emotionally to all we see and feel,
- rivets our minds to inquire regarding facts and science and truth,
- and doing so all while in the midst of beauty.

—David Washington Pipes IV
Nature center volunteer and
father of children aged 4, 5, and 10

### CHILDREN

How many childhood memories revolve around the old swimming hole, the hiking trail, the ditch, the river? How many of us prize these precious moments in nature, these intermissions between the acts of our lives? Cross-culturally, children are fascinated by animals and plants. From introducing urban and rural children to natural settings, it has become clear to us that children are inherently open to learning in natural settings, excited about the mysteries of life, curious about the individual lives and relationships in the environment. Children want to be outside, even in decayed inner-city areas with few trees or green spaces. They need the life-giving presence of the natural setting.

### TEACHERS

Teachers consistently report renewed enthusiasm in their students following nature center experiences. In 1895 Sarah L. Arnold of the National Education Association discussed outdoor educational programs: "The power of observation is developed; thought power is quickened; the child grows in accuracy of expression, he/she gains knowledge of fundamental facts of science; becomes interested in his environment." (See Appendix B: Publications, *Proceedings of the National Education Association.*)

In preparing the next generation for their future, teachers realize that their students will need a strong concern for their environment. The health of future families will depend on the health of our planet, and vice versa. Teaching farsighted thinking is perhaps the most important challenge of teaching.

Environmental conservation can be woven into any school curriculum. While students are learning about math, language, and history, they can also be developing an appreciation of the local ecology. Young people who are given the opportunity to enjoy and understand nature will be more responsible citizens tomorrow. Students who participate in community service activities in a public natural area are less likely to vandalize it, and—in our experience—more likely to actually protect it.

---

*M*oment: Some Students from the Inner City

A group of fourth graders from an inner-city elementary school came to visit the Cibolo Wilderness Trail. These children grew up in one of San Antonio's toughest neighborhoods, far removed from nature and the peace and quiet of the countryside. As I led my small group down to the creek, I pointed to the water and asked if anyone knew what that was. I expected some one to shout out, "Cibolo Creek!"—instead one bright-eyed young man shouted, "Freedom!"

---

## CHAMBERS OF COMMERCE AND LOCAL BUSINESSES

Nature centers bring their communities good publicity, which is always good for business. Local papers are always

**Native plant growers, crafts people, and artists sell their wares, network, and support their local nature center at the Mostly Native Plant Sale, an annual fundraiser for the Cibolo Nature Center.**

looking for stories that present a positive community image. Programs can be advertised at no charge through public service announcements and local newspapers. The more tourists you bring to your community, the more valuable the nature center will become.

Wildlife watchers represent 39 percent of the U.S. population and spend their money to visit natural attractions of many localities. Overall, about 40 percent of their expenses are trip-related, including meals, motel, gas, and other travel costs. Local communities will capture an average of $50 per day for each wildlife-watching visitor. According to the U.S. Fish and Wildlife Service, in 1993 approximately 76.1 million wildlife watchers spent $18 billion in the United States. In 1987 283 million visitors went to one of our 350 national parks. In

short, nature centers are good for local business. (See Appendix B: Publications, *Wildlife Planning for Tourism Workbook*.)

In the Rockport–Fulton area of Texas, public fascination with the whooping crane brings in more than $5 million each year. The Rockport Chamber of Commerce reports that its community gained over $1 million in revenues from the 1994 Hummer/Bird Celebration. In 1991 Texans alone spent $1 billion on food, lodging, and expenses for various wildlife appreciation activities. All over the country, communities are finding that ecotourism is a clean and profitable industry.

*M*oment in the
"Mostly Native Plant Sale and Festival"

Each April the Friends of the Cibolo Wilderness have a fund-raiser that brings an ever increasing number of visitors.

The "Mostly Native Plant Sale and Festival" features goods from small and large nurseries from the area, as well as other garden and nature-related items. The day starts off with a radio garden show featured by a San Antonio station, live from the Cibolo Nature Center (about 25 miles away). Magazines, newspapers, posters, radio—all bring visitors to the Cibolo Nature Center, and our town. Five thousand visitors have come to Boerne, a town of five thousand, for this one-day event. Two police officers are needed for traffic control, and fifty vendors offer plants and related products for sale, donating 20 percent of their sales to the nature center. The festival is anticipated by native plant enthusiasts, local gardeners, and outdoor lovers from a hundred-mile radius. Operational funds are raised for the nature center, and our community has a great party, celebrating life.

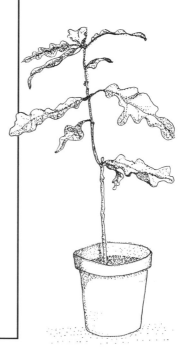

## TOURISTS

Nature-related travel is the fastest-growing segment of the travel industry. Wildlife viewing is the number one outdoor activity in the United States. There are about as many wildlife photographers in the country as there are hunters. Birdwatchers, hikers, bicyclers, anglers, sight-seers, photographers—all are looking for new places to go. Birds and wildlife are abundant in pocket parks and even small nature centers. Many communities are interested in attracting tourists by building expensive water parks or amusement centers. Nature tourism uses resources that already exist, boosting the local economy while improving the quality of life for neighbors.

---

*M*oment in the Life of a Tourist

A quiet place with room to recognize the majesty of earth. . . . Everything here—the earth, life, the arch of sky—all was senior to me. I stood, struck suddenly, with keen appreciation, close to worship, of the freedom of a snipe that took to the air from the far side of the pond. It left the memories of its call and the whistle of its wings—the zigzag pattern of its flight across a gray late-afternoon sky. (I have them still.)

—Jennings Carlisle, tourist

---

## CITY PLANNERS

Communities that provide green space for their citizens are becoming more and more desirable. A high quality-of-life factor includes not only roads, schools, and athletic facilities, but also open space for children to play in and for families to enjoy. A city or town with little park land can be intimidating and sterile. Green spaces can provide recreation and aesthetic experiences, make the climate milder, and provide habitat for wildlife. Service organizations and volunteers can work with local government toward conservation for future generations. Some nature centers go beyond the preservation of wild space

$\mathcal{M}$oment in the Life of a City Planner

"What if . . . ?" "Have you or the city ever considered . . . ?" These questions frequently make those of us who know better shudder, or wish it were 5 pm, or that I really had gone fishing. But, a walk in Boerne City Park in the spring of 1988—with a young lady who wanted something better and someone who saw, beneath the piles of fill material, fallow fields and a creek—led to the establishment of the Cibolo Wilderness Trail (CWT) and Nature Center, which has turned into a gem for the City of Boerne.

In the evenings you can sit at the Nature Center and watch the sunset over a recovering tall grass prairie. Many people in the Boerne area felt that the tall grass reclamation project was a waste of space that could be better used as baseball/softball practice fields. The Boerne City Council designated the area as a primitive area following a heated public hearing. This action solidified the CWT as a permanent facility in Boerne City Park, with the following happy results:

1. The CWT has provided the city with an alternative form of passive recreation that will assist us in meeting the needs of our area residents, now and in the future, as over 48 percent of the Kendall County residents are 45 years of age or older.

2. It has received a great deal of publicity, which has been excellent for the city.

3. It has provided an additional attraction for tourists in the Boerne area, making Boerne a destination point rather than a day trip.

4. It has joined forces with city government in the maintenance and construction of the trail and nature center. This joint venture of city government and civic volunteers has given the community a good feeling about the city.

—Mr. Chris Turk
　　Director of Planning and Community Services,
　　City of Boerne

and education, and even set aside a portion of their park for community gardening.

## FARMERS AND RANCHERS

Educational programs on local conservation can provide valuable information to landowners. Workshops on native grasses, organic farming and ranching methods, watershed protection, soil conservation, wildlife management, and local gardening tips are of great interest to those who work the land.

**Long-time rancher teaches identification of native grasses. "Our soil is our wealth."**
**—Hilmar Bergmann**

---

### ℳoment for a Rancher

Hilmar Bergmann, who is now pushing eighty, began working for the Soil Conservation Service in the fifties. He still lives in the country on the ranch where he was born. In 1993 he was honored by the people of Boerne by having the Cibolo Nature Center's preserved prairie named in his honor. A number of old-timers and new ranchers turned out for the event, as they do for every program he presents. Mr. Bergmann had volunteered many hours at the Cibolo Trail, documenting plant life and producing a brochure describing grasses found on the preserved prairie.

Noting the importance of native grasses and plants, Bergmann said, "In this prairie, you can find around sixty different grasses. . . . Our soil is our wealth." Ranchers and farmers throughout the region know and respect Mr. Bergmann. His involvement enriches the nature center, and the nature center enables his retirement to include valuable community service.

---

## CONSERVATIONISTS AND ENVIRONMENTALISTS

Citizens interested in conservation or environmental improvement find nature centers to be settings that can demonstrate good stewardship of the land and provide educational programs for the public.

With most of humanity living in cities, cut off from contact with nature, and with traffic congestion, mounting population numbers, polluted air and water, overcrowding, violence, and decay, there is an obvious need for nature centers. We live like aliens upon the land, in air-conditioned homes, moving about in climate-controlled private cars and public transport. We have separated from nature to a large extent—building, developing, paving, and "improving"—leaving most of nature worn and torn.

It is not only the quality of life that is jeopardized by overpopulation and habitat destruction: Many biologists claim that we are currently endangering our oceans, our soil, our water, our atmosphere, and the diversity of plant and animal life all over the globe. The level of environmental degradation is becoming critical. The history of civilization is filled with stories of collapsed cultures that depleted the very ecosystems they had depended upon. The greatest threat to our way of life, and perhaps our survival as a species, may be our own tendency toward "progress" at the expense of the natural world. These are issues that many members of your community are thinking about and would like to learn more about.

An educated citizenry can make decisions, whereas uninformed voters tend to be complacent about issues of profound importance. A nature center can serve the public interest by providing authoritative educational programs and forums for the discussion of local environmental concerns.

The conservation ethic does not suggest that blind opposition to progress is the answer, but it does assert the dangers of blind progress. To educate the public, to engender a more cooperative relationship with nature, and to encourage wise stewardship of the land, our communities need a natural place to fall in love with, a place in which to learn how to live more harmoniously with the natural world. As communities become more aware of their natural heritage, and its fragility and potential, our neighborhoods and countryside can become more beautiful and more sustainable. Thinking globally and acting locally can start with a nature center.

### GARDENERS

Gardening is the most popular form of recreation in the United States. Nature centers can provide programs tailored

## *M*oment for a Hawk Lover

As I watched the Birds of Prey program, I felt such admiration and respect for the magnificent birds in the show. Most of the birds used in the program cannot be released or rehabilitated, owing to severe injuries or human bonding. However, they brought a young hawk to be released in the tall grass prairie that day. This red-tail had been with "Last Chance Forever" for almost a year, since it had been found as a chick. When John Karger brought the brave survivor out, he asked if I would like to be the one to release it. I held the fragile little bit of feather and fluff in my hands and felt a tenderness and compassion so strong, my heart nearly burst.

Then I looked this creature in the eye, and got a fierce glare in return. He was no cute and fluffy Disney character. No, this creature was a survivor, a warrior, ready to battle for a free life. I raised my arms and let him fly, and he did fly, circling high over the prairie. We hoped he would call it home. Then he was off to perch in a tall tree with a good view. A part of me soared that day, and I will always feel a kinship with the grand and noble hawks.

to the local interests, such as xeriscaping, butterfly gardens, wildscapes, and solving local gardening problems. Community gardening can feed people, soften the world, and bring folks together. Those interested in native plants find a nature center the perfect place to study and learn. Herbalists can have their meetings at a nature center and become avid supporters of the project.

Gardeners tend to have a feel for nature that will render them likely allies with nature center developers. Many garden clubs are composed of interesting, educated, and enlightened gardeners who have a wealth of information and good will.

*When the world wearies
And society ceases to satisfy,
there is always the Garden.*
—Anonymous

Gardeners are natural friends and allies for developing nature centers.

---

### *M*oment for a Gardener

Our nature center has a Wildscape Demonstration Site. It is a quarter acre of land surrounding the Nature Center that has been planned to encourage native plants, birds, and other wildlife. Some of our volunteers live in apartments, and this is their only chance to get their hands in the soil—they love it. Others have gardens of their own, and still want more. We have built two ponds, left a pile of brush, set out bird feeders, and grown plants that feed hummingbirds, butterflies, wildlife and bird species. The site is becoming an inspiration to people who want to have interesting yards, to landscape with native plants, and to encourage their wild friends.

---

## MINISTERS, CHURCH MEMBERS, AND SPIRITUAL SEEKERS

The natural beauty of wild area is often found to be inspiring to visitors. Members of churches, synagogues, mosques—any spiritual group—often seek the sanctuary of natural settings. Throughout history, spiritual prophets have taken their pilgrimages to nature: a desert, a mountain, a river, a forest, a tree, a cavern—somewhere untouched by civilization. The Christian Bible notes that Jesus went to a desert, a garden, a mount, and to the sea for inspiration. Buddha went to the Bodhi Tree. Abraham went into the wilderness. Moses went to the mountain. Native American holy persons speak of power places where the Spirit speaks. For many, wilderness is hallowed ground. "Speak to the earth, and it will teach thee" (Book of Job, 12:8). For a history of how organized religions

---

*M*oment Remembered
by a Thirty-Six-Year-Old Musician

My father had just finished constructing a beautiful home on about twenty acres of woodland. Unfortunately, the atmosphere within was anything but peaceful, because my parents fought continually. I felt very lonely.

Yet I always loved being outside, and I would look with longing at the tall pine trees that surrounded our backyard. One day, I felt enough courage to slip away from my mother's watchful eye and walked alone into the woods. It was there that I found the joy I had been disappointedly seeking in my own family. The woods felt peaceful and loving, and there I felt really at home.

. . . as I kept walking deeper into the woods, the more wonderful it became. After exploring and talking happily with everything I could see, I lay down under a big pine tree. From its many-rooted base I could see straight up to the sky and feel its branches dancing with the wind. I knew that I was safe, and more than that, I felt loved by all that was around me. I felt connected to the plants, trees, animals, and even the insects, and I fell asleep surrounded by love. . . . For me, it has taken years of spiritual searching to understand fully the natural simplicity and perfection of my childhood episode in the woods.

—*Visions of Innocence,* Edward Hoffman

have approached treatment of animals, nature, and conservation, see *Replenish the Earth,* in Appendix B.

For us, saving a spot of paradise and helping people find its magic and wonder was the goal. We just loved to watch people fall under nature's spell. We were vague about what we wanted, but ten years have certainly helped clarify the possibilities. That goal can be summarized in the words of Albert Schweitzer, in 1915. He was on the Ogowe River, pondering the troubles of his times, watching four hippopotamuses and their young: "The only way our culture can be brought into greater moral depth and energy is through gaining 'reverence for life.'" A nature center can be more than a natural science center that teaches facts and figures. A nature center can inspire the visitor to develop a humane relationship with all living creatures.

## SPECIAL NEEDS POPULATIONS

**Special needs will become apparent as your nature center develops. Grants for accessible trails are readily available.**

> The best remedy for those who are afraid, lonely, or unhappy is to go outside, somewhere where they can be quite alone with the heavens, nature, and God. Because only then does one feel that all is as it should be . . . amidst the simple beauty of nature. . . . I firmly believe that nature brings solace in all troubles.
>
> —Anne Frank

Troubled teens and children, the blind, the physically handicapped, the deaf, the mentally challenged, the emotionally disturbed, hospice residents, and citizens recovering from illnesses—all need and respond to outdoor recreation. While the appeal of nature is universal, access to nature in the modern world is not. But it can be. With good planning, any nature center can bring these populations to the green space. (See Chapter 4: Facility Options; Chapter 5: Program Possibilities; and Chapter 11: Managing Land Without Managing to Ruin It, "Trail Building.") The results of putting special needs populations in touch with nature have been documented to be enor-

> $\mathcal{M}$oment in the Life of Helen Keller
>
> What a joy it is to feel the soft, springy earth under my feet once more, to follow grassy roads that lead to ferny brooks where I can bathe my fingers in a cataract of rippling notes, or to clamber over a stone wall into green fields that tumble and roll and climb in riotous gladness!
> —Helen Keller, *The Story of My Life*

**A nature center outreach program brings tabletop gardening to a nursing home.**

mously therapeutic. (See Appendix B. *People–Plant Relationships: Setting Research Priorities.*)

## SENIOR CITIZENS & NURSING HOME RESIDENTS

Gardening and nature programs for seniors can create inspiring moments in beautiful natural settings. Elders tend to enjoy meditative activities and quiet recreation. A short stroll or wheelchair ride down a trail can be the highlight of a

> $\mathcal{M}$oment in the Life of a Nursing Home Resident
>
> When local nursing home residents heard about an inner-city fourth-grade class whose garden had been twice vandalized, they wanted to do something. Through the nature center, they sent a care package: decorated potted plants ready for transplanting. The giant poster, onto which all their Polaroid portraits and notes of encouragement were attached, read "Never Give Up!" The children were thrilled, and they replanted their garden. Later that year the children traveled to the nature center to meet and thank their new "foster grandparents."

nursing home resident's week, and an enjoyable outing for the staff or family of the elder as well.

## HEALTH CARE PROVIDERS

Those responsible for helping special needs populations have developed a number of creative outdoor approaches for rehabilitation and recreation. The American Association of Horticultural Therapists and the American Association for Experiential Education provide excellent information regarding the development of such programs (see Appendix A to contact organizations). Opportunities for positive community service and rehabilitative activities abound in a nature center environment.

Researchers have found that plants in our surroundings can improve our mood, help us heal faster from surgery, and reduce vandalism in cities. A study at the University of Illinois indicates that landscaped housing projects (with as few as four or five trees) have significantly fewer incidents of vio-

---

*M*oments in the Lives of Troubled Teenagers

The SEED (Self-Esteem Through Ecological Dynamics) Program of Charter Real Hospital in San Antonio, Texas, often took adolescent patients to the nature center. Said one teen about the experience, "I realized that I too could play an important role in helping our environment—which is struggling to survive. Through your teaching, caring, and guidance, I too have been implanted with the desire to become involved—and that is something for which I will be forever grateful." One boy expressed his feelings this way: "In the past when I was depressed, I didn't know what to do except to lie in my room in the dark with the music turned up loud. Now, I take off for a walk on the nature trail, and I feel so much better."

*Now I see the secret of the making of the best persons. It is to grow in the open air, and to eat and sleep with the earth.*

—Walt Whitman,
*Leaves of Grass*

lence and more congenial relationships among residents. Residents of the greener housing projects reported feeling safer and more positive about their living quarters, and they also reported more visitors and better relationships with their neighbors than residents of the nongreen areas. They were found to be more likely to use reasoning to discipline their children and less likely to use physical violence with adult partners. The study, reported in the November 1995 News Edition of *American Horticulturist,* the publication of the American Horticultural Society, was conducted by William Sullivan, assistant professor in the Department of Natural Resources and Environmental Sciences at the University of Illinois.

## FUTURE GENERATIONS

Envisioning the future for most communities means anticipating growth. As populations expand, land will be developed more extensively, and the opportunities for preserving our natural wonders will gradually disappear. Just as we take our National Parks for granted, we pass by local greenery and

**Carolyn, son Jonah, and grandfather August Herff at the marsh.**

## $\mathcal{M}$oment in the Life of Carolyn

When my great-great-grandparents came to this land, the wilderness seemed endless. But with each passing generation the wilderness grew smaller and smaller. When my children were young, I would take them to the same creek that their ancestors had enjoyed, but it was no longer the pristine, clear running creek of the past. No, it was littered with garbage of every sort, and children could no longer wade without fear of cut feet, or worse. But my grandfather remembered, and told me how the creek used to be. It was for my children, and all children, that I vowed to protect this wild and beautiful place. It is their birthright.

natural beauty every day. It is hard to imagine that the world population will double in the next generation's lifetime. What kind of world will our progeny inherit? Where will the children play?

## A NONHUMAN POINT OF VIEW

We *Homo sapiens* often ask the question "What good is that species?"—meaning, "What good is it to us?" The question exposes our sense of being the center of the universe. Nature is often viewed as merely a stage for our drama, all other species being seen as just supporting actors. Spending time in nature can change that perspective. A nature center serves not only humans and their interests, but also the interests of the flora and fauna of the region.

---

*M*oment in the Life of a Commuter

As I was driving to the city of San Antonio, over Sheep Dip Crossing at the Cibolo Creek, I noticed a great blue heron flying low, heading for the marsh that our group of volunteers had restored. I wondered about this fellow commuter, his work, his family, his drama. That evening, on my way home, there he was again, flying back over Sheep Dip Crossing, heading home from his day of fishing at the marsh. I laughed at the synchronicity of our paths that day and realized that the nature center means much more to him than it ever will to me. To life! You Great Blue! To Life!

---

A NATURE CENTER can enrich the local environment, and the lives of every member of the human community. To witness the thriving of wild beings is certainly good medicine for us. But for some living creatures in our world, preservation of such habitats is simply vital.

# Chapter 8 Getting Your Organization Organized

*We owed it to do, not what was to perish with ourselves but what would remain, to be respected and preserved into other ages.*

— THOMAS JEFFERSON

## PHASES OF GROUP DEVELOPMENT

As you consider embarking on this journey of nature center development, it is vital that you enjoy each step of the process, and not become impatient or overwhelmed with the number of steps to come. Your project is unique, and it does not have to emulate the course of other centers. It can be as large or small as you want it to be. Nature center developers need to grow with their project and should be careful not to let the organization evolve so fast and furiously that it becomes unmanageable. As you read through the various phases of group development, remember to simply appreciate the phase you are in, and anticipate enjoying the next one you envision.

Phase 1: "The Seed." Someone has an idea about starting a nature trail or nature center.

Phase 2: "Planting." The idea person starts spreading the word to likely cohorts.

Phase 3: "Sprouting." Interest builds, and everyone is friendly and agreeable.

Phase 4: "Semiharmony." Conflict exists but is glossed over.

Phase 5: "Sparring." Conflict develops between individuals, and issues of ego and pecking order emerge. This can be a time of polarization and competition, with chaotic interpersonal dynamics.

Phase 6: "Cohesion." The productive, group-centered phase begins, in which conflict is addressed directly, worked through, with real agreement concerning the overall mission of the group. Individuals learn to communicate interests and feelings without manipulation and games. The group truly "gels."

**Phase 7: "Adolescence."** The organization has fits and starts of growth and regression, in membership, finances, or facilities. The board may begin taking on more responsibility, rewriting the director's job description, or redefining the mission of the organization.

**Phase 8: "Maturation."** Stability is established, in which continued effort yields predictable quality programs that are appreciated by the surrounding community. Membership and funding are a continual issue, but not a source of panic and turmoil.

Here are some other possible scenarios.

**Phase 9: "Midlife Crisis."** Major funding loss, internal divisions, or community upheaval results in threat to the existence of the organization, or to important programs or staff positions.

**Phase 10: "Compost Happens."** Even in the worst-case scenario, in which a nature center is lost, lives have been touched, and new beginnings ("seeds") can emerge. So forget about worst-case scenarios and get on with it!

You may be the originator of the nature center idea in your community, or be wanting to join in at some other stage of development. If you are joining an existing organization, explore its history sufficiently to clarify in your own mind what stage it is currently going through, so that you can gauge how to involve yourself most effectively. You may best serve as a volunteer trail guide, community organizer, mediator, carpenter, or program presenter. Ultimately, your interests should determine your function.

## HOW TO ORGANIZE VOLUNTEERS

As people start to become interested in the project, you will hear the phrase "Let me know if there is anything I can do." Or someone might have a very specific way in which they would like to help. The opportunity presented by their simple offer should not be lost. Even in the early stage of organization, developing your volunteer base is vital. Volunteers come with their own needs and ideas. They also have an opening in their life that will not last forever. Life fills all vacuums, and soon they will find meaningful activity to be involved with if they do not find it with your group. Therefore, carry a notebook at all times. When someone offers help, act immediately. Get their name and phone number and note their interests and strengths. Discuss ideas, offer suggestions, make an action plan, but keep in mind that volunteers must be inspired about what they are doing, or they won't last.

## WORD TO THE WISE

Some of our first volunteers came from our local high school, when an environmental science teacher grew tired of teaching the bad news side of the environment story. He felt that his students only grew discouraged about the environment as they plowed through the huge textbook that described the horrors of air pollution, water pollution, overpopulation, deforestation, and so on. His solution was to activate the students. Instead of just sitting around with a sense of "it's no use," he put them to work.

Ten years ago Mr. Chuck Janzow started requiring his students to "volunteer" eight hours a year to an environmental or conservation organization of their choice. The Cibolo Wilderness Trail received most of the students because of its proximity and Mr. Janzow's passion for the project. Each year 125–150 students work locally to help our environment. They have been the backbone of the CWT. They have cleared trails, built paths, planted trees, dug ponds, painted signs, designed brochures, and much, much more. What we have gained is thousands of hours of volunteer labor that actually built the CWT. What they have gained is the realization that they can make a difference, and that the solution to our environmental crisis lies within each of us.

**Volunteer activities can be fun and productive, if careful planning is used.**

Volunteers come from many sources. A garden club tour can inspire someone to join forces with you. Presentations to service organizations help build support and often inspire volunteers, who join in either as a club or individually. Boy and girl scouts often need projects for badges; retired persons often want to be of service; church youth groups and high school clubs can be of great help. Volunteers are the heart of your community. Their time is a precious gift.

A volunteer information sheet is an effective way to sign up volunteers, keep track of who can contribute what, and ensure that some folks don't just fall through the cracks. Having a central file of volunteer sign-up sheets will provide organization and a ready bank of helpers for future projects that have not yet been conceived. Most of all, you will ultimately need a volunteer coordinator, because managing volunteers is a vital and time-consuming job.

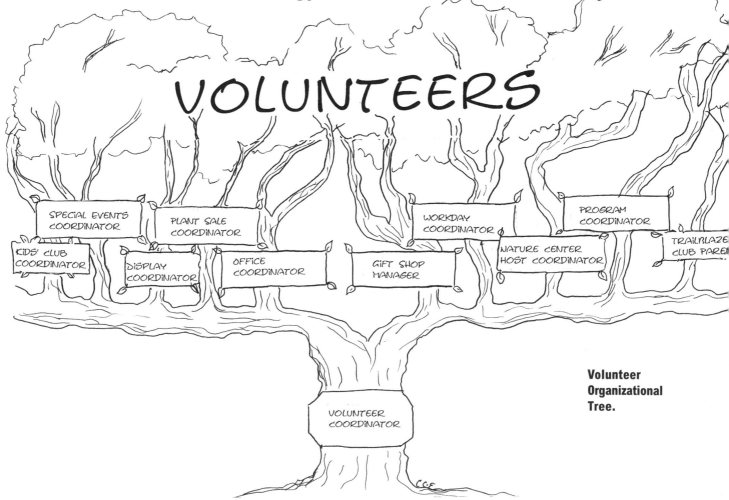

**Volunteer Organizational Tree.**

**Scout leaders are always looking for great outings and outdoor projects for earning achievement badges.**

The Appalachian Mountain Club has developed a step-by-step program for grassroots conservation action groups, entitled *Organizing Outdoor Volunteers* (see Appendix B). This is a valuable resource for details about recruiting, planning fund-raisers, organization, and many other practical considerations.

## HOW TO KEEP HAPPY VOLUNTEERS

- Help them understand organizational goals and their assignments.
- Give them meaningful and fulfilling jobs. No matter how small, show them the importance of doing it.
- Put *fun* in the job.
- Make them feel needed and wanted.
- Encourage ownership of the nature center by involving them in program decisions.
- Recognize them publicly and privately.
- Listen to suggestions and ideas.
- Don't overload one volunteer.

- Don't waste their time.
- Thank them time and time again. Surprise them with small gifts, birthday cards, flowers in the office, candy in the jar, and so on.
- Build community among the volunteers; have parties, pot-luck dinners, etc.
- Keep them abreast of organizational goals and changes.

Another thing to keep in mind is the importance of recognition. Although many volunteers have no burning desire for fame and glory, they do like to be appreciated. Recognition in the form of newspaper articles and pictures, thank-you notes, mention of appreciation at get-togethers—all help create a feeling of community within your group. As your organization develops, you may even create certificates of appreciation, with phrases like "Outstanding in Her Field."

The Points of Light Foundation publishes the *Volunteer Community Catalog* with products and publications for volunteer coordinators (see Appendix B). A good resource for rec-

**Ellie Dillon, our office Mom, and Larry Roos, the accountant with a heart.**

**Volunteer Murray Winn receives a bronze wood duck with the inscription, "Friend of the Cibolo."**

*Friends of the Cibolo Wilderness News*
An Abundant Spring, May 1996

It seemed a sparse spring at first. The obvious absence of rain, the pitiful little wildflowers bravely attempting to come up, the hungry wildlife, all weighed on my heart. I was born at the end of the terrible seven-year drought that killed ancient giant cypress trees and crippled the region. All my life I have heard stories of the drought, so it is easy for my imagination to fly. As I watched the marsh drop down to a puddle, and the creek slow to a crawl, I felt the uneasiness of scarcity.

Meanwhile, however, I was experiencing an abundance of generosity. This spring was like a renaissance for the Cibolo Nature Center. Many talented people gave their time and energy tirelessly to many different projects. Although there are hundreds of people I would like to thank here, there are a few who really have put their souls into creating a nature center with a heart.

There were those who created the plant sale. I call them "The Dream Team." Every Wednesday for months, we met at the Bear Moon Bakery to whittle away at the mountain of details involved in a project of this scope. Thanks, Dream Team: Jill Mason, Chuck Janzow, Georganne Taylor, Nina Nye, Alice O'Grady, Vivian Rule, Deb Boerner, Mary Morton, Paula Hayward, Susan Gross, Brent Evans, Steve Bonner, Joel Handley, Meg Grier, Barb Jeffries, Heather Segovia, Delia Jobst, Mark Mason, and Ellie Dillon. This was an inspiring group of people to work with, smart, energetic and committed. No one can deny the profusion of talent and good nature.

We had a busy spring with other projects as well. With a grant from the City of Boerne and the Lower Colorado River Authority we were able to complete the back and side porches of the nature center. The Lion's Club and Boerne High Environmental Science Students worked with David Pipes. Paul Schuetze of PJ's Painting and Marty Carroll of Sterling Electric donated time also. And Col. Milt Hawkins made us all stay on task.

Other unsung heroes of the Trail are Col. Lola Ball, who cares for all the creatures who live at or near the nature center. She fills the hummingbird feeders, feeds meal worms to the snapping turtles, waters trees, and so much more. Thank you, Lola, for your tireless commitment.

Also I want to thank Ms. Herbst and Mr. Janzow and their 120 or so environmental science students from Boerne High School. These students have cleaned the creek and trails, built a new pond, worked at the plant sale, mulched trees, moved displays, cleaned aquariums, planted native plants, and much, much more. Each of them has made a great difference at the Cibolo Wilderness Trail and we all thank you.

Meanwhile Trail guides led 2,700 children through the Trail throughout the school year. Thanks to them for sharing their talent for teaching with these eager young people.

Our gift shop is open, thanks to a grant received this spring, and help from Dick Gross, Robin Bastien, Vivian Rule, the Nature Center Hosts, and Larry Roos. We now have nature items, books, tee-shirts, caps, rocks, and more.

We are currently building our outdoor stage, to be finished just in time for our Father's Day concert. The stage will provide us with a place for outdoor theater, concerts, slide shows, and lectures.

Thanks to this incredible wealth of support and care, the feeling of scarcity was overcome with a sense of abundance. It is a wonderful thing to see such a community of caring, involved, diverse people come together to work toward the dream of a kind, beautiful world.

—Carolyn Chipman-Evans

PS: We did receive a rich and luxurious rain. However, we are still in drought conditions, so remember, water is precious and even with abundance of generosity in the air, we still need to conserve.

ognition ideas is *Beyond Banquets, Plaques and Pins: Creative Ways to Recognize Volunteers*, by Sue Vineyard, which lists hundreds of great tactics and solid advice for understanding the needs of volunteers.

Keep records of who helped with what and for how long. These records can come in handy for some grants that accept in-kind contributions toward matching funds. These records are also useful at newsletter time when you want to thank every volunteer. It is critical to thank and thank and thank. Never take your volunteers for granted or expect them to work forever. Always appreciate them.

Remembering that volunteers are participating out of a giving spirit, the crucial ingredient of fun must be emphasized and called upon frequently. Nature lovers are going to need access to nature. If your nature center land is not yet available for immediate enjoyment, excursions to other areas of natural beauty and interest can help solidify your group. Some volunteers are looking for new social contacts, so get-togethers are important. The love of nature is what attracts some volunteers, while others are sincerely interested in helping with envelope stuffing and communing with computers.

**Trash pickups can be extra fun if they are followed by picnics or adventures in nature.**

Look in Appendix A for a list of helpful organizations. Some, like the National Audubon Society or the Sierra Club, may have local chapters with potential core group members. You never stop building your core group, because it will constantly change. People don't always have time in their lives for community service. Five years into the project you may have an entirely different group, so it is vital that you keep your eyes open for sincere, energetic doers.

## DEVELOPING A "VISION"

In the early meetings of your core group, questions will naturally arise about the group's purpose. What do we hope to accomplish, and why? It is helpful in the early stages of development that the group clarify the ends that the group is striving for: the vision. This can be arrived at through a process that allows each member of the group to express ideas, hear differing points of view, and seek common ground.

Know where your group is generally heading, before you set sail. Invite your prospective core group to a meeting

---

A Letter from Jennings Carlisle
A Friend of the Cibolo Wilderness

Dear Carolyn and Brent:

. . . The first time you and I talked, I told you that I had mixed feelings about wishing you well. My fear for such things is that success results in destruction. The things we treasure (high on the list are silence and solitude except for bird songs and the sound the Cibolo makes . . . ) and want to share are fragile and easily "loved to death."

---

after individual contacts have convinced you that each person has potential for being helpful to the cause. Explain that the purpose of the meeting will be to share ideas about the possibility of starting a nature center. Each person's idea will be different, so it is vital that members understand and respect each other's differences. Consensus building is the process through which the group will evolve in the most fruitful way. If consensus is not achieved, the group will be working at cross-purposes. Only when there is general consensus about the group's vision should you start planning action. The vision can be broad, with room for change and "revision," and should not stifle the creativity of your group.

As your group works to secure land, the hurdles will become clear. If the property is privately owned, will the owner sell? If the owner will sell, will the community resist or promote the project? Are there public or private funds available to purchase the land for this purpose, or will funding sources have to be developed? If the land is publicly owned, what is currently planned for its future? What governing body controls the land, and who has the power to make new plans? Moving from the drawing board to issues "on the ground" will definitely change the project in unplanned ways, with unexpected twists and turns. Now your group can move beyond its beginnings, learn from encounters with reality, and adapt.

If your vision was to encourage a city or county government to independently develop and operate a nature center, and the community convinces its representatives to do so, then the future of the nature center will be in the hands of that governing body. If you are comfortable with this, then everyone is happy. However, even when cities or counties decide to develop nature centers, they usually want to do so with the assistance of a "Friends" organization. This will enable the center to maintain its link with interested citizens, facilitate grants from foundations, and provide a ready group of volunteers that can substantially reduce the costs of operation.

## THE ACTION PLAN

Once a group has a clear vision, individual members will begin imagining what they can do to further the cause. If they act independently and without coordination, efforts can be duplicated, and major areas of vital concern may be ignored, or left all in the hands of one person. The action plan is your group's means of creating a clear and coordinated method of achieving its goals. The group's action plan does not need to precisely describe every step to be taken in the weeks and months to come, but it does need to clarify areas of interest and responsibility and the expectations the members should have of each other.

Group communication is essential. A contact person with an available phone and post office box will enable the group to receive mail and phone calls and to distribute a newsletter and other information to each other when necessary. Often this person is the natural leader of the group who is the primary founder of the organization. Having simple means to make contact with your group will be increasingly important as your project builds momentum and members want to get in touch with each other. Have enjoyable meetings and get-togethers, cafe chats, picnics, outings, and creative ways of coming together to further the cause.

The action plan should be generated through brainstorming and consensus building. The action plan meeting will be a crucial step for the group. A list of vital activities should be generated, along with names of volunteers agreeing to take responsibility for particular actions and time lines.

A community has a formal and informal organization. The formal organization is the structure of positions in public offices and businesses. A city has formal positions such as a mayor, and perhaps a city administrator, a city clerk, a police chief, and a city council with city staff. These are important positions, with specific functions and responsibilities. But equally or even more important are the informal relationships within a community. Sometimes the most powerful decision makers in a community hold no public office, but know all the right people. The most influential person in town may be the newspaper publisher, a lawyer, a teacher, or a grocer. "Insiders" in the community are the well-connected folks who know everyone and can be of invaluable help. Charting the informal and formal systems in your community will help clarify who you need to approach, and why.

At this stage you are mapping the community, not approaching everybody you can. You are seeking out likely collaborators and a clear idea of who is who in the community. The core group should agree on who wants to approach whom, to prevent duplication and overdoing it. Document who is approached and what their reaction was, and collect all this information in a centralized place, like an outreach folder. As your organization expands, this folder can become quite valuable. One helpful way to do this is to write a thank-you letter to the individual contacted, noting the main points of the discussion, and thanking them for their input. They appreciate the thoughtfulness. A copy of the letter goes into the outreach folder and documents the contact. In other words, it's time to get organized!

These early contacts will suggest who else to talk to, what problems you might encounter, and other valuable information. Listen carefully and appreciatively, even when you disagree. Out of these contacts you will be able to map your community in terms of power, likely support, and likely opposition. You will discover who owns the land, and who else might want it. You will learn the history, as well as the political and economic influences, in this locale.

A formal survey of the community may help define the project in terms of community needs. This does not mean that the direction needs to be altered from the vision, but a community survey may reveal some unidentified needs and notions. The Louisiana Nature Center found that a questionnaire distributed throughout the city became a persuasive tool with philanthropists, corporations, and city leadership.

## HOW TO START A NONPROFIT ORGANIZATION

Whether your vision is to develop a nature center on private property or in conjunction with a city or county government, you will want to grow into a nonprofit organization. This will enable your group to seek funding from foundations, charitable organizations, and private individuals who can make tax-deductible donations. The nonprofit organization becomes a more stable entity, not dependent on any one individual for its survival. At the state level, your nonprofit status can enable your organization to make tax-exempt purchases for the nature center.

Don't be intimidated by the idea of incorporation or nonprofit status. Although the terminology used may be unfamiliar, there are simple steps that can enable your group to realize its vision by utilizing the legal system. The laws that govern nonprofit organizations vary from state to state. An attorney's assistance will be required (try to find a good-hearted one who will donate his or her services). You will need

---

**Advantages of Creating a Nonprofit Organization**

- Many individuals, foundations, and corporations will give only to an entity that is considered a publicly supported, tax-exempt organization.

- Nonprofits can act more quickly than the government can.

- Nonprofits can obtain donations more easily than can local government.

- Nonprofits qualify for gifts that can be deducted from federal income taxes.

- The corporate entity in itself may provide certain protections for the organization's volunteers and staff from liability, although personal liability varies from state to state. The purchase of relatively inexpensive fiduciary insurance is suggested.

a board of trustees, officers, and bylaws. Many nonprofit organizations state their purposes broadly so that they may expand their activities in the future. However, if a large part of your organization's activity will consist of lobbying, it will not qualify for tax exemption. In order for the IRS to recognize your organization as tax-exempt, you must file an application with the IRS. It is not a complicated process. It just takes eliciting help from the legal profession. Remember, the thousand-mile journey is taken one step at a time.

## BYLAWS AND ARTICLES OF INCORPORATION

Bylaws are the legally required operating rules of your incorporated organization, which cover everything from the selection and terms of board members to legal structure and tax status. Bylaws can be quite general in the early stages and revised as the need arises. They are easily assembled by an attorney with experience in nonprofit law.

A nonprofit organization must also have articles of incorporation, which is a short legal document describing the purpose of the organization, place of business, and how it will be run. When you are creating your nonprofit organization, you will need to obtain a tax status of 501(c)3, which shelters the organization from taxation and allows contributors to deduct donations from their income tax. A statement of "exempt purpose," citing activities such as educational programs or conservation of natural resources, will facilitate a 501(c)3 status. Both bylaws and articles of incorporation are required to incorporate at the state level, and then the tax-exempt 501(c)3 status is applied for at the federal level, through the IRS. *How to Form a Nonprofit Corporation* is a good resource for the beginner, including tear-out forms for all fifty states (see Appendix B: Publications).

## BOARDS

Your founding board will need to develop a mission statement, goals, objectives, and methods of money management. A sympathetic nonprofit organization may already exist in your community, which you can work through. However, if you want to have continued control of your project, create your own organization (it's not that hard). To create a board from scratch, you can have a meeting of your core group, even if it's only a few people, and begin forming a board. The bylaws adopted will determine how future boards will be chosen, such as election by the general membership, nomination by the board, or other means.

If you are creating a nonprofit organization, it will have a board of trustees that makes the decisions for the organization, and may or may not have an advisory board that makes suggestions and serves in a variety of non-decision-making functions. It is often helpful to include on your advisory board influential community members, donors, experts, and talent, while keeping your board of trustees reserved for members who will give time and effort toward vital tasks and provide leadership. A board of trustees with less than twelve members can act swiftly and still represent a broad spectrum of the local community. Committee meetings will also be involved throughout the year, as various board members assume specific areas of responsibility.

The founding group may or may not be the best group to comprise your board of trustees. Often the "best birder" and "best native gardener" are best used on an advisory board, while a banker or CPA may better serve on the board of trustees. Many nature centers have the following:

- a board of trustees (10–50 members);
- an executive committee (usually officers, committee chairs, and maybe a few at-large members);
- an advisory board (from community leadership);
- a president's council, composed of former board presidents, as a way of keeping old leadership involved; and
- standing committees that may include non-trustees from the community, giving the center a chance to broaden its base as well as to "try out" a potential trustee.

In order to keep these folks informed, though not overworked, the following is a good schedule of meetings: board of trustees (four to six per year), executive committee (monthly), advisory board (biannually), president's council (as needed), and committees (varies depending on their work at the time, but at least once between board meeting months).

Board meetings need not be boring. Plan some light time, some fun. You don't want bored board members.

New members of the board should be welcomed with an adequate introduction to the organization, explaining history, bylaws, mission, and master plan, as well as current issues under consideration. Keeping up an orientation packet will ensure that this occurs as new members come onto the board. An executive committee can be created that is empowered by the board to meet between regular meetings, and act on behalf of the board.

If your organization is to work in conjunction with another governing body, such as a city or state parks department, then your entire organization may be functioning in an advisory capacity for the center, but maintaining control over programs and funds of its own creation.

## WHO'S ON FIRST:
## SHARING THE PIE OF RESPONSIBILITY

[The following article, written by Robert A. Thomas, then executive director of the Louisiana Nature and Science Center in New Orleans, appeared in the ANCA newsletter *Directions*, in September of 1990. It demonstrates how a well-established nature center in a large community divides responsibilities between its board and its staff.]

Most nature center professionals view Trustees and staff as separate operations within their scheme of activities. In a healthy, well-managed organization, the Trustees, with the staff, make policy, and the staff, with the Trustees, carries it out. Though they work hand-in-hand, the overall responsibilities of Trustees and staff may be defined and the division of labor that does exist must be understood by all concerned.

In order for a Board of Trustees to adequately support its organization (in our case a nature center), it must have excellent composition. The particular people, businesses, other organizations, and social mix will be different with peculiar needs of various communities. Boards, however, have commonalities that can be briefly summarized as follow: they must have a good balance of wealth, wisdom and workers. An imbalance in any direction can result in confusion and disaster.

Trustees should represent a cross section of the community, yet be strong enough ( = possess clout) to open key doors and attract a full range of support from the community. . . . There are two old clichés that still apply:

- they must give, get, or get off!;
- they must share wisdom, wealth, or work.

Trustees should be held accountable in ten major areas of responsibility:

1. Assure compliance with all tax-exempt laws, keep records of meetings, and maintain bylaws and articles of incorporation.

2. Raise money to meet the annual budget (by developing a plan, delegating, contributing and soliciting); approve annual budgets; recommend investments; and approve wages, contracts, and fees.

3. Develop (with staff) the long-range, operational, and marketing plans (together serving as the nature center's 'strategic plan'); review and approve mission and vision statements, and all other components of the above.

4. Identify, nominate, train, and nurture new members of their body in order to perpetuate and improve the nature center organizationally.

5. Select and evaluate the Executive Director, approve wages and benefit packages recommended by the Executive Director, and approve all personnel policies.

6. Set policies and procedures under which the nature center operates.

7. Interpret and sell the nature center to the community.

8. Evaluate services to the visitors, visitor satisfaction, and performance of the Executive Director and the Trustees themselves.

9. Be thoroughly familiar with the breadth of programs of the nature center and their relevance to its mission and the community.

10. Every effort should be made to attend as many functions as possible. It is impossible to accomplish all of the above if you are not there.

It is obvious that the staff must have all the talents necessary to meet the nature center's mission. Staff educational background, experience, and capabilities should be dictated by the community's needs and there are no rules about ratios of teaching to support personnel. Whatever works well for a given nature center is what is right for that organization. It is this balance of staff and the plan of work that govern overall professional duties of the staff. There are, however, a number of responsibilities to the Trustees that diverse staff will have in common.

1. Make increased Trustee involvement in the nature center one of the staff's goals.

2. Implement actions approved by the Trustees and keep all work within the policies and procedures set forth by the Trustees. If your Trustees have no such written policies and procedures, see that they are developed. It is your right to have stated guidelines.

3. Provide the Trustees with all necessary information needed to understand the problems in the field and the program of work of the nature center in the community.

4. Provide excellent staff service to the proper Trustee Committee Chairs who rely on you for staff backup. Be prompt!

5. Devise a plan to communicate to the Trustees (repetitively) activities of the program of work of the nature center.

6. It is your responsibility to ensure that the Trustees clearly understand staff's evaluation of organizational needs and priorities and that the Trustees address them in the proper sequence. Realize that the Trustees have the power to alter them, but they must take staff suggestions seriously.

7. Help identify points of view and talents that are necessary for the Board and/or its committees to function properly. These requirements change over time under differing situations and both Trustees and staff should be attentive. Actually, this duty is usually attended to by the Executive Director, but other staff should funnel their observations and suggestions to him/her.

8. Know the related services that exist in your area. You must constantly assess the "competition" if you are to be a lean and mean nature center that is functioning at its peak efficiency in and for your community.

9. One of the most important staff roles is to have a thorough understanding of sources of information. Though most of us constantly look for the glamorous, exciting projects, the basis of our day-to-day operations is answering questions. We seem to be plagued by telephone calls, letters, etc. Most staffers complain about these questions taking them away from what they are supposed to be doing! Nature centers should function not as a primary source of new-found information, but as a conduit for and interpreter of information between laymen and scientists.

10. Make planning a priority. We all fuss about having to take time for meetings, but without adequate planning, our nature centers become inefficient.

11. Build flexibility into your planning. If staff doesn't insist on flexibility to take advantage of serendipitous situations, it risks losing the excitement that keeps the nature center throbbing. But be careful that the new opportunity is within the organization's mission and, for the sake of all involved, that adjustments are made in other work assignments.

12. Recognize that staff is the key link between the community at large and the nature center since staff are "full-timers" and normally easily recognizable as representatives in the community. Your Trustees will function this way, too, but most of them have a lower profile with the nature center and many will be involved in more than one civic endeavor.

13. Keep the dream alive! Don't get so run down with the day-to-day drudgeries that you fail to remember the importance of the nature center's mission. See that staff stays on task with goals.

14. Provide all possible credit, thanks, and satisfactions for Trustee activity. This will require a good deal of subordination of your own ego, but your goal and your satisfaction must be measured by the degree and kind of Trustee effort achieved.

Remember that a fledgling nature center has plenty of time to develop. The level of organization described by Mr. Thomas has taken years to achieve. A good resource for understanding dynamics of boards is *Executive Leadership in Non Profit Organizations,* by Herman and Heirnovics (see Appendix B).

## COMMITTEES

Committees are the most important bridge between the staff and trustees, as well as the nature center and the community. Standing committees are those that address continuing projects, such as membership, finance, education, and so forth. Ad hoc committees are formed to address specific projects, such as construction projects or specific events, and then disbanded after completion. Giving a group the opportunity to solve problems and complete tasks builds ownership and keeps the organization from leaning too heavily on staff or one or two hard workers. If you are just joining the organization, ask about the standing committees in your area of interest.

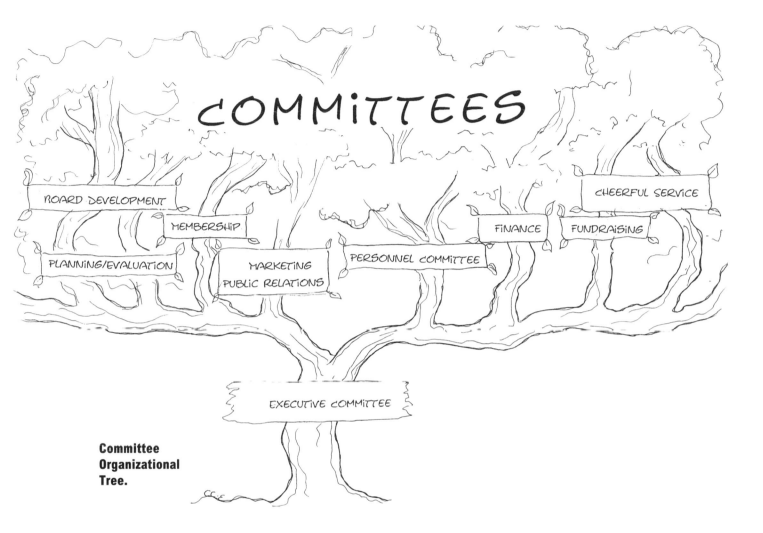

COMMiTTEES

BOARD DEVELOPMENT

CHEERFUL SERVICE

MEMBERSHIP

FINANCE   FUNDRAISING

PLANNING/EVALUATION

MARKETING
PUBLIC RELATIONS

PERSONNEL COMMITTEE

EXECUTIVE COMMITTEE

**Committee Organizational Tree.**

Create job descriptions for each committee in order to ensure effectiveness. In large organizations each committee should have one staff member as a liaison. The board president should meet with or phone the committee chair at least once a month to check on progress and offer suggestions and moral support. The executive director should be on all committees, but may choose not to attend if provided an immediate report from the staff liaison person. Each year committees should set annual goals and write them down. The important point is that each committee knows what they are responsible for and gets it done. A committee can be a fun group that forms a "dream team" or "lunch bunch" that makes amazing things happen. If you listen to and encourage new and creative ideas, and bend the rules a little, masterpieces will evolve.

## THE MISSION STATEMENT

To develop the guiding principle of the organization, the mission statement, a board meeting should be facilitated by someone who is a good communicator, respects different viewpoints, has a good sense of humor, and hopefully has had some experience at consensus building. Next, the group is asked to suggest ideas about what they envision the group is to be working toward. Participants are encouraged to present ideas without evaluating them. The purpose of brainstorming is to create a safe atmosphere for creative exploration of ideas, without criticism or competition. Gradually participants will begin understanding each other's interests, and areas of common ground will emerge.

Often groups will discover that some participants are primarily interested in preserving a piece of natural wonder, while others are interested in using the setting for educating the public. If the differing parties can come together to see the value of each other's ideas, a nature center with both purposes can emerge. If the group primarily wishes to preserve the area, it may be that a nature preserve will be the ultimate vision of your organization, and public access to the area will be minimized. Some participants may want to research the ideas of nature preserve versus nature center in more detail, before making a decision about what the vision of the group should be. Don't hurry the process. Each group needs to work at its own pace.

We recommend working toward a very concise mission statement with broad possibilities. This simple statement may be the product of weeks of thinking and dreaming, so that its meaning to the participants is more profound than the words might imply.

### Examples of Mission Statements

The mission statement that the group adopts will give direction to future plans. The mission statement should be a general declaration of purpose. Here are some examples:

* *Aullwood Audubon Center and Farm:* "A regional facility of the National Audubon Society for environmental education and organic agriculture, provides activities that increase understanding and preservation of the planet by children and adults through education, research, and recreation."

- *Fontenelle Forest Nature Center:* "To provide the highest quality natural science and educational programs to the community, and to preserve our land and wildlife in a natural state."
- *Pine Jog Environmental Education Center:* "To provide educational programs which foster awareness and appreciation of the natural world, promote an understanding of ecological concepts, and instill a sense of stewardship toward the earth and all its inhabitants."
- *Hashawha Environmental Center:* ". . . is a 320 acre preserve which is devoted to the goals of environmental education, conservation, and outdoor education."
- *The Wilderness Center, Inc.:* ". . . is dedicated to nature education, wildlife conservation, natural history research, and community service."
- *Treehaven Field Station:* "To support the teaching, research and outreach programs of the College of Natural Resources–University of Wisconsin/Stevens Point. To manage land and operate programs with the primary objective of developing an environmental ethic and philosophy of integrated resource management."

## Membership

Your members provide the money and energy for your organization. Members demonstrate public support, provide a fund-raising base, create a volunteer pool, and flex political muscle. Starting with your earliest gatherings, use a sign-in sheet with name, address, and phone number. These pioneers can become your first members. Send your newsletter to members, to your family and friends, to community leaders, and to everyone who has shown interest or been at a program. In your newsletter, always have a membership form included. Look over other newsletters; there are numerous clever ways to encourage new members. Your chamber of commerce can be a great help with mailing lists and ideas. Garden and civic clubs, as well as the Junior League, have funded many nature centers across the country.

Members join for a variety of reasons. Some just want to support your cause because they believe in what you're doing. Some join for contact with like-minded people, some for programs for their children, and others because they want to receive discounts, newsletters, and special offers. When planning your membership campaign, consider all these reasons.

## *Friends of the Cibolo Wilderness*
## MEMBERSHIP AND SPECIAL GIFTS

❑ I would like to be a new member and help Cibolo Nature Center continue to improve its programs and facilities through membership in one of the following categories:

| | |
|---|---|
| ❑ Kids' Club | $10 |
| ❑ Senior/Student | $15 |
| ❑ Individual | $20 |
| ❑ Family | $30 |
| ❑ Pecan | $100 |
| ❑ Live Oak | $500 |
| ❑ Benefactor Club | $1,000+ |
| ❑ Legacy Club | $5000+ |

❑ I would like to make a special gift to the Cibolo Nature Center in one of the following areas:

❑ Memorial or Honor Gift(please include name of honoree and family to be notified).

❑ Partner in Education (sponsors school field trips).

❑ Hill Country Conservation Fund (toward Rain Harvesting Demonstration).

❑ Camp Scholarship Fund (sponsors under privileged campers).

Name _____

Address_____

City _____State_____ Zip_____

Home Number _____

❑ Renewing Member
❑ Contact me to help you by volunteering my time/talents
❑ My address has changed, see below.
❑ I receive duplicate newsletters, delete one listed below.
❑ I would like to be removed from your list, delete name listed below.
Name _____
Address_____
City_____State_____ Zip_____
Home Number _____

### *The Cibolo Nature Center now accepts Visa, Mastercard and Discover.*

Card #_____ Exp. Date_____
Cardholder's name (print or type)_____
Cardholder's signature_____

❑ Check enclosed

Try to find ways to meet the desires of your members. For example, offer member walks at your park or tours to other beautiful natural places. Get a volunteer naturalist to lead the walk and have a brown bag picnic afterwards. This will get your members bonding and provide a way to get to know who will be a potential volunteer, board member, or funding source contact. Eventually you can offer member discounts for programs, gift shop items, tee shirts, and so forth. Staff and volunteers can sell memberships to each visitor, offering rebates of admission payment if they join immediately.

Membership campaigns can evolve with your organization. However, if you don't have a computer for your project, get one. They are relatively easy to have donated or funded, and they are not that hard to find. Just make sure the computer is in good working condition and someone knows how to use it. There are many membership software programs available; they don't need to be complicated or expensive. You will need to enter name, address, phone, date of renewal, giving record, and special notes, such as: volunteer, board member, honorary member, and so forth.

Use your database. Don't let your members wait while their checks sit in a pile. At least once a week someone will need to enter the data, make bank deposits, and write thank-you notes to new members. Members need to know they are appreciated, and they expect to stay informed. A short form letter can do both. Always thank new and renewing members in your newsletter. Someone will also need to send out the renewal notices. Don't expect your members to remember when their commitments are due. Phone banks can contact members for renewal. Most members will renew if reminded, but if you lose them, they can be hard to get back.

You will need to be able to print mailing labels for your newsletter or notices. Make sure the computer program has the capacity to sort in a variety of ways. For example, you will need to be able to sort according to zip code for bulk mailing discounts. If you can't sort, you will be spending many hours trying to separate all those zip codes. You may also want to send a notice to just volunteers and therefore want to print only the volunteer list. Again, look for a program that allows you to sort. We use "Now Contact."

Membership growth can be greatly enhanced by the media. You may want to create a campaign that lasts a month or two with special events, discounts, and media stories on your great work. Of course, those who come to your programs are perfect candidates for membership.

We usually send out two or three newsletters to prospective members, but if there is no response after that, we remove their name from the list. Some people should receive complimentary member status, such as community leaders, school board members, some key teachers, principals, your grandmother, and so forth. It creates good feelings and a sense of recognition.

If you are a new volunteer or contributor, by all means become a member. You will be updated by the newsletter on a regular basis, be invited to member functions, and channel yourself into the mainstream of the organization.

## HIRING A DIRECTOR

Our research and personal experience have convinced us of the importance of hiring a director. There have been nature centers that evolved from self-motivated volunteers who did not require financial support, but they are the exceptions. For continuity of service and quality, a nature center needs a director that its membership can count on. It is our position that a paid director should be the first item on your wish list, with the possible exception of newsletter funding for fledgling organizations. This is the single most important job of your board: hiring a director who will be your center's public image, responsible for direction, goals, funding, hiring of additional staff, and so on.

## INTERNS

Universities and colleges are often eager to develop intern programs for biology, agriculture, earth science, and environmental science students. Individuals preparing for careers in nature interpretation or related fields often seek apprenticeships. Many nature centers provide internships and reap great advantages from highly educated and motivated students who may need nothing more than college credit for pay. Students can be involved in all aspects of nature center operations, from caretaking and maintenance to administra-

**Children's presentations attract their parents to the nature center and introduce them to your programs.**

tion, interpretation, wildlife management, research, gift shop operations, and so on. Some centers provide lodging, uniforms, and weekly stipends. These details can be customized to fit the requirements of the college, the student, and the nature center involved. For more information about intern programs, write to the Sanctuary Manager, C. E. Buckley Wildlife Sanctuary, 1305 Germany Road, Frankfort, KY 40601, the Hashawha Environmental Center in Maryland, or the Pennsylvania State University Department of Recreation and Parks.

## LIABILITY AND SAFETY

Because we live in the age of litigation, your organization will need to have insurance. Many foundations, governmental entities, and funding sources will require proof of liability insurance, fire and theft coverage for buildings, and fiduciary and other coverages, depending on the risks associated with your particular locale (flood, earthquake, etc.).

The National Center for Community Risk Management and Insurance is a nonprofit organization that provides community service organizations with advice and information about insurance, including a variety of related publications (see Appendix A: Organizations). Use a local insurance agent—they have access to all types of insurance.

Your individual liability may be protected by the umbrella of the nonprofit corporation—check with your insurance agent or attorney. The organization can be devastated by one lawsuit over an injury occurring to a program participant. Most organizations require participants of adventurous outdoor activities to sign a waiver. Talk to your attorney.

The Association for Experiential Education has developed publications describing the practices commonly considered safe and responsible for adventure programming, such as hiking programs, river journeys, mountain climbing, swimming, and many other outdoor recreational activities (see Appendix A). Following these procedures is no guarantee against lawsuits, but greatly increases the likelihood that your actions would be considered responsible by others.

The best rule of thumb is to take reasonable precautions to prevent injuries, and explain all possible risks involved. Lawsuits are decided by individuals who will ask the question, "Did you take common-sense precautions?" Here are some examples:

- Avoid attracting visitors to dangerous areas, such as cliffs, slippery creeksides, poorly designed steps, very challenging climbs, avalanche areas, bogs, or snow and ice hazards.
- When working with groups, help parents know when to caution children about certain hazards, such as slippery footing, steep grades, reaching into small animal dens, and so forth.
- Public should be made aware of hazardous flora and fauna: (a) poison oak, poison ivy, poison sumac; (b) venomous snakes; (c) outbreaks of rabies in skunks, foxes, etc.; (d) ticks, mites, fire ants, "killer" bees, mosquitoes.
- In large parks, help visitors gauge their excursions in terms of time and difficulty. Provide information about availability of water, weather hazards, and clothing suggestions.

# Chapter 9  Building Community

*Community means strength that joins our strength
to do the work that needs to be done.*

— STARHAWK

ONE OF THE GREATEST JOYS in nature center development is participating in the birth of a community. A nature center not only conserves natural resources but creates fabulous human relationships. As your core group develops its vision, a special intimacy can develop. As public awareness grows, new energy is recruited, and new friendships are found.

If you are attempting to create a nature center from scratch, learn who is influential in the locale you wish to serve. Learn who makes decisions about the fate of the land you may be eyeing, who controls potential funding sources, and who is likely to help or hurt your cause. Now it is time to create an

**Donations make everyone feel good.**

action plan for building support. It is time to move into the mainstream of local citizenry, contacting the formal and informal leaders, service organizations, parties who might be affected by your plans, potential allies, and local experts. Again, document contacts. Your group needs to remember who has been contacted and be kept up to date with public reactions. Choose your spokespersons carefully, with diplomacy in mind.

## COMMUNITY RESOURCES

Any local institution can become involved. Nature centers, like politics, can make strange bedfellows. Groups that normally do not have anything to do with each other can find common ground in the creation of a local nature center. As you size up your target population, don't underestimate the power of nature in attracting support from diverse institutions:

- Families
- Schools
- Religious organizations
- Day-care centers
- Hospitals
- Colleges or universities, alumni, and faculty
- Service clubs, civic groups, and garden clubs
- Businesses and corporations: executives, boards of trustees, employees
- Unions
- Professional organizations
- Recreational clubs: bicyclists, hikers, etc.
- Fraternities/sororities
- 4-H clubs
- Boy scouts and girl scouts
- Youth organizations
- Senior citizens organizations and retirees
- Nursing homes
- Probation and community service systems
- Law enforcement
- News media
- Agricultural groups
- Military organizations
- State or federal departments
- City or county government
- Gardening clubs
- Audubon Society or Sierra Club members
- Foundations
- Other nonprofit organizations

Collect letters of support every chance you get. When someone likes your idea, ask them to write a letter, identifying themselves and documenting their sentiments. Letters from citizens, local experts, community leaders, educators, and "insiders" can give you an edge in recruiting others. Your growing file of letters will demonstrate support for your idea. A good way to increase the likelihood that someone will write a letter is to give them a self-addressed, stamped envelope with a written request for the kind of letter you are looking for.

## SAMPLE LETTER OF SUPPORT

Hello:

   We need your help. (Name of your organization) is trying to preserve a little pocket prairie that has a wonderful variety of native plants and grasses. This 35-acre prairie is in need of protection from competing community interests. We envision developing a nature center at this location that conserves the natural resources and provides education to the public about our natural heritage. We need letters on file that support this dream to convince officials that the public is indeed interested.

   If you could help us with a brief letter, we would greatly appreciate your efforts. Please address the letter to (your organization's address), and include your address and phone number, and why you are interested in supporting this project.

   Thank you,

   _____

## GETTING THE WORD OUT

   There are a number of ways to get the word out: newspaper stories, public service announcements, press releases, presentations, mailouts, door-to-door campaigns, posters, church bulletins, newsletters of local organizations, and word of mouth.

### Word of Mouth

   Probably the most important outreach technique is personal. The enthusiasm expressed by yourself and your core group will be contagious. Friends listen to friends. Challenge members of your group to bring one friend into the fold. Talk up the project wherever you go, because potential volunteers and donors can be anywhere. Your approach should be casual and full of fun. This is not an occasion for high-pressure salesmanship. Your scrapbook with pictures of activities can be worth a thousand words.

## The Newsletter

The best tool for communicating what you have done and where you are going is the newsletter. It recognizes efforts of volunteers, clarifies your vision of the future, lists names of supporters, advertises a wish list, and promotes causes dear to your heart. The newsletter facilitates communication of essential information to your group members, potential members, interested citizens, and potential supporters. In short, it inspires interest and makes your organization look real. Your image is largely created through the newsletter. An attractive and creative newsletter will propel your programs and activities. Take time to develop a top-notch publication. Never settle for rushed, sloppy, or disorganized work. Good newsletters have lively articles that focus on developing support and informing the readers. People like reading about other people. Stay positive, and remember that negative comments can come back to haunt you. Newsletters are the perfect place to highlight your volunteers, staff, board members, and supporters.

Invite participation from your readers. Members will appreciate a calendar of events that they can put on their refrigerator. Include your volunteer openings and wish list. These are ways to involve people and make them feel more invested in your organization.

Newsletters should be fun, attractive, and easy to read. They should contain photos or artwork and plenty of open space. Copyright-free clip art is available in bookstores. These graphics can illustrate ideas or simply beautify the newsletter. There are "clip art" books with thousands of images of animals, birds, insects, children, cartoons, you name it. Copy the format of another newsletter you like, or ask for a graphic artist to donate time toward creating one for you. There are many computer software programs available for creating newsletters. You might want to ask around about simple, effective ones for your needs. *Simple* is the key word here; unless you are a whiz on the computer, it can take days of train-

# Friends of the Cibolo Wilderness

# News

Volume 5, Number 2      Boerne ~ Texas      Summer ~ 1994

## Field Notes

This is the year of the wildflower. This is one of those rare and wonderful years when the many colored jewels bespeckle the ground as if simply for our delight. Wildflower books get dusted off and left out in the rain. Names like blue-eyed grass and golden-eye phlox and pearl milkweed paint pictures in our minds, to help us remember, to help us notice.

The time spent on slow strolls through wood and prairie and marsh, help us remember our ancestral appreciation of beauty. Wildflowers with names or no, do shout out to our inner wildness, calling us home to a place where all is as it should be.

When I spend time with small children at the Trail, I feel their fresh experience fill me with wonder all over again. I never tire of touch-me-nots closing right before my eyes and graceful barn swallows dipping into the mirror pond . We all feel the awe and something deep inside stirs.

These are the experiences that shape our future. Simple appreciation of nature molds lives, and caring for what we appreciate, comes naturally. ∞

## What's News

The Cibolo Kids' Club took it's first field trip. We went to Dave McKelvey's farm where they had a hands-on experience in animal communication and care. We had a wonderful time and the kids were so much fun, we'd take them again anytime.

Members went on a beautiful summer morning walk along the Guadalupe River, as part of our Watershed Series.

Our Herff Spring signs are completed, thanks to the fine work of sign painters John Bridges and David Doss.

The first session of our Nature Adventure Day Camp just ended and we are still floating from the great time we had. The campers had the rare and delightful experience of being able to explore and fall in love with the Cibolo Creek. We had many scholarships donated. Children who needed the opportunity to succeed and flourish could do so, naturally. A special thanks to Kendall Co. Family Services, The Optimist Club of Boerne, Parkway Automotive, Boerne Chrysler-Plymouth-Dodge and The United Way of Kendall County. ∞

*Carolyn Chipman-Evans*

## Fun on the Trail

This was our biggest and best year ever. During the 1993-94 school year 2350 students from Bandera, Boerne, Comfort and Northside Independent School Districts and St. Mary's Hall visited the Wilderness Trail. They played games, wrote poetry, saved a 'poison river', measured a tree, chased insects, tested the water and got their feet wet, all the while learning important ecology concepts such as bio-diversity, watershed conservation, nature's cycles and recycling.

I want to give special thanks to our incredible volunteer trail guides, who give of themselves to turn our trail into an enchanting outdoor classroom - a place of authentic discovery and true delight. Everything that the education program accomplished is thanks to:

Anne Adams, Theresa Brown, Linda Chalberg, Lora Carlisle, Kim Clogston, Chanda Day, Mary Dillard, Barb Herbst, Clayton Hodges, Jody Jones, Darrah McCammon, Ann Meyer, Lottie Millsaps,

ing to learn how to use a program. We suggest you find someone who will help you at first, by teaching you to work the
program while creating a newsletter.

You will need money for postage, paper, and printing—
it's the best investment you'll ever make. If possible, print a
few hundred extra in order to leave some with the chamber
of commerce, schools, nature stores, your local library, and
so forth. In the early stages of organization, your first contributors should be asked to help support the newsletter. Some
nonprofit organizations actually print advertisements of local
businesses in their newsletters to help defray the publication
and postage costs. Start small and simple but be consistent in
your mailings. It's important to present an image of reliabil-
ity. When you get enough names on your mailing list, around
three hundred, check with your post office about the benefits
of bulk mailing. It can save you money, but plan on having
volunteers help in the sorting and bagging. Bulk mailings also
go slower through the mail, so be sure to mail your materials
in plenty of time for the event calendar to be current.

**Making national network news, the Cibolo Nature Center planted trees with visitors from the Soviet Union on the day before Earth Day, 1990, when news organizations were hungry for such stories.**

When you go to the printer, ask for "postconsumer" recycled paper options: The colors are beautiful. If you go to a local printer, they may give you a discount on printing for a mention in your newsletter. Shop around. Prices vary, but the cheapest may not be the most sympathetic to your cause, and it may be more expensive in the long run. Don't be afraid to ask for help. Our local "Mom and Pop" printing business has donated posters, given us discounts on newsletters and been tremendously patient, giving us hours upon hours of advice, skill, and expertise. We wouldn't use anyone else.

### The Media

When starting out, it is important to inform the media in a professional manner. Journalists like positive stories, and a service project in a beautiful setting in nature can make a great news story. However, approach the media with respect, and without a sense of entitlement. Rubbing the local media the wrong way can result in a severely handicapped grassroots movement. Stay positive in your story. Don't make wild claims

**WORD TO THE WISE**

**Newsletters have hidden work in store for you. In addition to the writing and designing, there is the planning of the calendar, the bulk mail sorting, the printing of mailing labels, the sticking on of labels, the mailing. Get volunteer help! It's work, but it is worth it.**

---

### A Press Kit

A press kit is a good idea when you are just starting out. Basically it includes the following:

- a press release announcing the organization's purpose, and details about the campaign—
  list who is to be contacted, and how, for more information;
- a fact sheet detailing your project, location, progress, and anything else you want the media to know;
- good black and white photos of your nature center location; get the best photos you can;
- quotes from prominent people saying good things about you and your cause;
- a list of your board of trustees and staff; and
- a personal invitation for a tour of your site.

or exaggerate the facts. Give the media representative written information with essential facts to minimize their work and avoid inaccuracies in reporting.

Carefully choose who will represent your organization to the media. They should be clear thinkers with personality and organizational skills. They must be informed about the organization's agenda, and what sensitive areas to avoid.

Be flexible with your time, understanding that reporters' schedules are hectic and demanding. Be available for visits with reporters, and offer dates when things are happening at your trail, such as a "trailblazer" crew cleaning up a creek. Often times they will prefer to see people in action, but let them know what to expect. Some reporters may show up in dress clothes or high heels. They would not enjoy bushwhacking through dense vegetation to follow your scout troop on a river clean-up.

Small local papers are often weeklies, with firm deadlines concerning news stories or public service announcements. Your organization must learn what their schedules, deadlines, and idiosyncrasies are.

News stories need to be interesting to the public that patronizes the newspaper or broadcaster in question. Stories should be unusual, capture the imagination, and have a simple basic message. You may want to take advantage of local television and radio stations that offer talk shows or public information programs. You can request a public service announcement, or you may do better to strike up a relationship with a producer and find out what the opportunities might be.

Established nature centers have ongoing public relations activities that must be maintained, to continue active community involvement. At the Cayuga Nature Center in Ithaca, New York, with an annual budget of $420,000, the public relations coordinator spends ten hours per week on public relations, public education, and program marketing.

## HOW TO COOPERATE WITH CITY HALL, SERVICE ORGANIZATIONS, SCHOOLS, BUSINESSES, AND EVEN YOUR FRIENDS

A community-based nature center must reach out to as many groups as possible. Each community is a system composed of many elements: government, schools, churches, busi-

Media attention to conservation issues can increase public support to nature centers. Cartoonist John Branch of the San Antonio Express News raised public awareness of the monstrous growth of San Antonio (S.A.) and its encroachment upon the Boerne community and the countryside.

nesses, service organizations, clubs, and families. Each of these elements can be of potential help to the center.

### City Hall

Approaching local government is best accomplished informally. Talk to those in official positions as people, and seek their advice and support. Citizens often go to officials with complaints or hare-brained schemes. Therefore, many officials have learned to say no first, even when an idea sounds good. So don't give up at the first sign of resistance. Address objections with intelligence and calmness, with a determination that is sincere. Government officials are most often well-intentioned individuals who want to leave behind a lasting legacy of public service. Invite them to visit the proposed site with you. Let nature do the sales job. Help them visualize what a nature center can be. Pictures can be very helpful. For this reason, we have included photographs and other illustrations in this book to help you inspire your target individuals.

### It's Your Chamber of Commerce

Nature tourism is big business. Often times the chamber of commerce will help promote nature centers because they bring visitors to the community. In our case, the director of the chamber helped us create our newsletters, provided us with media mailing lists, published our programs in the calendar of events, made posters, sent us magazine contacts, and much more. If you can nurture a relationship with your chamber of commerce, by all means do so. Again, personal contact is the key. Go talk to your chamber director.

The chamber is your best bet for meeting the business community. Offer to present a short slide show and talk at a chamber luncheon. It is a great way to win support from local businesses. Have your facts in order; speak from the heart.

Recruiting business support will be vital to the success of your project. Keep your eyes open for business owners who are sympathetic to your cause: They are potential board members. They can open doors for you. The business owners are usually community-minded and care about their image. Therefore they can be great support in outdoor education campaigns or special events. Just remember to thank every contributor publicly in as many ways as possible.

## Businesses

Businesses exist to make money, but businesses are also run by people who can be inspired. In addition to liking your project, businesses can benefit by the positive public relations and advertising that can result from involvement with a popular community project. There are tax benefits for contributing to nonprofit organizations. Businesses can be recognized for their contributions in your newsletter, on plaques or signs, in the local newspaper, and in other media.

## Schools

Your local school system can find tremendous benefits from a local nature center. Field trips, science projects, and customized curriculum can excite teachers as well as students. And, having the support of your local schools greatly enhances the prestige of your project. Also many businesses will be likely to support your cause if the schools are involved. A Partners in Education campaign can elicit funds from otherwise reluctant sources.

Find a few key teachers or administrators who can see the value of a nature center. This group can become your base of power within the school system. Having advocates from within the school system will dramatically increase your

After a recycling effort at their school, inner-city students enjoyed an outing at their local nature center.

**Our local Optimist Club helps with construction of the nature center. Optimist Clubs serve the youth of their communities.**

chances of involvement. Some school districts support nature centers in substantial ways, providing ongoing funding for staff or programs, while others pay for field trips per student or per class. Some districts need to be educated about the advantages of providing such curriculum enhancement.

### Religious Organizations

About 40 percent of the U.S. public are affiliated with a religious organization, so churches, synagogues, and other local religious groups are of potential help. Their newsletters and bulletins inform members of upcoming community events. Some organizations will see the value of the nature center to their own congregation and may want to provide service or use the facilities for gatherings.

### Service Organizations

Service organizations and clubs in local communities are constantly approached for help with good causes. You will need to explain how a nature center can benefit the community and its special needs populations and what kind of recognition the service club will receive. Make a few acquaintances with these organizations, so that you have a sense of what kinds of projects get favorable response. For example, Optimists Clubs typically like youth projects. Lion's Clubs often focus on the needs of handicapped children.

It is also advantageous to know how much to ask for when seeking funds, since there is no sense in "pricing yourself out of the market." Some groups have very little capital but can offer skilled and unskilled labor for projects at your site. Remember that recognition, such as a picture in the local paper, helps the service organization and encourages more contributions in the future.

### Friends

Working with friends can be one of the great joys of nature center development. Here your friends can join in fun and meaningful activities, and have a lasting impression on your community. And having friends on your board of trustees is essential. Some founding directors have discovered themselves crosswise with their own board, finding that they did not have a basic *simpatico* relationship that could help them weather storms and difficulties. Besides, bonding in nature is jazzy!

Working with friends also has potential problems. Friends can join your efforts out of friendship and end up regretting how much time they are giving to the project. Friends can disagree about how the project should develop. Some friends may feel you are too radical about environmental issues, while others may feel that you are not radical enough. It is natural to seek the help of friends, but overtaxing your best relationships with your pet projects can severely test friendships. Make sure your friends are actually wanting to be involved, rather than just having difficulty saying no to you. Working on projects of mutual passion can actually be the most exhilarating times for friendships. But when you start sensing fatigue or resistance from friends, pay attention. You need volunteers who are happy doing what they are doing. And you need your friends, whether they are volunteers with your project or not!

### DEALING WITH OPPOSITION AND CONFLICT

It can be hard to imagine who would oppose the creation or expansion of a nature center, when the benefits seem

Our children and their friends on a community outreach project, along with strange superhero, "Garbage Man."

*Every progressive spirit is opposed by a thousand men, appointed to guard the past.*

—Maurice Maeterlinck,
*The Blue Bird*

so obvious. Since every member of the community can enjoy such a facility, natural resources will be preserved, and tourists can add revenue to local businesses, where would the opposition come from? There are several likely sources: neighbors who fear congestion, citizens who favor using the land for other purposes like golf courses or residential development, or people who have philosophical objections.

The Fort Worth Nature Center and Refuge went through a period of conflict of interests in the early seventies. Many activities such as hunting, fishing, picnicking, camping, dumping, gravel mining, motor biking, and running hounds had gone on for years with little or no control. This resulted in large sections of land being abused. Adjacent to the center, there were dog kennels, boat landings, a police pistol range, dumps, the Fort Worth Rehabilitation Center, and housing developments. To cope with these problems, issues of zoning, roadway and land use, park policies, and overall planning had to be addressed. Imagine your local fire department using part of your sanctuary for bomb disposal explosions. It happened at Fort Worth, because of disagreements over land use. This nature center now has one of the most sophisticated five year strategic plans in the nation (and a small and fabulous buffalo herd), thanks to the expertise of its director, Wayne Clark, and a farsighted board and city council.

A conflict can also develop within your own organization. In any group, it is inevitable that some conflict will occur. This is the result of diversity; it is not a bad thing. Through expressing different points of view, members of a group can develop a common bond and a common core of beliefs. Even power struggles can be healthy if mutual respect is maintained, because natural leaders emerge.

The first rule of dealing with conflict within the community is to respect the differing opinions and attempt to work out compromises. Even when others become emotional or provocative, your demeanor must remain calm, friendly, and mature. When some residents of our community favored using a native prairie for ball fields, the city government eventually worked hard to find and finance new park land for ball fields, so that the native prairie could continue to exist. Instead of vilifying your opponents, or using confrontational tactics, you may be able to win new allies by finding ways to help them achieve their purposes also. Nevertheless, you cannot please everyone, and choices must be made.

The next rule is to deal with the opposition in person, rather than through the media or third parties. By being available and personable, you minimize conflict and maximize chances for an agreement. Politicians may say things that sound like they support your project, and then later take less than supportive positions, owing to pressures from other sources. Continued contact with politicians throughout a political process is suggested.

Even after compromising and attempting to consider other viewpoints, conflicts may have to be resolved through the political process: city council decisions or even a referendum election. The problem with this kind of victory is that someone loses and can become a lifelong opponent of the project, sabotaging you at every opportunity. Therefore, consensus building and compromise are the preferred courses when possible. However, at times it is necessary for the elected officials to see a "show of support," such as a meeting room filled with supporters, or petitions signed by local voters.

What about when there seems to be no "rhyme or reason" to the opposition, such as "I just hate environmentalists," or "Trees are good for one thing—firewood!"? In certain situations, there is no reasoning with the opposition, because it is coming from an emotional or philosophical position. Face it, some people just have axes to grind and may decide that your project is their problem. When you attempt to do good in the world, you will get the flack that comes with creating social change. There is always some resistance to change, so greet the resistance as evidence that you are making a difference, and do not let the negativity of others infect you. Unless you are extremely blessed, you will lose some battles. It is vital to keep your perspective about your long-range goals, not allowing the inevitable defeats to discourage you. When wounded in such a battle, let nature heal your wounds. Take a walk in some natural beauty, and you will be soothed and renewed.

Developers have long held a powerful and revered position in our culture. When in conflict with developers, you are at a profound disadvantage, even when public opinion is on your side. Never underestimate the power of economics. Woo the developers in your community, asking them where there might be a good site for a nature center, inspiring them with photos (and projections of increased property values). Credit them for their help. There are often sites that developers have abandoned because of "drainage problems." Such plots of land may be exactly what you are looking for. If, on the other hand, you are competing with developers for the land in question, respect their knowledge and experience. They may respond to public pressure by donating or saving the most environmentally sensitive part of a recently purchased property—they have to live in your community, too. (At least, some of them do.)

## POLITICS

Although conservation issues can become political, our nature center project has been multipartisan. After all, these days many people in our country think of themselves as "conservationists." Concern for our world and its future is something that can bring us together. Traditional political terms like liberal, conservative, Democrat, and Republican do not seem to be as significant as personal interests. If self-interest is at stake, the political wheels can start turning. As Mark Twain said, "You show me where a man gets his cornpone, and I'll show you where he gets his opinions" (cornpone being symbolic of a person's basic means of survival). For example: Some real estate developers may imagine that taking land off the market to create a nature center will result in a loss of revenue, until they discover how property values actually increase near nature centers. Therefore, see past the usual political boundaries, and show individuals how a nature center can benefit them personally. And do not expect to find your support in only one side of the political field, because some of the greatest accomplishments in the conservation movement have been unlikely coalitions of property owners, businesses, government, and individuals.

Some organizations, such as the National Audubon Society, take strong political positions on issues—like strengthening the Endangered Species Act. Other groups keep a lower profile, working to inform the public on issues without advocating particular political action. This becomes a decision for the membership of each organization to make, within the parameters of the mission and bylaws of the organization. As your community of nature center supporters grows, it will take on a life of its own.

---

### NAIVE NOTIONS

1. Everyone will fall in love with the idea as quickly as I did.
2. Things will progress at a predictable pace.
3. This will be a problem-free project.
4. Introducing the public to a natural area can be done without damage.
5. People will use common sense.
6. People will do what they say they are going to do.
7. Money is no big deal.
8. Bigger is better.
9. It can't be done.
10. I remembered to thank everyone in the newsletter.

# Chapter 10
# Money Matters: Costs, Budgets, and Funding

*Dream, diversify, and never miss an angle.*

— WALT DISNEY

THE NITTY-GRITTY DETAILS of operating a nature center involve money. However, your project can grow at its own pace, without being a slave to the dollar, if you are careful to understand costs, develop a realistic budget, work out a fund-raising strategy that fits your community, and remember to get outdoors a lot. Especially before and after number crunching, take to the wild.

## COSTS

How much does it cost to run a nature center? According to the *Directory of Natural Science Centers* (see Appendix B), less than 10 percent of nature centers report annual budgets of less than $25,000, and a similar proportion report budgets in excess of $1,000,000. More typically, centers fall into three categories of budget size: 23 percent have budgets between $25,000 and $100,000; 35 percent report $100,000 to $250,000 budgets, and 31 percent administer annual budgets of between $250,000 and $1,000,000. Don't let these numbers discourage you. No nature center began with money in the bank. Each community is unique, and any community can create its own nature center.

*Most important advice:* Keep records of all financial activity. From the very beginning, keep receipts from all purchases of goods or services for the project. Keep a record of all volunteer time or materials donated to your project. Keep a record of your own time and activity. These records become a vital tool in selling your project, keeping it alive, and helping it prosper. This chapter will discuss the kinds of records you should be keeping and methods of fund-raising.

Your organization will need a budget, which is a financial plan of what you expect to receive and spend in the next year. You will also need a record of actual income and expenditures: a financial statement. These two documents will form the basis for all financial decisions. These documents provide members and potential fund sources with a clear understanding of what you intend to do and what you have done.

## BUDGETS

As you are starting out, you will realize that any budget you imagine is just a dream, but it helps to have an idea of what you would like to do in the first year, and how much it might cost. You have nothing more than projections and income targets, but those figures are markers for measuring your progress and knowing where you are at any given time.

It's good to have an idea of where you are striving to go, but it's also important to be flexible. In the early stages of the Cibolo Nature Center's development, we were suddenly given a building to move onto the property and renovate as our headquarters. Obviously this was not part of our projected budget. However, with the new vision of a headquarters, we were able to gather the funds and help necessary for the move and renovation from private individuals and a grant obtained from the Texas Parks and Wildlife Department through the City of Boerne.

The opposite development occurred for the Riverside Nature Center in Kerrville, Texas. Their dream building burned down before it could be renovated. They rose from the ashes, found a new site, gathered help from local businesses and individuals, borrowed money, and purchased structures to be moved to the new piece of property. Your budget projects what you think will happen. Your creativity and adaptability will create your reality.

Your initial budget will be dictated by the goals you have established through your mission statement and the action plans you have made. As you try to put a price tag on projects like trails, interpretive signs, educational programs, and improvements, we suggest having two budgets: a dream budget and a bare-bones survival budget. You can begin the dream

**A WORD TO COMFORT YOU**

**If you are feeling intimidated by the size of the task or the complexities of dealing with budgets, understand that a nature center project begins small and usually grows in manageable steps. You can grow with it. The momentum created by the person-to-person contacts you make will generate some of the funds you need. If you don't try to grow too fast, you will learn where moneys are available and how to access them. Try not to go into debt. Let the nature center support itself as it grows.**

budget by constructing short-term and long-term wish lists. When speaking with potential large contributors, you can ask for state-of-the-art signage detailed in catalogues. But also keep in mind the very real possibility that you may end up building the signs yourself out of donated or recycled materials. In this way, you cast seeds in all directions and find out later which landed in fertile ground.

Your budget can address short-, intermediate-, and/or long-term goals. Some more established nature centers publish a five- or ten-year strategic plan, while others are surviving on a year-to-year basis.

Bookkeeping for a nonprofit organization can become complicated, because you must account for different groups of funds: foundation grants, membership fees, program income, shop income and expenses, donations, building funds, and on and on. You should be able to track where your funds came from and how they were used, on a month-to-month basis.

If a foundation grants your organization $15,000 for building a discovery room, you will need detailed receipts and statements that document how the money was spent, showing that indeed the money was used for the purpose for which it was intended. Obviously you don't use such dedicated funds for other purposes. If you accept a matching grant, which carries an expectation that you will generate additional funds, you must document that you have in fact matched the grant. One answer is a separate checking account for each major fund your organization has. Another option is to develop a separate budget for each program and operation component, and then use a spread sheet to combine them into an overall budget. In this way you can allocate overhead expenses to each program, according to percentage of use. A cash flow budget can predict problems during the fiscal year, so that you can prioritize your fundraising activities to meet your projected needs.

The need for a professional accountant with some nonprofit experience becomes clear as your project expands. A part-time bookkeeper with occasional help from the accountant and yearly audit may be sufficient. This is where the dreaded Peter Principle (advancing your career into areas you are not competent in) can play havoc with novices. If you have

### Table 1. Friends of the Cibolo Wilderness 1993 Operational Budget

| OPERATING INCOME | | Actual | *In-kind |
|---|---|---|---|
| *Contributions* | Individuals | 15,000 | |
| | Foundations | 12,000 | |
| | Business | 3,650 | |
| | Total | 30,650 | |
| *Other Income* | Fundraising (net) | 5,000 | |
| **Total Operating Income** | | 35,650 | |

| OPERATING EXPENSES | | Actual | *In-kind |
|---|---|---|---|
| *Education* | Honoraria/professional | 5,700 | 300 |
| | Printing | 1,440 | |
| | Supplies–materials, printing | 850 | |
| | Bus transportation for schools | – | 500 |
| | Dues and publications | 250 | |
| | Program coordinator | – | 1,000 |
| | Salaries–director | 10,000 | |
| | Total | 18,240 | 1,800 |
| *Development* | Printing newsletter | 1,100 | 200 |
| | Postage | 200 | |
| | Supplies | 400 | 500 |
| | Hospitality | 300 | |
| | Development | 500 | |
| | Salaries–director | 5,000 | |
| | Total | 7,500 | 700 |
| *Nature trail and center* | Trail maintenance/supplies | 300 | |
| | Center maintenance | 500 | |
| | Student volunteers | – | 3,000 |
| | Adult volunteers | – | 5,000 |
| | Utilities | – | |
| | Total | 800 | 8,000 |
| *Administration* | Accounting | – | 2,000 |
| | Office Supplies | 50 | |
| | Postage | 600 | |
| | Telephone | 600 | |
| | Insurance | 900 | |
| | Salaries–clerical | 2,400 | 2,000 |
| | Salaries–director | 3,000 | |
| | Payroll taxes | 1,560 | |
| | Total | 9,110 | 4,000 |
| **Total Operating Expenses** | | 35,650 | *14,500 |

*"In-kind" figures are donated services or materials. It is important to document these donations and to demonstrate community support.

Note: the director listed in categories is one person.

**The generosity of this local professional painter resulted in the saving of thousands of dollars through his in-kind donation of services.**

advanced beyond your personal level of financial competence, get an accountant! Recruit a competent volunteer treasurer with bookkeeping experience. Look among yourselves for the most qualified person. Ask around for referrals. Many financial professionals are willing to volunteer if asked. Some people actually *love* bookkeeping; you can help them shine, while saving yourself from hair pulling and teeth gnashing.

In-kind contributions are services or items of value that are donated in lieu of monetary gifts. Our center was entirely painted by volunteer labor and donated paint.

Tables 1 and 2 provide a sample budget of a small, five-year-old nature center (Cibolo Nature Center) in 1993. This is divided into two sections: the operational budget, which funds ongoing functions of the center (Table 1), and the capital improvement budget, for new construction (Table 2).

**Table 2. Cibolo Nature Center 1993 Capital Campaign: Construction Detail**

| Costs | Cash | In-kind |
|---|---|---|
| Porch roof construction | 5,000 | 700 |
| Porch screening | 4,150 | |
| Paint | 1,000 | 1,000 |
| Floor refinishing | 1,500 | |
| Library shelving | 3,000 | |
| Shelving | 1,000 | |
| Landscaping | 500 | 1,500 |
| Closet addition | 7,200 | 1,000 |
| Permanent porch railings | 1,500 | |
| Porch steps | 1,200 | |
| Heater/AC installation | 500 | 1,000 |
| Signage | 250 | |
| Plumbing | 400 | |
| Electrical fixtures | 500 | |
| Total | 27,700 | 5,200 |

For purposes of comparison the following budget categories are presented to illustrate the operations of a larger nature center:

Revenues *(note whether the amount is guaranteed or potential)*
        Membership fees
        Donations
        Events income
        Interest income
        Gift shop revenue
        Grants
                    *Total revenues*

Expenses *(note whether the amount is fixed or adjustable)*
        Printing and promotional materials
        Professional fees
        Staff salaries and benefits
        Office expense
        Meeting expense
        Exhibits
        Events expenses:
                Arts and crafts fair
                Enchanted Forest
                Native Plant Sale
                Public educational programs
                Bird seed and feeder sales
        Banquets
        Bus trips
        Membership
        Miscellaneous
                    *Total expenses*

Each nature center adopts its own system for accountability, and no two budgets will be alike. As you begin attracting volunteers, keep your eyes out for people with bookkeeping and/or accounting experience. The importance of accurate records cannot be overemphasized. Foundations and agencies that donate money will not tolerate inaccurate or incompetent accounting and will stop funding groups that fail to keep adequate financial records. The above examples are simple, while larger centers will have more complex and sophisticated budgets. As your organization grows, you can consult with larger organizations regarding budget development.

## FUNDING

Fund-raising strategies vary widely among nature centers and have involved both traditional and innovative approaches. The basic rule of thumb that seems to run through most of the responses to our survey suggests that nature centers take their funding where they can get it, and usually that means locally. Sometimes the donor of the land for the nature center also offers a grant or endowment. Sometimes a governmental entity commits to funding the operations or particular programs offered by the center. Most often, numerous funding sources, rather than one primary source, support the project. The majority of nature centers we surveyed are partnerships between "Friends," (nonprofit) organizations, and public entities, relying on public funds, private donations, program fees, contracts, endowment income, annual giving programs, grants, fund-raising drives, nature shops, and memberships.

Another important piece of advice we can give is that you will not receive any funds from any source unless you ask. This fact seems simple enough, but is often overlooked by timid activists. The reality of the need for a direct and often bold approach will eventually dawn on every nature center administrator and board member. We have found that asking friends and family does not create hard feelings and does engender support. When you give talks to organizations, ask for funds, or in-kind help. Do not assume that people understand your needs. Ask for the amount that you believe a group can provide, and define how the funds will be used. Knowing your target audience will help you gauge your request to their abilities and interests. Public approaches vary by community, traditions, and the creativity of the organization.

We suggest that you be direct when you approach an individual, without apologizing or pressuring. "Toot your own horn." Tell of your accomplishments. Ask for what you hope for, and know your budget well, so that you can answer questions knowledgeably. After asking for help, allow the person to respond, without expecting rejection. Remember that "no" may mean "not now." Ask again at a later date. Know who to approach for special projects, endowments, capital drives, or in-kind contributions. Have written information to leave with the person, detailing the possibilities for giving and how the gift can be used. Stay optimistic, and view each rejection as one more step toward a jackpot!

**The Large Gift and the Four Rs of Fundraising: Research, Romance, Request, Recognition**

When searching for major gifts for your nature center, plan to be patient and persistent. The first step is finding out who is a potential donor. It takes understanding what the *donor* is interested in to understand how to ask for a gift. This is where your research comes in. Find out as much as you can about who this person is. What have they given to in the past, what are their favorite hobbies, what do their children like to do, are they linked to your organization, who are their friends? Be gracious and polite, but ask questions. If at all possible, find a personal connection through someone who knows the donor or the donor's spouse. This will help tremendously. Never make a "cold call" and ask for a gift right away.

If you have no contact, send a personal letter from a volunteer fund-raiser. The letter should express the writer's personal commitment to the organization, the organization's mission, perceived link to recipient, and the next projected step contact (a phone call).

Formulate a plan to contact your potential donor. Select the best volunteer for the prospect, hopefully someone who has had some connection with the donor and someone who understands the financial workings of the organization. Fund-raisers are the ambassadors of your organization. Choose them carefully. A first meeting will not be to ask for anything. When you call prospective donors, let them know you want to tell them about your organization, let them know about new developments and dreams. Often, asking for advice is a good way to start a relationship. The easiest prospects are those who have given some small gift in the past, sent their grandchild to summer camp, or at least received your newsletter. You need to create a bond between prospective donors and your organization. Spend most of a first meeting finding out about their interests and values. Most people give major gifts to perpetuate their values. This is where the romance comes in. Help them understand how your nature center can help them express themselves.

Perhaps you will find that your prospect's deceased wife loved birds, or that in his youth he was a great outdoorsman. Be all ears. Your job is to find out what *they* need and help them find a way to get it.

Involve your prospect in your project. Invite her to events of interest, send her publicity you have received, newsletters, and notes. Ask her for feedback on how your organization is doing.

A good way to develop a relationship with donors is to invite them to an exclusive party for your benefactors. When they call to RSVP set up a meeting time to follow the party. Make your party small enough so that you can follow through on each one.

Make your request. Procrastination kills the process. After developing a relationship with your prospect, it is time to decide how much to ask for and how. You will know when the time is right. If you don't know how much a donor is capable of giving, present your budget and goals. You can say, for example, "In order to accomplish the educational goals we have talked about we need a total of $_____. Would you be interested in helping us with a gift in one of these categories?" Show a list of options; don't be afraid of listing large and small amounts. Special funds can be created to honor the donor. Think creatively about what your organization does that fits the prospect. But, never accept a gift with strings attached that are not compatible with your mission or that will build something you can't care for.

Once you receive a gift, it is very important to find out what kind of recognition is appropriate to your donor. Not everyone wants the world to know about their gift, but even anonymous givers still want attention. If they are receptive to publicity, have their pictures in the local newspaper giving you a check, put their names on a plaque or building, thank them in your newsletter, and always keep them in your mailing list. Be receptive to their needs. Do not forget about your donors until next time you need money. After the meeting in which the gift is agreed upon, write a letter of agreement along with a heartfelt thank-you note. Thank and thank and thank until they give again.

If you get the dreaded "No," treat it as a "Not now." Find out what they are saying no to. Ask about your prospect's concerns, and be gracious. Tell them "thank you" for their help in the past, and let them know you will keep them posted about new developments.

Study the art and skill of fundraising. It is essential to any nonprofit organization to have people who can get their heart into asking for gifts. The beauty of getting large donations is how good it makes the donors feel. To help someone fulfill their desires to leave a mark in the world is noble work. It makes everyone happy and good things become possible.

A fund-raising plan can clarify for your group who are the target populations for future nature center patronage, and how to approach them. Look up the names of individuals and organizations that have donated funds to other organizations in your community. These names can be found through your local funding information center, or a foundation directory, and often on plaques on the walls of libraries, community centers, and hospitals.

Your plan can also indicate who will approach these individuals or groups and what they should ask for. This involves everything from public relations with local news media to membership drives, annual fund drives, corporate grant solicitation, individual donations, and school outreach. Young nature centers are usually not so systematic. After all, people who start nature centers are often creative, right-brained people, who do not think in such pragmatic, linear terms. This is why nature center founders often seek help from professional administrators who are more experienced with systematic planning.

The Association of Nature Center Administrators is the best source of information about specific fund-raising strategies, marketing plans, and development plans; it has compiled a pamphlet entitled *Fundraising for Nature Centers,* which is provided to new members. Volume 1 includes the following tactics:

- Completing a Successful Capital Campaign
- Rent-a-Bucket
- Flight into Fashion
- In-Kind Instead of In-Cash
- Robotics Exhibits for High-tech Fundraising
- Guidelines for Operating a Nature Center Shop
- Cash for Trash: Trash-a-Thon
- Direct Mail Campaigns
- Starting and Running a Planned Giving Program
- Customer Service: Concessions
- A Phantom of a Fundraiser
- Corporate Investment in Community Interpretive Programs
- Bird-A-Thon
- Adopt an Animal

Attending an ANCA Annual Summit can be particularly helpful. Meeting other administrators and sharing ideas can help the novice learn from the trials and errors of the experienced veterans. In 1996 the Summit was conducted at the Aullwood Audubon Center and Farm in Dayton, Ohio. Topics at this conference included:

- Creation, Care, and Feeding of Special Interest Clubs
- Collaborative Fund-Raising
- Getting to Know Your Market
- Building Endowment Funds
- Institute of Museum Services—Information to Help Nature Centers
- Standards for Nature Centers and Residential Learning Centers
- LeadTeam
- Managing Multiple Sites
- Integrating Evaluation into Your Entire Program

Nonprofit organizations receive about 85 percent of their financial support from individuals through annual giving and endowments, the remaining coming from foundations, corporations, and bequests. Therefore, your organization should have a broad approach to fund-raising and not rely on single large entities, which can suddenly end support and shut down your center (all your eggs in one basket).

Nature center projects can start generating funds through program fees and memberships. Newsletters keep you in touch with membership and generate new members. Research suggests that the most effective method of solicitation is personal and face-to-face. Personal phone calls are half as effective, followed by personal letters, and then phone-a-thons. The least effective is direct mail. All approaches can work, and all should be tried.

A "Giving Club" of major donors is a popular method of generating capital. This involves approaching and maintaining contact with major target donors—individuals capable of and probably interested in helping with large donations ($100, $500, $1,000, etc.). This can be established by responding to larger gifts with thank-you notes, personal phone calls, invitations to special meetings, honorary advisory boards, personal visits, special dinners, requests for advice, and media events. The club can be organized by an annual contribution plan involving a certain amount of money, which can be paid annually or made in several payments. Some centers create several different clubs at different funding levels. Luncheons, dinners, seminars, or special parties can be used to bring interested persons together and motivate continued giving. Recognition in newsletters, special publications, plaques, or local newspapers can be arranged. However, make sure that your donors *want* to be recognized, because a few may not want their names publicized, because of the solicitation from other groups that may result. Some are simply humble.

### The Passionate Art of Proposal Writing

Approaching business, government, or foundations for grants involves the art of writing a proposal that describes a need and proposes a program to fill that need. Finding a volunteer or board member who is skilled in this area would be helpful. Hiring a grant writer can be expensive and is not always successful. The best proposals are written from the heart.

For a fledgling organization with novice grassroots organizers, usually the best alternative is to just learn how to do it yourselves. After all, you know the project, feel the passion, and can answer the questions. Most large communities have a central funding information center that can be helpful to nonprofit organizations. Two very helpful publications are

**Grant for nature center construction presented by the Lower Colorado River Authority to the City of Boerne and the Friends of the Cibolo Wilderness.**

*Successful Fundraising: A Complete Handbook for Volunteers* and *Professionals and Environmental Grantmaking Foundations* (see Appendix B). Another good source for learning grassroots fundraising techniques is *The Simple Act of Planting a Tree* by Andy and Katie Lipkis.

Before writing the proposal, you should write a letter of inquiry or call the funding source, and verify whether funds are available for such a purpose and if there is a specific proposal format to be followed. Most proposals include the following components:

1. *Summary Statement or Abstract:* tells the major features of the proposed plan, what is to be accomplished, how much it will cost, and how long it will take.

2. *Introduction:* describes the organization's qualifications or "credibility."

3. *The Need:* is a defense of why the plan is necessary and why no other organization can fulfill this specific need.

4. *The Objectives:* are the proposed outcomes of the project stated in clearly specified, measurable terms. Usually an objective is provided to meet each major need.

5. *The Method:* is a statement of how objectives will be accomplished. Each objective should be followed by a procedure.

6. *The Evaluation:* details the means by which the organization and the funding source will know the project has accomplished its objectives within a definite time frame.

7. *Future or Other Necessary Funding:* describes a plan for continuation beyond the grant period and/or the availability of other resources necessary to implement the grant.

8. *Cost/budget:* presents a financial outline of what you expect the expenses of the project will be. It is necessary because it helps you to limit your expenditures and it reinforces the ideas presented in the proposal. An annual budget, and possibly a three-year projected budget, will be required.

9. *"People give to people."* Personal contact with the funding source is highly recommended. Who you know is important; relationships make or break the project.

## Support from Local Government

Soliciting a governmental entity, like city hall or the county commissioners court, is certainly a lesson in political science. All governmental entities are made up of people who can come to see the value of your project, and eventually find ways to help fund it. There is enormous competition for tax dollars, but many politicians and citizens do appreciate the value of nature centers. The solution involves education and perseverance. Approaching politicians or civil servants should be done with a combination of respect, patience, and a good sense of humor. Governments usually operate on annual budgets, so you should start your education program in a timely manner, perhaps six months in advance.

Many nature centers evolve through years of gradually expanding community support before local governments decide to participate in funding. Successful inclusion of governmental support begins with person-to-person contact. Find folks who like your project and involve them in it. This is like planting seeds rather than pushing a button. If a piece of land suddenly is available, and you don't have time to cultivate relationships, then a large show of community support, through letters, petitions, and public hearings can sometimes influence your local leaders.

**Other Good Ideas**

Someone may offer to donate land for your nature center. In such circumstances they may have a vested interest in seeing the nature center succeed and may be open to discussing endowing the project with operational funds as well. Sometimes an individual is interested in donating real estate in return for tax advantages and the lifetime use of the property: a life estate contract, or charitable remainder trust (see Appendix B: Publications, *Preserving Family Lands: Essential Tax Strategies for the Landowner*).

A real estate donation can be one "bucket of worms." Gordon T. Maupin of The Wilderness Center, Inc., describes several of the complications in the ANCA Newsletter *Directions* (vol. 4, no. 3). Land can be encumbered in a number of ways, through legal restrictions, donor requests, building problems, and so forth. In short, consult your experts. There are few entanglements more complex than those in real estate, and jumping at a gift horse can create huge problems for the impulsive recipient. What about utility easements, restrictions, taxes, liens, or deed complications? On the other hand, a gift of land may be a tremendous asset for your organization. Look closely. Land offered with no endowment can be risky. Be open-minded, but smart. Develop a land acquisition policy.

The avenues to funding are many and varied. Tactics for generating funds have included parties, summer camps, overnights, canoe trips, workshops, door-to-door canvassing (local regulations may require solicitation permit), telethons, payroll deductions, memorials, bequests (through a donor's will), charitable gift annuities, charitable remainder trusts (a donation of property that becomes available to the center after the donor's death), charitable liens trusts (a donation of property or stocks that the center can use for a specified length of time), donated securities—even "laser rock concerts." Talk to financial experts. Basically, you are developing relationships and trust. Patience, persistence, and perseverance are the keys to fundraising.

Approach state fish and game departments, parks and wildlife departments, private preserves, public parks, school districts, universities, foundations, businesses, and individuals —try them all. But keep in mind that your dream will really be driven by your enthusiasm, and the tenacity of your spirit.

In Minnesota an innovative approach is being undertaken by five nature centers—a cooperative fund-raising effort to develop a coordinated environmental education system for all audiences in the state. This enables the centers to cooperate in a fund-raising effort, rather than competing for funding. For more information, contact the Greenprint Council or Project Earthsense.

Nature centers tend to grow. As citizens discover the value of their nature center, adjacent properties sometimes become available through bequest or sale: The Chippewa Nature Center in Midland, Michigan, started out in 1966 with three acres and now has 885 acres, with a membership of fifteen hundred and an annual operating budget of $700,000. What's more, "seed moneys," or grants for the initial development project, do eventually run out. With an austere economy, it is more and more vital that nature centers nurture their members for local support. Nature centers that depend on political entities or single sources for funding are more vulnerable than others, so diversifying sources of income is usually the wisest path. There are a few centers, like the Max McGraw Wildlife Foundation, that have been so well endowed by the original donor that they are financially independent and need not even charge for their programs. This is the exception. Most centers must keep an active fund-raising campaign going, if they are to survive.

Several of the administrators we surveyed mentioned being careful about what money you agree to accept. Strings can be attached to funds that require more conditions, or documentation, or a greater surrender of your ideals than you want. Read all grants and financial documents thoroughly, and be clear about the requirements. You can receive a large grant for a building that requires a particular level of maintenance and staffing but no funds for such purposes. A large membership may be able to provide the extra funds needed, but a small membership in a small community may not be able to. There are facilities we have visited that are no longer open to the public, because the project development got ahead of itself. For example, we have seen an extensive live animal demonstration facility fallen into disrepair, with no animals in it, because the original grant was restricted to "bricks and mortar," and the board had assumed that operating funds could be obtained. Be cautious.

If your nature center is operated by a small group of very interested people who do not reach out to the surrounding community, it is vulnerable. A community-based center, supported by a broad spectrum of the citizenry, is much more likely to weather hard times and have sure and steady growth.

## What About Earning a Living?

Can you create a nature center that might eventually pay you a salary? Yes. Some founders eventually do wind up on the payroll of a nonprofit organization. There is nothing wrong with making a living by doing what you love and helping save natural resources. The board of trustees of your nonprofit organization can hire you so long as this is not expressly forbidden by your bylaws. This means that they can also fire you, so maintaining congenial relationships is a survival issue.

If your nature center is owned by a governmental entity, you may develop such good working relationships with the officials that they may create a position and hire you to administrate the park. Being instrumental in creating a nature center, even on public land, can demonstrate your abilities and prove as valuable on your resume as a college education.

How much do nature center administrators make? The salary range among administrators is broad. In 1993 Robert A. Mercer of the Silver Lake Nature Center completed a survey of fifty-eight members of the Association of Nature Center Administrators. He presents his findings in the newsletter *Directions* (vol. 5, no. 2, 1995). Fifteen reported salaries of less than $30,000, three of whom received supplemental housing. Twelve administrators made more than $45,000, and twenty-eight fell somewhere between $30,000 and $45,000. ANCA is conducting another survey that will compare the whole range of positions and salaries. This can be deceiving, because of the varying cost of living around the country. Nature center employees do not get rich, but conscientious directors are working to raise salaries of employees.

A large community can provide a healthy budget. The Milwaukee area supports the Riveredge Nature Center with a

$650,000 annual budget, paying its executive director up to $65,000, with health insurance, tax-deferred annuity, vacation, sick leave, and other benefits. Qualifications for the position include the following:

- Master's degree (or equivalent combination of education and experience) in business administration and management and/or environmental science, natural science, or a closely related field;

- a minimum of five to seven years of proven successful experience in leading and administering an environmental education center; and

- contagious enthusiasm, creativity, and common sense.

If your community is small, you should keep your expectations modest. We had no training, no money, and not enough time. The community itself provided the expertise. We just nurtured the land and the people the best we could. If your community wants a nature center, it will eventually learn that volunteers can usually do only so much: For continuity and accountability, centers need a paid administrator and links to professional organizations. A small nature center with a small budget, an administrator, and just a few volunteers can create a sustainable enterprise.

Many centers evolve to the point of staffing several positions in addition to administrator, such as naturalist, education director, office manager, secretary, wildlife rehabilitator, maintenance coordinator, and so forth. Hiring staff defines the character of the nature center. Knowledge is important, but personality is even more so. Nature center employees should love nature *and* people. Your staff is the critical ingredient that will help your community fall in love with your center. Their ability to teach and inspire will access visitors to nature's lessons and build a community that is sensitive to planetary issues.

---

*Perseverance furthers.*    —I Ching

---

# Chapter 11 Managing Land Without Managing to Ruin It

*This we know—the earth does not belong to man,*
*man belongs to the earth. . . . So, if we sell our land,*
*love it as we've loved it. Care for it as we've cared for it.*
*Hold in your mind the memory of the land*
*as it is when you take it. And with all your strength,*
*with all your mind, with all your heart, preserve it*
*for your children, and love it . . . as God loves us all.*

—CHIEF SEATIIL*

ONCE THE LAND has been entrusted to you, you have a responsibility to the land, to your membership, and to future generations. Stewardship includes being mindful of legal issues, so that you do not end up with a piece of land that is so legally encumbered that it is unusable. You will need a clear board policy for dealing with offers of land, and an organizational structure that can implement it. Find a board member who is well versed in local real estate law as soon as possible.

Severely damaged land must be *rehabilitated* by bringing in new soil and replanting. If land is moderately damaged, it can be *reclaimed* by bringing in a few historic species. To fully *restore* a piece of land, soil must be intact, exotic species are removed, and extensive replanting and reintroduction of close genotypes are carried out. (See Appendix B: Publications, *Environmental Restoration.*)

From the very start of your project, you need to be mindful of conservation issues. There are so many different ecosystems that are served by nature centers that it would be impossible to be specific about conservation measures for every possible project. *Full Circle: Restoring Your Habitat to Wilderness* is a good overview of restoring a wide range of habitats: wetlands, grasses and legumes habitats, old fields, crop fields, food plots, woodlands, shrub and tree areas, ripar-

*Attributed to Chief Seathl (Seattle) of the Suwamish tribe, in a letter to President Franklin Pierce, 1854

ian zones, perches and cavities, urban landscapes, and backyard habitats. Another useful resource is *The Earth Manual: How to Work on Wild Land Without Taming It.* (See Appendix B.) Many biologists spend a lifetime studying a particular habitat or subecosystem. Therefore this chapter will examine some basic generic considerations in the management of nature center properties.

There is a delicate balance between protecting the land and allowing people to enjoy it. If there is water on the property, people will find a way to get to it. You can provide access, or they will create it. Water is, after all, fun.

Safety is a vital concern, and a nature center can easily contain an "attractive hazard." Warnings of hazards should be clearly posted, and appropriate precautions taken. Examples of hazards include a lovely creek engulfed in poison ivy, a narrow trail along a steep cliff, a slippery path, or a wild bee colony in the wall of your headquarters. People will be curious and inquisitive, seeking adventure where better judgment leaves off. So, provide adventures of the safe variety, and use reasonable precautions, such as "caution signs" for challenging trails. See *Signs, Trails, and Wayside Exhibits,* of the University of Wisconsin's Interpretive Guidebook Series.

The Wilderness Center, Inc., of Wilmot, Ohio, has developed an excellent land management plan, with a detailed explanation of why a land management plan is needed, a history of land management, basic assumptions, objectives, policies on introduction of plant species, and management policies for the various zones within the park. When you are serious about developing your own land management plan, a copy of this plan would be most helpful (see Appendix C: Nature Centers Surveyed).

## FIRST STEPS

Our primary advice is to be humble in your approach, asking lots of advice from others and moving slowly and carefully in learning how to care for your piece of paradise. The steps involved in creating management policies actually begin at the moment of inspiration:

1. Fall in love with a place, or see its potential.
2. Get permission to take walks there.

A boardwalk provides access to the marsh without damaging the fragile habitat.

3. Take some naturalists for walks with you, and ask questions. Ask about the type of habitat, the native flora and fauna. Ask about the present condition of the prospective park, its health, its problems, its possibilities. It takes years to become knowledgeable about any habitat, so seek many sources for information and consultation.

4. A survey of the flora and fauna within the nature center boundaries is essential if you are to systematically approach the question of land management. This task is complex, and can often be accomplished by approaching local universities, wildlife management consultants, parks and wildlife departments, county extension agencies, or soil conservation services. If not done in the early stages, you can unintentionally destroy rare species.

5. Seek consultation regarding actions that would encourage native species, without dramatic disturbance of the local ecology. (*Example:* Think twice if you are advised to apply large quantities of herbicide in order to restore a "native" area—you may lose more than you gain.) Talk to local biology teachers, ranchers, farmers, agricultural advisors, Sierra Club members, Audubon members, bird watchers, game wardens, and naturalists. Look in the yellow pages of the nearest large city for a sympathetic collaborator under Land Planning Services, Landscape Architects and Contractors, Ranch Management, or Wildlife Management.

6. Investigate local colleges and universities for departments in earth science, biology, wildlife management, and geography, for assistance in early surveys, thesis projects, and local support.

7. Build your land management plan slowly. You will find a number of very confident experts, with differing points of view. Gradually, you will gather enough information to form your own educated opinion. Encouraging biodiversity, particularly native species, should be of primary concern.

8. Nature is constantly changing. Don't expect to achieve some kind of permanence in your conservation plan, because there will be changes! Storms, floods, droughts, fires, infestations, blights, diseases, die-offs, and the

inevitable invasion of humans are part of nature, too. Remember John Lennon's line: "Life is what happens to you while you are busy making other plans."

9.  Once you know what type of habitat you have, you can start studying how you can help, what aspects are more fragile, and how an influx of humanity might change the area you are considering. (*Example:* Keep in mind that people will come in cars with motors and radios, which can prove too noisy for certain nesting birds and beasts.)

10. Think in terms of high-impact and low-impact areas. High-impact areas will be near motorized traffic and parking areas, possibly having facilities such as restrooms and picnic tables.

11. Land management planning requires careful thinking through of the rules of behavior that you will need to ask of visitors. Issues such as the general paths you wish people to travel will be handled by careful trail planning and construction (see Trail Building and Trail Etiquette sections below). Different visitors are often going to want different services. Your center cannot be all things to all people. Will you provide facilities such as tables, litter barrels, and periodic litter cleanup? What about hunting, fishing, rock collecting, pets, boom boxes, four wheelers, motorcycles, bicycles, swimming, rock climbing, firewood cutting, camping, fires, and dumping? Posting rules is essential. Common sense is not that common in the natural setting when people live most of their lives indoors.

12. Questions about wildlife that your land management plan should address include the following:

    a. What local regulations exist regarding wildlife management?

    b. What must be done to preserve and improve the habitat for native species? For example: controlled burns.

    c. What wildlife, if any, should be introduced into the area?

    d. What do current surveys tell you about the status of species in the area, including numbers, problems, and recommended strategies?

There are different schools of thought about conservation. Some people are "purists" in terms of how "native" plants should be: Some folks want only pre-Columbian species; others feel that nature is in constant flux, and that some introduced species are fine as long as they are not aggressively invasive. Everybody has an opinion; you will most surely develop your own.

For additional information see Appendix B: Publications for resources that can help in developing a land management plan for your particular situation. Some examples: *Adopting a Stream, Environmental Restoration, Helping Nature Heal: An Introduction to Environmental Restoration, Prairie Restoration for the Beginner, Restoration and Management Notes, Sources of Native Seeds and Plants.*

Most of all, hold on to that magical feeling you had when you fell in love with that landscape. Preserve the feel of the place. Protect it from eyesores. A seemingly correct approach to land management can be aesthetically appalling. You are conserving not only species and ecosubsystems, but the wonder and beauty that touched your heart in the first place.

**You are conserving not only species and ecosystems, but the wonder and beauty that touched your heart in the first place.**

*Friends of the Cibolo Wilderness News*
September 1994, Field Notes

There was a day not long ago when I stood in the marsh and looked at the last remaining pool of still water. Tracks of bewildered animals patterned the dry ground. I imagined the loss we would feel if all the water sank deep into the earth, leaving no oasis for the heron, turtle or raccoon. I spoke to the trail guides in training about the natural cycles of marshes; sometimes they are wet, sometimes they do dry up. It's natural. Even if the children come to the Trail to find no water to dangle their fingers into, no water in which to dip nets and trays, it is all right. This is a place where we can see what is real. If we live in neighborhoods with green lawns and water continues to come out of our faucets, how can we feel the drought? How can we imagine a low water table?

When I stood on the boardwalk, once surrounded by clear water, now perched on dry ground, I felt the drought in my bones, in my heart. I quietly prayed for rain, looked wishfully to the sky and felt a certain uneasiness in the dry, clear, blue.

But I talked the brave talk, remained scientific in my explanation and convinced myself that it would really be all right if the 6th grade came through the dry marsh. There were still wonders around and they would definitely learn something. We could explain how the more water is pumped out of the ground, the less water there is for ponds, streams and marshes. Perhaps we could convince these students to conserve more water, be more aware, etc. It was really beginning to sound like a good activity.

The next morning was dark, as if the sun hesitated just below the horizon. The air was thick with moisture and promise. I must say I was not disappointed when all my plans for the 6th graders were washed away by a torrential downpour. The first rain only partially filled the marsh, but now the cycle of beautiful sunny days seems to be broken and we are brimming once again. The sky has become big in my eyes with layers of billowy clouds and a palette of color. I am celebrating the goodness of rain and it seems all's right with the world.

—Carolyn Chipman-Evans

**NURTURING NATURE**

Wildlife needs habitat that provides water, food, cover, and protection. Each habitat is a complex system of interdependent organisms. The basis of all life in an ecosystem is the interaction of soil, water, and atmosphere, which create the myriad of microscopic organisms that are the building blocks of the various food chains in the system. Well-intentioned stewards of the land can do considerable damage in the process of trying to "improve" a habitat. Land managers have introduced foreign species to areas to solve problems, only to discover that their introduced species have become a much larger problem than the original. In most situations, improving the habitat means manipulating the combination of water, food, cover, and protection in a way that gradually increases the native flora and fauna of the area.

Novices in nature center development may wish to put the public in touch with wildlife, and in the attempt apply inappropriate solutions. For example, telling local residents to release all their captured raccoons in the nature center area is not a good idea. Raccoons will soon overpopulate the park, attacking bird nesting areas and creating an imbalance in the natural system. Sound land management can help the public view wildlife without harming the ecosystem that they are coming to enjoy.

The now out-of-print National Audubon Society publication *Wildlife Habitat Improvement: Guidelines on Habitat Management Measures* suggested three types of zones for nature centers: intensive educational use areas, management demonstration areas, and natural areas. Each of these areas should be managed differently, in accordance with their purposes.

**Wildlife "management" requires in-depth knowledge of how all members of a biological community interact with each other.**

### Intensive Educational Use Areas

Intensive educational use areas are designed to provide teachers, students, and the public with structured naturalist lessons. These are often high-impact areas, including interpretive circles and areas that can accommodate large groups or classes who have come to experience wildlife. Many centers manipulate the natural setting to facilitate these experiences with wildscaping (planting food-producing plants that attract wildlife to easily viewed locations), bird feeders, nesting boxes, frog and fish ponds, floating logs or rafts for water fowl, spray fountains or dripping pipes, brush piles, viewing blinds, or even captive live animal displays.

## Management Demonstration Areas

Management demonstration areas educate the public about management techniques that can be used on private or public lands to promote wildlife habitat and improve the quality of local stewardship. Such projects can include wetland reclamation, ponds or marshes with controlled water levels, patches of food-producing plants, plant succession plots or strips, arboretums (demonstrating native tree species), open spaces for wildlife, salt licks, water "guzzlers" for wildlife, artificial animal dens, fence rows interspersed with vines, shrubs, and trees, wildflower demonstration plots, prairie restoration projects, forest replanting, artificial nesting projects for endangered birds, and so forth. In these projects, nature centers usually favor trees and shrubs with high wildlife value, such as plants that produce a large amount of seeds, berries, and fruit for wildlife consumption. Some recommendations for wildlife management are described below; they provide a good overview of some land management possibilities. (Thanks to our friends at the Texas Department of Parks and Wildlife.) Specific actions should depend on expert local advice.

*Brush management* involves the establishment, maintenance, or selective removal or suppression of targeted woody plant species (including exotics) to encourage the growth of native trees, shrubs, grasses, and forbs for forage and nesting or protective cover for selected wildlife species.

*Range or prairie management* involves the establishment of native plants, such as grasses and wildflowers, to provide food and cover for wildlife or help control erosion. Seeding mixtures should provide for maximum native plant diversity.

*Riparian management* focuses on protecting the vegetation and soils in low areas on either side of stream courses, as well as clean-ups.

*Forest management* encourages the growth of desirable trees, grasses, and forbs for forage and nesting or protective cover for selected species.

*Wetland management* provides seasonal or permanent water for roosting, feeding, or nesting for wetland wildlife. This

**WORD TO THE WISE**

**Providing natural foods for wildlife through planting native food crops is more ecologically sound than providing feeders, since animals become dependent on artificial feeding and can often suffer severe losses in bad weather or times of negligence on the part of those feeding. Bird feeders should be placed in viewing areas, with good ground cover. When visitors can view wildlife directly, the resulting thrill and sense of compassion for animals is rewarding. However, big game animals will concentrate in artificial feeding areas and can become susceptible to disease and parasites. Therefore, seek advice regarding artificial feeding in your area, to avoid potential problems and yet provide visitors with "close encounters of the wild kind."**

includes creating, restoring, or managing shallow wetlands, greentree reservoirs, playa lakes, and other moist soil sites.

*Grazing management* is needed by nature centers that maintain grazing livestock herds, such as buffalo or cattle. Livestock grazing is shifted to increase food and animal cover and to improve specific animals' habitat.

*Prescribed burning* is the planned application of fire to improve habitat and plant diversity, to increase food and cover, or to improve particular species' habitat. Your local natural resources conservation service, state parks and wildlife department, or fire department may have controlled fire experience.

*Habitat protection for species of concern* provides habitat for an endangered, threatened, or rare species. This may involve protecting nesting sites, feeding areas, and other criti-

**Prescribed burns require careful planning, firefighter backup, and an experienced "fire boss."**

cal habitat-limiting factors by fencing off areas, managing vegetation, creating firebreaks, and annual monitoring.

*Native, exotic, and feral species management* involves controlling the grazing and browsing pressure from native and nonnative wildlife (such as deer or hogs), to prevent overuse of desirable plant species and to improve the habitat and plant diversity for native animals.

*Wildlife restoration* improves a habitat for targeted species and reintroduces and manages native species within a habitat's carrying capacity.

*Erosion control* reduces soil erosion by the following means:

- Pond construction
- Gully shaping
- Streamside, pond, and wetland revegetation
- Establishing native plants
- Water diversion and dike or levee construction

*Predator management* is sometimes necessary to protect a vulnerable wildlife population from depletion. Such predators may include brown-headed cowbirds, feral housecats and dogs, wild mammalian predators, fire ants, or grackles and starlings.

*Providing supplemental water* increases wildlife populations through marsh or wetland restoration or development, provision of wells, troughs, and windmill overflow, and spring development.

*Providing supplemental food* is also a means of increasing wildlife populations; it can be accomplished though food plots (at least one-quarter acre per twenty acres of park land), feeder and mineral supplements, and managing tame pasture, old fields, and croplands near natural areas.

*Providing supplemental shelter* is the active creation or maintenance of vegetation or artificial structures that provide shelter from the weather, nesting and breeding sites, or "escape cover" from enemies. The best shelter for wildlife can be provided by a well-managed habitat. The following practices can provide shelter that may not otherwise be available in the nature center habitat:

- Installing nest boxes and bat boxes
- Brush piles and slash retention
- Managing fence lines
- Half-cutting trees and shrubs
- Establishing woody plants and shrubs
- Developing natural cavities and snags

*Census counts* are periodic surveys and inventories to determine the number, composition, or other relevant information about a wildlife population to measure if the current wildlife management practices are serving the targeted species. This can be accomplished through spotlight counting, aerial counts, daylight wildlife composition counts, harvest data collection and record keeping, browse utilization surveys, and monitoring of non-game, endangered, threatened, or protected species.

### Natural Areas

Minimal management is usually employed in these areas to allow the visitor to appreciate nature in its wild state. Some of the above-mentioned management techniques may nevertheless be necessary to preserve or protect the habitat. Primary consideration in these areas is to minimize the impact of visitors and maximize the natural character of the habitat. Therefore, springs and water seepage areas are left undisturbed. Dead and fallen trees are left to provide dens and habitat for little creatures. Sand and gravel are used in openings and along access roads and trails to prevent erosion in traffic areas. The goal is to keep the area ecologically natural.

### TRAIL BUILDING

Trail building is an art all its own. There are several sources listed in the appendix on trail building: *Lightly on the Land: The Student Conservation Association Trail-Building and Maintenance Manual*, *The National Park Service Trails Management Handbook*, and *Trail Building and Maintenance*. *Signs, Trails, and Wayside Exhibits: Connecting People and Places* is another excellent publication in the Interpreter's Handbook Series by the University of Wisconsin.

There are four types of trails:

1. *Interpretive trail* (up to 1 mile): Provides concentrated informational stops to explain ecological issues and natural features.

2. *Nature trail* (up to 2 miles): Provides an opportunity to walk and study interesting or unusual features at the user's own pace.

3. *Hiking trail* (2 miles and over): Provides long-distance walking experiences.

4. *Access trail:* Provides access between areas or from other types of facilities, like gardens or recreation fields.

When planning trail building, keep in mind these four points:

1. Water flows downhill and takes soil with it.

2. People will tend to take the path of least resistance, whether this tends to cause erosion or not.

3. Existing trails may not be the best for the future.

4. Professional consultation is just as important for your trail as for any complex construction project.

Here are some further considerations in regard to trail construction:

1. *Erosion control*—Water diversion methods, steps, drain tiles, improved surfaces for high-traffic areas or handicap access.

2. *Interpretive stops*—Accessing and educating the public without destroying or overdeveloping the attraction.

3. *Fragile areas*—Barriers and signs to discourage entry.

4. *Bridges and boardwalks*—Professional design for safety, accessibility, and proper functioning.

5. *Rest stops*—Professional design strongly advised, so that the facility meets codes for sanitation, accessibility, and safety, while maintaining aesthetic appeal.

6. *Signs*—Educational value, durability, clarity, and simplicity.

7. *Maintenance*—Ongoing expenditures of time and money.

8. *Vandalism*—Findings from the experience of other nature centers:

   a. Parking areas usually experience more damage.

   b. Access trails from public streets or other types of facilities can attract persons with no interest in nature.

   c. Interpretive displays are common targets.

   d. Immediate cleaning and repairing prevents copy-cat destructive behavior.

   e. See Appendix B: Publications, *Vandalism Control Management for Parks and Recreation Areas.*

9. *Littering*—More findings from the experience of other nature centers:

   a. Parking areas and roads experience the bulk of littering.

   b. Frequent litter clean-up reduces volume of litter.

   c. Picnicking should not be encouraged along trails, because picnickers inevitably litter, and litter barrels require service vehicles that will also cause erosion.

10. *Stopping places*—Just as highways need periodic turn-offs, so do trails of any distance. Hikers need to rest, and if no such stops are designated, your visitors may block the trail by sitting in the middle of it. Visitors may use rock outcrops or durable places, and even vegetated or fragile areas. Benches help direct walkers to such stops.

## TRAIL ETIQUETTE

At the entrance to Manyara National Park in Tanzania, visitors encounter this sign:

> Let no one say
> and say it to your shame
> that all was beauty here
> until you came

The rules and etiquette suggestions that you give to visitors will help protect the park and the visitors, and express your interpretive message. Rules should be clear and should be stated positively and explained when necessary. The following messages typically are found on nature center signs:

**Boardwalks should be designed with durability, safety, accessibility, and beauty in mind.**

- Please stay on pathways (fragile habitat).
- Shortcuts cause erosion—please stay on the trail.
- Pack it in, pack it out.
- Please, don't disturb the ecology.
- Keep your dog on leash at all times.
- Caution: Feeding wild animals ruins their survival habits. They carry diseases—and they bite!
- Swimming prohibited: Don't feed the alligators!
- Please, take only pictures, leave only footprints (on the trail).
- Please do not disturb wildlife.
- No fires!
- Please allow the sounds of nature to be louder than your own.

**Top, opposite page: Vandalism can be minimized by prompt repair, which often prevents copy-cat behavior.**

Left: Signs can be expensive and durable, or they can be simply laminated paper on plywood.

Landscaping timbers are set to control erosion and provide an easily traversed sloping trail.

For multiuse trails, these signs are often appropriate:

- Hikers, wheelchair-bound visitors, bicyclers, and motorized trail users: Please stop and give horseback riders right-of-way (some horses spook easily).
- Horseback riders: When encountering motorized vehicles, bicyclists, hikers, or wheelchair-bound visitors, "collect" your horse, wait for them to give right-of-way, and proceed cautiously. Your mount may spook at unfamiliar sights and sounds.

Ask children to think of themselves as visiting their grandmother's home. "You wouldn't pull up her rose bush, would you?" Other statements can help: "Wild beings belong here. We are the guests. Try to leave nature a little better than you found her! Pick up litter, and help us keep this place forever wild."

The population explosion has reached our parks and wilderness areas in such a dramatic fashion that campers and hikers all over the country are now being asked to use "minimum impact" techniques and attitudes. The National Outdoor Leadership School has published *Soft Paths,* which is an excellent resource for describing these techniques and the reasons for them (see Appendix B: Publications).

**WORD TO THE WISE**

**Horse manure can contain grass seeds of any variety. If you are attempting native plant restoration and are concerned about indiscriminate seed dispersal, horseback riding may have to be banned.**

# Chapter 12 Planning: Making the Dream Come True

*In our every deliberation, we must consider the impact*
*of our decisions on the next seven generations*
*. . . on those faces that are yet beneath the ground.*

— **THE GREAT LAW OF THE SIX NATIONS**
**IROQUOIS CONFEDERACY**

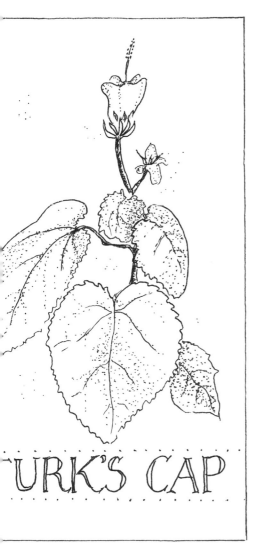

URK'S CAP

AS YOUR PROJECT EVOLVES, the need for a master plan will arise. This is an issue for fledgling nature centers and particularly for organizations that are ready to begin applying for large donations and grants. For the nature center pioneer who is excited, motivated, imaginative, and vibrant, writing a master plan would be about as much fun as doing taxes. Never fear! Magically, a worthy volunteer will appear, perfectly happy to be a systems person, who can put your wild ideas into clearly worded goals, objectives, and the like—if you live right.

Governmental entities, foundations, private contributors, members, and visitors will want to know what the final product will be. As your membership grows, a sense of direction and purpose will be needed to focus the efforts of your group. Without a master plan, one segment of your organization can be planting wildflowers in an area that another group wants to use as an interpretive circle. If your group works in partnership with a governmental organization, the master plan can facilitate cooperation and unity of purpose and prevent many conflicts. Furthermore, your master plan can sell your project to potential supporters.

The master plan is the dream. The overall plan usually contains the mission statement and a proposed management plan, describing the interpretive strategy, the facility options, the operations and maintenance policies, budgets, funding approaches, and land management policies. It may also contain a marketing plan. It usually includes a map of the major features of the proposed nature center, showing land formations along with current and projected facilities, with explanatory notes. A master plan map should lay out the locations of all existing and proposed trails, buildings, roads, parking areas, facilities, exhibits, fragile areas, points of interest, utility lines, watershed areas, and hazards. Often an architect will provide this pro bono, since it may eventually generate business.

## DEVELOPING THE MASTER PLAN

The first step in constructing your master plan is to decide upon the interpretive goals and strategies that you will use to accomplish the mission. As you decide which strategies will best suit your situation, your facility and trail plans will emerge.

Advice from experienced nature center operators, or the Association for Nature Center Administrators, is strongly suggested at this stage of development. Private consultants can be expensive, but when a nature center receives generous financial support, this is money well spent. (See Appendix A: Organizations, ANCA and InsideOutside.)

**Don't forget to consult the real experts.**

Usually nature centers start out poor, just as ours did. We couldn't afford a professional consultant any more than we could afford to buy signs or pay for the newsletter. Gradually we did buy signs and pay for newsletters by begging for funds anywhere we could. Business-minded donors will often see the value of early professional consultation and donate funds to ensure a viable project. We recommend that you actively search for professional help. Some consultation will be freely given by local experts with community spirit. Get all you can for free. However, you are likely to receive more comprehensive help from a paid "pro." If you can afford professional advice, get it. You can always ignore their advice if you don't like it. Remember your thank-you notes.

The master plan map can be constructed by a friendly architect or surveyor. Landscape architects are often ideal for the job. Check with the local city or county offices for maps that you can purchase or copy, which can be enhanced with additional information that you gather. The map you create should be checked with the actual situation on the ground. Walk every area noted. Some maps are not accurate or up-to-date. Aerial photos or contour maps will be quite helpful when you start serious planning of building sites and trails. Remember to be flexible in your plan. Often things change, or new ideas come to light.

Your master plan, like all aspects of your project, will evolve through time. Some master plans can be quite extensive and expensive, while others may be short and stated quite generally. For example, the modest plan for the Cibolo Nature Center was entirely donated work, except for the final architectural drawing, which cost $750.

The Master Plan for Ijams Nature Center commissioned a team of architects, landscape architects, and interpretive exhibit planners to develop a market analysis, interpretive plan, site master plan, building concept, and interior exhibit plan. A five-year budget, staffing, and attendance projection was created, and a consulting group was hired to assist with planning and implementation of the capital campaign, which raised a total of $3.4 million between October of 1994 and June of 1995. Of course, this is a thirty-two-year-old organization with a $370,000 annual budget and more than two thousand active members.

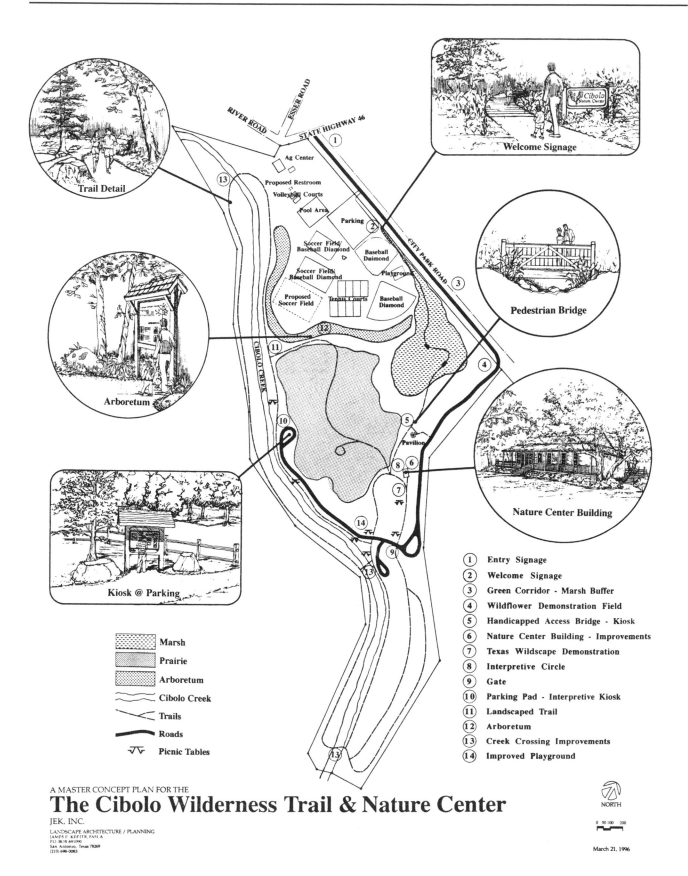

Trail Detail

Welcome Signage

Pedestrian Bridge

Arboretum

Nature Center Building

Kiosk @ Parking

RIVER ROAD
ESSER ROAD
STATE HIGHWAY 46
CITY PARK ROAD
CIBOLO CREEK

Ag Center
Proposed Restroom
Volleyball Courts
Pool Area
Parking
Soccer Field/ Baseball Diamond
Baseball Diamond
Soccer Field/ Baseball Diamond
Playground
Proposed Soccer Field
Tennis Courts
Baseball Diamond
Pavilion

Marsh
Prairie
Arboretum
Cibolo Creek
Trails
Roads
Picnic Tables

1   Entry Signage
2   Welcome Signage
3   Green Corridor - Marsh Buffer
4   Wildflower Demonstration Field
5   Handicapped Access Bridge - Kiosk
6   Nature Center Building - Improvements
7   Texas Wildscape Demonstration
8   Interpretive Circle
9   Gate
10  Parking Pad - Interpretive Kiosk
11  Landscaped Trail
12  Arboretum
13  Creek Crossing Improvements
14  Improved Playground

A MASTER CONCEPT PLAN FOR THE
# The Cibolo Wilderness Trail & Nature Center
JEK, INC.
LANDSCAPE ARCHITECTURE / PLANNING
JAMES F. KEFFER, FASLA
P.O. BOX 691090
San Antonio, Texas 78269
(210) 698-0083

NORTH

0  50 100    200

March 21, 1996

There is no standard master plan. The master plan of the Runge Conservation Nature Center in Jefferson City, Missouri, is laid out as follows:

1. Area information
   a. Area and vicinity map
   b. Length of planning cycle and management intensity
   c. Background
2. Area expansion plans
3. Area resources and management
   a. Existing natural resources
   b. Management history and potential
   c. Goals
   d. Objectives and strategies for resource management
   e. Public use and access, including:
      Target audience objectives
      Visitation objectives
      Programming/delivery objectives
      Volunteer objectives
      Promotion objectives
      Evaluation objectives
4. Implementation schedule and management costs

The Ijams Nature Center master plan is structured as follows:

1. Introduction
2. Membership and attendance projections
   a. Membership
   b. Attendance projections
3. Interpretive concept
   a. Mission statement and goals
   b. Story line
   c. Interpretive characteristics

**Opposite page: Master plan for the Cibolo Wilderness Trail and Nature Center.**

4. Master plan

   a. Site assessment

   b. Interpretive experience

   c. Arrival

   d. Trails and interpretive notes

5. Headquarters building

   a. Designing criteria

   b. Space utilization

   c. Square footage breakdown

6. Exhibit hall: Interior exhibit description

## STRATEGIC PLANNING

The strategic plan is a long-range plan for an organization, including organizational issues, marketing strategies, communications, and advertising. It details the process that is initially laid out by the master plan. If you are joining an existing nature center, ask about the existence of a strategic plan, or the plans to create one. Strategic planning will determine the future path that the organization follows, and you may want input. As Tim Merriman noted in *Directions* (vol. 3, no. 3), key questions need to be addressed:

- What is to be obtained or done?
- What are the financial considerations?
- How will the goals be accomplished—what tasks are involved?
- Who will do the work—make definite assignments?
- How will the organization provide support?
- How will the work be completed?
- When will the work be completed?
- How will tasks be measured or judged as done?
- Why should these be done? Do yields outweigh risks?

### Steps in Strategic Planning

1. Organization of the process

   a. Decide to develop a strategic plan.

   b. Get commitment.

    c. Determine if outside assistance is needed.

    d. Outline a planning process that fits.

    e. Form a planning team.

2. Situation analysis

    a. History.

    b. Mission.

    c. External opportunities and threats.

    d. Strengths and weaknesses.

    e. Critical issues for the future.

3. Strategy

    a. Choose a planning approach.

    b. Identify and evaluate alternatives.

4. Drafting and refinement of plan

    a. Agree on format.

    b. Develop first draft.

    c. Refine the plan.

    d. Adopt the plan.

5. Implementation

    a. Implement the plan.

    b. Monitor performance.

    c. Take corrective action.

    d. Update the plan.

For our young organization we began strategic planning in 1990 with a statement of mission, goals, purposes, and methods. The plan continues to evolve.

## CIBOLO NATURE CENTER: STRATEGIC PLAN 1990

### Mission Statement

The Friends of the Cibolo Wilderness is committed to preserving greenspace and recreational lands in an effort to maintain the high quality of life in the Hill Country. We intend to continue to support the City of Boerne in their efforts to preserve and extend the Cibolo Wilderness Trail.

## Goals

1. To establish a long-term commitment to the preservation of the Cibolo Wilderness Trail and Prairie and other areas as discovered and acquired.

2. To develop research and educational programs based on tours and studies of the Cibolo Wilderness.

## Goal 1 Objectives

- To seek a legislated long-term commitment by the City of Boerne to preserve the Cibolo Wilderness Trail and Prairie.

- To continue developing a Board of Trustees willing to support the organization's mission and long-term goals.

- To develop an effective community of support providing funds to preserve, restore, and sustain the Cibolo Wilderness and educational programs utilizing its resources.

- To develop and expand a growing community of volunteers.

- To recruit and organize an Advisory Committee to provide expertise in the effective preservation of the Cibolo watershed; identify plants and wildflowers; interpret the trail and advise as needed.

## Goal 2 Objectives

- To develop a curriculum for area schools using the Cibolo Wilderness Trail as a living classroom, and to subsidize transportation for the schools to the site.

- To seek, develop, and accommodate university-level research programs utilizing the resources of the Cibolo Wilderness Trail.

- To develop a Docent Training Program to give tour guides the tools they need to interpret the Cibolo Wilderness Trail.

- To develop a program of public information to raise awareness of the Cibolo Wilderness Trail and promote community wilderness preservation.

- To continue monthly education programs at Cibolo Wilderness Trail and the newsletter.
- To develop an advisory committee to share ideas and needs for a nature center.
- To build a nature center at the Cibolo Wilderness Trail to accommodate information exhibits and educational programs.

## Methods (Action Steps)

In order to fulfill our goals we will:

1. Establish a membership with dues and fund-raising activities.
2. Hire a director and recruit a very dedicated volunteer director.
3. Move a building donated to the CWT to the site, renovate it, and equip it as a nature center.
4. Provide 36 general educational programs/activities throughout the year serving approximately 2,000 people of all ages.
5. Provide curriculum materials and teacher training for teachers who will influence approximately 2,000 students, including field trips for Kendall County schools.
6. Supervise trail maintenance and improvement by volunteers.
7. Provide public presentations for local and regional groups requesting information on environmental concerns.
8. Provide a clearing house for environmental information.
9. Provide newsletters and educational publications.
10. Interact with communities through Texas, the nation, and the world in support of community-supported natural area preservation.
11. Promote the concept of "setting aside" undeveloped natural areas and providing comprehensive support, to include management, of such areas in the Boerne/Hill Country region.

What kind of strategic plan does an established nature center need? The Aullwood Audubon Nature Center, an established center since 1957, has a well-developed nature center, working farm, and trail system. Aullwood must now focus its efforts on advancing the dream that its pioneers worked so hard to achieve. Its strategic plan is structured in the following way:

1. **Building understanding and support for Aullwood Audubon Center and Farm in general.**

    a. Active association with local civic organizations such as Rotary, Lions Club, Chambers of Commerce, Optimists, etc.

    b. Participation in community events.

2. **Recruiting the kind and quality of members that the Friends of Aullwood can best serve.**

    a. Ongoing membership drive.

    b. Annual corporate membership drive.

    c. Market study of community needs which can be met by Aullwood.

3. **Obtaining financial support for current operations, major maintenance, special activities, endowment, and capital growth.**

    a. Annual membership solicitation—"Light a Candle" campaign in December.

    b. Fund-raising with special activities: Wildlife Festival, Earth Rhythms, Apple Fest, Quilt Auction, Happy Bird Day, etc.

    c. Grants.

    d. Capital or endowment campaigns.

    e. Deferred giving/estate planning for bequests.

The strategic plan also addresses the target audiences, primary responsibilities that will be assumed, and an action plan. Aullwood's director, Charity Krueger, told us that keeping an established nature center going and growing can be as challenging as creating one in the first place. Indeed, the network established during the creation of a nature center becomes its backbone. This family tree of relationships will need

**WORD TO THE WISE**

**If all this sounds absurdly regimented, understand that funding sources want information presented in this way. You will never receive substantial funding without strategic planning. Again, do not be intimidated by any task before you. We promise that if you have been good, you will indeed find someone to help. It is a law of the universe that we have discovered. So, have faith and proceed.**

to continue branching outward. The group's ability to be far-sighted and focused determines longevity.

Local planners can be helpful, such as a Nonprofit Resource Center. The Association of Nature Center Administrators has a good track record for helping nature centers develop customized strategic plans. The long-term viability of your organization depends on sound strategic planning.

## OPERATIONS POLICIES

When a nature center is created as a grassroots movement in the community, many people are involved, each with well-meaning ideas and energy to expend. Without careful guidelines, some volunteers can be undoing the work of others. Conflicts can be avoided and a well-coordinated center can emerge. There are many vital issues that must be addressed by the guidelines you create for the operation and maintenance of your center. At the time of this publication, ANCA is producing a manual for nature center administrators, which will be particularly valuable to administrators with less than five years' experience.

When you finally get a building to deal with, and land to steward, the excitement is overwhelming. The last thing you will be thinking about is writing up procedures. But this project may last hundreds of years, and as it develops, you will gradually find a need for having policies and procedures written down, even if you are a one-person operation. The following is a list of issues that usually have to be addressed sooner or later as a nature center matures. Again, do not worry. (This is a lengthy list, and our nine-year-old center has not completed half of these items yet.)

Some essentials:

- job descriptions for staff positions, docents, or volunteers
- lines of authority—an organizational chart
- membership policies
- rules for representing the nature center to the media (communications plan)
- rules regarding nature center financial transactions
- land management plan
- land acquisition plan

Operational issues to consider:

- hours of operation
- rules for use of facility
- guidelines for public events
- techniques for interpretation
- building repair and maintenance, records, and procedures (For example, if volunteers are staffing your center, they need to know where the water turn-off and the electricity breaker box are located. These little details can be outlined in a manual that volunteers are trained to use.)
- guidelines for special facility management, for example:

    book/nature shop

    live animal exhibits

    office

    discovery rooms or discovery boxes

    outdoor classroom programs for schools

    fund-raising events

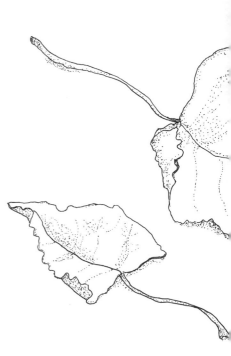

At some point the nature center will have a thick policy manual, addressing the specific concerns of your particular organization. Crises often give birth to policy statements, but good policies can prevent crises.

# Chapter 13 Hope

*In my own experience, nature was encountered
most intimately when I left the city to go to our ranch.
Once there, I quickly fell in tune with the great
rhythms of life. I knew whether the sky held
a new moon or a full moon or the dark
of the moon. When storms came, I thrilled to
the crackle of lightning and the majesty of
thunder. I rediscovered a sense of caring and
a sense of smell from the perfume of blossoms
and grasses after a rain. This participation
in the seasons and the weather is one of the
most vital and renewing experiences of life—too
important to be reserved for vacations for the few.*

—LADY BIRD JOHNSON,
*HEARTLAND NEWSLETTER*

THE PROCESS OF NATURE CENTER MIDWIFERY and care
is now, hopefully, less of a mystery. We trust that by laying
out the broad picture of nature center development we haven't
frightened you off. We were not skilled in organizational development or volunteer management. We were not trained
naturalists or professional nature center administrators. And
we did not have the time to begin a grassroots community
project. Our lives were busy enough already. We lived in a very
conservative community. We must have been out of our
minds. Thank goodness! Throughout the project we have had
the privilege of creating programs that brought people into fun
and meaningful relationship with nature. This was the pay-
off. Here, before our eyes, was that "reverence for life" that
Schweitzer talked about.

**Moments of discovery create lasting memories.**

The shrieks of children, the joy in the eyes of the elder, the visitor's sense of peace discovered—these moments are so precious and important that they propelled us along this journey, giving the little town of Boerne a sanctuary that can be forever wild, and an education center that promotes conservation. The nature center phenomenon is gaining ground as a grassroots movement. Your center does not have to become a $1,000,000 annual budget monster that consumes your life and relegates you to an office. You can stay small and manageable or grow as opportunities arise.

As your project evolves, so does your message, the lesson you wish to teach. As your love of nature deepens, you will begin to sense how vital it is that you act upon your beliefs.

Our task must be to free ourselves . . .
by widening our circle of compassion
to embrace all living creatures and the
whole of nature and its beauty.
—Albert Einstein

Until he extends his circle of compassion to all living things, man will not himself find peace.
—Albert Schweitzer

How can humans learn compassion for other species, or even each other, when we have so severely divorced ourselves from nature? As long as we see humanity as so different from other species, we will probably continue to miss this essential lesson that animals in zoos have shown us: We need a relationship with nature, not just for food, or water, or raw materials, but for more subtle yet powerful reasons. Ecopsychologists claim that we need the invigorating influence that only nature can provide, just like any other animal on the planet. We all need some contact, some personal relationship, with nature: just a garden, a pet, a vacation, a park, a walk in the woods. Saunters in nature are symphonies for the soul, medicine for the heart.

Signs of change are in the wind. Lots of people are connecting with nature at some level: gardening (the most popular leisure activity in the United States), camping, hiking, bicycling, water recreation, golf, other outdoor recreation, and television programs about nature. Parks are busier than ever. We seem to be instinctively drawn to places of natural beauty, in spite of our social programming. These places seem to rejuvenate and invigorate. Vacations are often pilgrimages into natural settings, and we never get enough. We decorate apartments with simulated wood-grained trim, real or artificial plants, pictures of natural settings, and *windows.* Windows are the most sought-after commodity in office space for city workers, and workers with windows clock fewer "sick days." Few people indeed would prefer a home without natural light, regardless of the neighborhood.

In the city we continue to instinctively seek out that bond to the earth, through landscaping, tree planting, progressive city planning that respects natural resources, indoor plants, architecture that works with nature, and interior design based on natural colors and forms. But how barren is the home of the average child in a housing project, or even in a middle-class suburb? Where is the adventure and wonder that nature offers when a child is caged in a back yard with a manicured lawn and fenced-off property lines?

The average suburban neighborhood divides up the "lawn" space with a checkerboard of sidewalks and fences, so that children are taught to stay off other people's lawns and play on the asphalt. No wonder the children watch six to eight hours of television a day: It is the most interesting stimulation they can find in their worlds. Yet they are drawn to the drainage ditches and parks, where life is more abundant and free. Perhaps the answer is right before our eyes, in those forgotten wild gardens that still survive in our neighborhoods.

As we learn how to nurture our planet, we will learn how to heal ourselves. A nature center can have a staff of one and a humble facility, and yet touch the lives of your entire community. Nature centers become popular and vitalizing components of town or city life. The nature center phenomenon is poised to blossom into a myriad of diverse and exciting places, with thousands of small local programs and pocket parks promoting environmental awareness. Surely an ethic of conservation can grow wide and strong as nature centers spread across our lands. As our communities develop an educated respect for life, diversity on this planet can be preserved, and our own internal wildness and creativity can survive.

This book is like a tiny seed that contains information from thousands of lessons learned from thousands of good-hearted pioneers. There is still fertile ground in our world for many nature centers to be planted and nurtured. We pray this seed finds its way to the hands of a faithful gardener.

## STAYING MOTIVATED

> This is the true joy in life: the being used for a purpose recognized by yourself as a mighty one; the being thoroughly worn out before you are thrown on the scrap heap; the being a force of Nature instead of a feverish selfish little clod of ailments and grievances complaining that the world will not devote itself to making you happy.
>
> —George Bernard Shaw

Keep in mind that being a positive force in nature will require you to run into negative forces. Avoiding discouragement is a survival issue for the nature center fanatic. Get lots of exercise, eat healthy, and save time for yourself. Fun and play, *time in nature,* and an appetite for small victories are important allies.

Some "final advice" from two late conservationists:

> Do not burn yourselves out. Be as I am—a reluctant enthusiast . . . a part-time crusader, a half-hearted fanatic. Save the other half of yourselves and your lives for pleasure and adventure. It is not enough to fight for the land; it is even more important to enjoy it. While you can. While it's still here. So get out there and hunt and fish and mess around with your friends, ramble out yonder and explore the forests, encounter the grizz, climb the mountains, bag the peaks, run the rivers, breathe deep of that yet sweet and lucid air; sit quietly for a while and contemplate the precious stillness, that lovely, mysterious and awesome space.

> —Edward Abbey

> Let me offer a final thought. For all the darkness that presently confronts us and our descendants, there is no reason to give up. There is every reason to take up the fight, because we have within our grasp the power of the people to force the right decisions. The more people, the more power, the more hope.

> . . . We can take our inspiration from the dolphins, who defend themselves and their offspring through an instinct to mass together in the face of danger . . . and to attack power with wisdom.

> —Jacques-Yves Cousteau

**Helping children fall in love with nature can lift your spirits— sometimes right off the ground!**

# *Appendix* A Organizations

NOTE: *There are a number of organizations that can be quite helpful to nature centers. The following organizations have been leaders in providing assistance to grassroots activists as well as established organizations throughout the country.*

*American Association for Botanical Gardens and Arboreta:* improves professional standards, increases public awareness, and facilitates communication between botanical gardens and arboreta.
*Contact:* American Association for Botanical Gardens and Arboreta, 786 Church Road, Wayne, PA 19087; (215) 688-1120.

*American Association of Museums:* has promoted interests of the museum profession since 1906, maintaining professional standards.
*Contact:* American Association of Museums, 1575 Eye Street NW, Suite 400, Washington, DC 20005; (202) 289-1818.

*American Association for Zoological Parks and Aquariums:* offers conferences, education, funding, policy, publications, and research advancing the role of zoological parks and aquariums in conservation.
*Contact:* American Association of Zoological Parks and Aquariums, Oglebay Park, Wheeling, WV 26003-1698; (304) 212-2160.

*American Birding Association:* devoted to helping individuals increase the enjoyment of birding.
*Contact:* American Birding Association, PO Box 6599, Colorado Springs, CO 80934; (800) 634-7736.

*American Community Gardening Association:* for gardening and open space volunteers, with publications on the creation and maintenance of community gardens, including the *Community Greening Review.*
*Contact:* American Community Gardening Association, 325 Walnut Street, Philadelphia, PA 19106; (215) 922-1508.

*American Horticultural Therapy Association:* much information about therapeutic work with special needs groups and plants.
*Contact:* American Horticultural Therapy Association, 362A Christopher Avenue, Gaithersburg, MD 20879.

*American Nature Study Society:* has supported educators with publications, meetings, conferences, and field trips since 1908.
*Contact:* American Nature Study Society, 5881 Brook Road, Homer, NY 13077; (607) 749-3655.

*Association for Experiential Education:* has its roots in adventure education and is committed to the development, practice, and evaluation of experiential learning in all settings. The AEE provides publications on theory, ethics, and trends, and publishes the *Journal for Experiential Education.* Of particular value is *Common Practices in Adventure Programming,* a $25 publication that outlines procedures that provide for safety and enjoyment for a variety of activities in nature. Following such procedures would increase safety and decrease liability in case of injuries. *Contact:* Association for Experiential Education, 2885 Aurora Avenue #28, Boulder, CO 80303-2252; (303) 440-8844.

*Association of Nature Center Administrators:* is the single most important national organization for nature center pioneers or veterans to belong to; ANCA addresses the professional needs of nature center administrators. ANCA acts as a forum for improving communications among nature center administrators, government agencies, and other nature-center-oriented organizations. *Directions,* a digest of the ANCA, is an excellent compilation of cutting-edge information and advice from leading nature center movers and shakers. Since 1992 ANCA has completed sixteen Peer Consults for different nature centers, offering expert advice at a minimal cost. A manual for nature center administrators is available. *Contact:* Association of Nature Center Administrators, c/o Aullwood Audubon Center, 1000 Aullwood Road, Dayton, OH 45414; (513) 890-7360; FAX (513) 890-2382; or 1-800-490-ANCA.

*Association of Science-Technology Centers:* publishes a variety of bulletins of interest, such as *Marketing Basics, Creating Visitor-Friendly Spaces, Critical Issues to Consider, Exhibits for Sale,* and other offerings about museum stores.

*Contact:* Association of Science-Technology Centers, New Science Centers Support Program,1025 Vermont Ave. NW, Washington, DC 20005-3516; (202) 783-7200.

*Boy Scouts of America:* Contact BSA for names and locations of local groups, many of which are looking for outdoor activities and service projects. *Contact:* Boy Scouts of America, 1325 Walnut Hill Lane, Irving, TX 75015-2079; (214) 580-2000.

*Brazos Bend State Park:* For information regarding a state-of-the-art accessible trail. *Contact:* the park superintendent at Brazos Bend State Park, 21901 FM 762, Needville, TX 77461; (409) 553-5101; TDD/TTY (telephone access for the deaf): (409) 553-5105.

*Camp Fire, Inc.:* Contact Camp Fire, Inc., for names and locations of local groups, many of which are looking for outdoor activities and service projects. *Contact:* Camp Fire, Inc., 4601 Madison Ave., Kansas City, MO 64112-1278; (816) 756-1950.

*Delaware Nature Society:* in cooperation with the University of Delaware, has offered an Environmental Institution Management class for the last fourteen years. This intensive, month-long graduate-level course is specifically designed to enable participants to develop and maintain a nature center. A week-long Professional Leadership Institute for managers is also available. The DNS operates the Ashland Nature Center, a 600-acre facility with

nineteen full-time staff and educational programs for the public, interns, and schoolteachers. *Contact:* EIM Coordinator, Delaware Nature Society, Box 700, Hockessin, DE 19707; (302) 239-2334.

*Drapers Super Bee Apiaries, Inc.:* manufactures observation bee hives of superior quality. *Contact:* Drapers Super Bee Apiaries, Inc., RR 1, Box 97, Millerton, PA 16036-9737; (800) 233-4273

*Ducks Unlimited:* one of the leading organizations in wetlands conservation; can be of help to nature centers that focus on wetlands. *Contact:* Ducks Unlimited,1 Waterfowl Way, Long Grove, IL 60047; (708) 438-4300.

*Environmental Media:* works with a host of public and private agencies to manage the design, production, and distribution of media to support environmental education. *Contact:* Environmental Media, PO Box 1016, Chapel Hill, NC 27514; (919) 933-3003.

*The Foundation Center:* a clearing-house for over 170 libraries around the country that are geared to assisting grant-seekers. Your nearest will be a precious resource if you decide to form a nonprofit corporation. *Contact:* The Foundation Center, 79 Fifth Avenue, New York, NY 10003; (212) 620-4230.

*4-H Youth Development:* Coeducational program for ages 9–19, stressing leadership development, agriculture, family, and community. Local chapters often looking for outdoor activities and service projects for its members.
*Contact:* 4-H Youth Development, Cooperative Extension Service, US Department of Agriculture, Washington, DC 20250; (202) 447-5853.

*Girl Scouts of the U.S.A.:* Contact Girl Scouts for names and locations of local groups, many of which are looking for outdoor activities and service projects.
*Contact:* Girl Scouts of the U.S.A., 830 Third Avenue. New York, NY 10022; (212) 940-7500

*Global Releaf:* the national tree-planting program of the American Forestry Association, designed to help community tree-planting groups, with publications on tree planting and care, urban reforestation, and so forth.
*Contact:* American Forestry Association, PO Box 2000, Washington, DC 20013; (202) 667-3300.

*Greenprint Council:* In Minnesota an innovative approach is being undertaken by five nature centers —a cooperative fund-raising effort to develop a coordinated environmental education system for all audiences in the state. This enables the centers to cooperate in a fund-raising effort, rather than competing for funding.
*Contact:* Pam Landers, of Greenprint Council, Department of Natural Resources, Box 46, 500 Lafayette Road, St. Paul, MN 55155; (612) 282-5788; or Leon

Cooper, of Project Earthsense, 4609 Century Plaza, 1111 Third Avenue South, Minneapolis, MN 55404; (612) 321-9190

*InsideOutside:* a private organization that provides state-of-the-art assistance with master plans, as well as interpretive planning and design projects, site planning and landscape architecture, exhibit design, facility design, and construction administration. Lisa Brochue, author of the 1988 market study and action plan that helped create ANCA, has joined forces with other experienced and talented professionals to serve nature centers, museums, and state and federal agencies.
*Contact:* InsideOutside, Route 1, Box 172AA, Elgin, TX 78621; (512) 285-3801; FAX (512) 285-4105.

*Institute for Conservation Leadership:* provides research and training for grassroots leaders to help them reach their goals more effectively.
*Contact:* Institute for Conservation Leadership, 2000 P Street, NW, Suite 412, Washington, DC 20036; (202) 466-3330.

*Institute for Earth Education:* supplies materials based on the innovative work of Steve Van Matre and associates that create a complete environmental education program, with the goal of lifestyle change for the student.
*Contact:* Institute for Earth Education, Box 288, Warrenville, IL 60555.

*Institute of Museum Services*: has announced a program to grant up

to $1,000,000 for research into learning in museums, including nature centers. The organization is interested in how to create and maintain quality educational programs and facilities.
*Contact:* Institute of Museum Services, 1100 Pennsylvania Avenue, NW, Room 609, Washington, DC, 20506; (212) 606-8539; TTY (202) 606-8636; e-mail: imsinfo@fed.us; web site: http://www.ims.fed.us/imsresearch.html.

*Izaak Walton League of America:* provides a wealth of information about adopting streams and rivers. The IWLA fights for conservation at the local, state, and federal levels. Its Wetlands Watch program educates people about the plight of U.S. wetlands and provides suggestions about how to get involved to preserve them.
*Contact:* Izaak Walton League of America Endowment: PO Box 824, Iowa City, IA 52244; (319) 351-7037.

*National Arbor Day Foundation:* promotes tree planting in the United States. This nonprofit organization offers ten Colorado blue spruce trees (six to ten inches tall), with planting instructions and a copy of *The Tree Book,* with each $10 membership contribution (people in southern and West Coast states receive ten bald cypress trees.)
*Contact:* National Arbor Day Foundation, 100 Arbor Ave., Nebraska City, NE 68410; (402) 474-5655.

*National Association for Environmental Education:* supplies publications and conferences for

environmental educators of diverse backgrounds.
*Contact:* National Association for Environmental Education, PO Box 400, Troy, OH 45373; (513) 698-6493.

*National Association of Interpretation:* for naturalists, historians, park rangers, educators, museum technicians, curators, administrators, recreation specialists, authors, volunteers, and nature center folks. Publishes the bimonthly *Journal of Interpretation.*
*Contact:* National Association for Interpretation, PO Box 2246, Fort Collins, CO 80522; (970) 484-8283 or (970) 491-6434. NAI jobs hotlines: jobs, (303) 491-7410; interns, (303) 491-6784.

*National Audubon Society:* the national leader in nature center development, published the first how-to books on nature centers and trail development in the 1960s. The NAS currently encourages member chapters to adopt wildlife refuges, and operates numerous nature centers. Environmental education is used to develop a culture of conservation, through its network of Audubon Centers, Audubon Adventure Programs, Audubon Ecology Camps and Workshops, sanctuaries, education centers, *Audubon Magazine, World of Audubon* television specials, and *Audubon Adventures,* a bimonthly newspaper for elementary grade students who are studying the environment.
*Contact:* National Audubon Society, 700 Broadway, New York, NY 10003 (212) 979-3000.

*National Bird Feeding Society:* a consumer organization for people who feed wild birds.
*Contact:* National Bird Feeding Society, 1163 Shermer Road, Northbrook, IL 60062; (708) 272-0135.

*National Center on Accessibility:* an excellent resource for accessibility information.
*Contact:* 1 (800) 424-1877.

*National Center for Community Risk Management and Insurance:* a nonprofit organization that provides community service organizations with advice and information about insurance, including a variety of related publications.
*Contact:* National Center for Community Risk Management and Insurance, 1824 I Street NW, Suite 505, Washington, DC 20036; (202) 785-3891.

*National Center for Nonprofit Boards:* has an extensive catalog available, including books, pamphlets, and self-assessment guidelines. Also offers customized workshops and retreats and has a newsletter and a toll-free "Board Information Center" for its members.
*Contact:* National Center of Nonprofit Boards, 2000 L Street NW, Suite 411, Washington, DC 20036.

*National Consortium for Environmental Education and Training:* program at the University of Michigan's School of Natural Resources and Environment, funded by the U.S. Environmental Protection Agency in 1992. Works

to support, enhance, and extend effective environmental education in grades K-12. Produced the *EE Toolbox,* including a workshop resource manual, an EE reference collection, a slide resource kit, a national survey of EE teacher in-service education, and a guide for bringing environmental education into your classroom for teachers of all subjects; makes environmental education materials and resources more accessible to teachers and students. Anyone with a computer and a modem can access a wide variety of resources through NCEET's EE-Link, a service on the Internet. NCEET develops programs for environmental education to traditionally underserved audiences, such as Native Americans and inner-city youth, and it works with environmental education leaders to assess the ecological knowledge of schoolchildren and the environmental education needs of teachers.
*Contact:* National Consortium for Environmental Education and Training, School of Natural Resources and Environment, University of Michigan, 430 E. University Ave., Dana Building, Ann Arbor, MI 48109-1115; (313) 998-6726.

*National Outdoor Leadership School:* has taught wilderness skills, conservation, and leadership since 1965 to more than 30,000 students.
*Contact:* National Outdoor Leadership School, 288 Main Street, Lander, WY 82520-3128; (307) 332-6973.

*National Volunteer Center:* a clearinghouse that provides technical assistance and training, operates a library service, and distributes publications. They can refer you to your local center, which could be a valuable resource for project volunteers.
*Contact:* National Volunteer Center, 1111 N. Nineteenth Street, #500, Arlington, VA 22209; (800) 637-7799.

*National Wildflower Research Center:* founded in 1982 by Lady Bird Johnson and dedicated solely to conserving and promoting the use of native plants in North America. The center provides information state by state on habitat zones, species selection, planting techniques, and wildflower management. Its library and clearing house compile and disseminate information on native plants to individuals and organizations, including over 250 fact sheets, bibliographies, and recommended species charts, as well as lists of commercial sources of native plants, related groups, and resource people around the country. The data base here, as well as field research under way, makes this organization a vital source for any nature center in the country.
*Contact:* National Wildflower Research Center, 4801 Lacrosse Avenue, Austin, TX 78739; (512) 292-4200.

*National Wildlife Federation:* sponsors a wide variety of educational workshops and publications, including *Ranger Rick, Your Big Backyard, National Wildlife,* and *International Wildlife.* The *Conservation Directory* ($15 per year), by the National Wildlife Federation, annually lists a large number of environmental organizations. *Nature Scope* is a fifteen-volume curriculum for elementary students, and the *National Wildlife Federation's CLASS Project* is a curriculum for middle school students.
*Contact:* National Wildlife Federation, 8925 Leesburg Pike, Vienna, VA 22184; (703) 790-4100.

*National Wildlife Rehabilitation Association:* best resource for learning about the possibilities of training and programs in wildlife rehabilitation for a nature center.
*Contact:* National Wildlife Rehabilitation Association, 525 S. Park Blvd., Glen Ellyn, IL 60137.

*Natural Area Association:* publishes the Natural Areas Journal, which consists of technical information presented in a scholarly format.
*Contact:* Natural Area Association, 320 S. 3rd St., Rockford, IL 61104; (815) 964-6666.

*Natural Science for Youth Foundation:* For over fifty years John Ripley Forbes and this group led the nature center movement, providing a variety of services and publications, all aimed at promoting and developing centers and the staff who are the online professionals of our field. The *1990 Directory of Natural Science Centers* is available to the public through the foundation for $75 plus $3.50 postage and handling fee. This is the most extensive information available on nature centers throughout the United States and Canada. For fledgling nature centers, this organization holds a grant that enables such centers to order the *Directory* at $50, plus $3.50 postage and handling. The Proceedings reports that grew out of the Natural Science Centers Conferences in the 1970s are instructive in elaborating on the nature center movement of the time, its triumphs, and its problems.
*Contact:* Natural Science for Youth Foundation, 130 Azalea Drive, Roswell, GA 30075; (770) 594-9367.

*The Nature Conservancy:* The mission of The Nature Conservancy is to preserve plants, animals, and natural communities that represent the diversity of life on Earth by protecting the lands and water they need to survive. This organization is responsible for the protection of millions of acres of land in fifty states, Mexico, and Canada, and manages more than one thousand preserves. The Nature Conservancy is the largest private owner of nature preserves on earth. It maintains a data base, the Heritage Network, that is a national inventory of species in each state.
*Contact:* The Nature Conservancy, 1815 North Lynn Street, Arlington, VA 22209; (703) 841-5300.

*North American Association for Environmental Education:* assists and supports environmental education, research, and service, including curriculum development, monographs, conferences, and up-to-date solicited papers.

This group can assist with on-line resources.
*Contact:* North American Association for Environmental Education, PO Box 400, Troy, OH 45373; (513) 698-6493.

*Outward Bound:* the premier practitioners of the therapeutic wilderness experience.
*Contact:* Colorado Outward Bound School, 945 Pennsylvania, Denver, CO 80203.

*Permaculture Institute of North America:* Permaculture, modeling natural ecosystems, harmoniously integrates landscape and people to provide food, energy, shelter, and other needs in sustainable ways.
*Contact:* Permaculture Institute of North America, 4949 Sunnyside Avenue North, Room 345, Seattle, WA 98103.

*Renew America:* gathers information on U.S. environmental problems and what's being done about them. It identifies programs and projects that work through the Environmental Success Index and Searching for Success programs. Services include publications, conferences, demonstration projects, and education.
*Contact:* Renew America, 1400 16th Street NW, Suite 710, Washington, DC 20036; (202) 232-2252.

*Rodale Institute:* a nonprofit educational and research organization based in southeastern Pennsylvania that works closely with farmers, scientists, and extension personnel in the United States and around the world to develop new gardening and farming methods that protect the

land, improve productivity, and reduce or eliminate the need for costly chemical fertilizers and pesticides. Publishes *The New Farm* magazine, *Organic Gardening* magazine, and many books.
*Contact:* Rodale Institute, 222 Main Street, Box KS, Emmaus, PA 18098; (215) 683-6383.

*Rodale Institute Research Center:* The 333-acre Rodale Institute Research Center is one of the world's leading centers for the study of organic horticulture and sustainable agriculture.
*Contact:* Rodale Institute Research Center, 611 Siegfriedale Road, Kurtztown, PA 19530; (215) 683-6009.

*Roger Tory Peterson Institute of Natural History:* famous for Mr. Peterson's field guide series, RTPI is dedicated to connecting people of all ages with their natural world. Besides publishing the premier field guides, the organization works for the advancement of nature in education and has developed a 27-acre Wildlife Sanctuary and Outdoor Learning Center. In 1989 the RTPI sponsored a meeting of twenty national leaders with expertise in nature education, and produced *American Nature Centers: Guidelines for Leadership in the Nineties,* covering topics such as funding, learning, and designing with nature, choosing architects, goals, guidelines, and so forth.
*Contact:* Roger Tory Peterson Institute, 110 Marvin Parkway, Jamestown, NY 14701; (716) 665-2473; FAX (716) 665-3794.

*Sierra Club:* formed by John Muir in 1892, has been at the forefront of the environmental movement for a century of service. Local chapters all over the country will be keenly interested in the creation of a community-based nature center.
*Contact:* Sierra Club, 30 Polk Street, San Francisco, CA 94109; (415) 776-2211; ask about the nearest local chapter.

*Society for Non-Profit Organizations:* distributes numerous references about nonprofit management issues.
*Contact:* Society for Non-Profit Organizations, 6314 Odana Road, Suite 1, Madison, WI 53719.

*Soil and Water Conservation Society of America:* promotes soil conservation, publishes *Sources of Native Seeds and Plants,* a list of many of the native plant providers around the country. Also has inexpensive educational resources in comic book form, the *"Environmental Adventures"* series, with teachers' guides.
*Contact:* Soil and Water Conservation Society of America, 7515 NE Ankeny Road, Ankeny IA 50021-9764; 1 (800) THE-SOIL

*TreePeople:* dedicated to promoting personal involvement, community action, and global awareness of environmental issues. Efforts include teaching people how to plant and maintain trees, as well as environmental leadership. Publications include *The Simple Act of Planting a Tree and Seedling News.* Founded by Andy and Katie Lipkis, who are dynamite speakers.

*Contact:* TreePeople, 12601 Mulholland Dr., Beverly Hills, CA 90210; (818) 753-4600.

*Trust for Public Land:* works nationwide to protect land as parks, gardens, recreation areas, and wilderness. Publishes regional newsletters, as well as *Land and People,* which highlights the TPL's work and increases awareness of land conservation issues.
*Contact:* Trust for Public Land, 116 New Montgomery Street, 4th Floor, San Francisco, CA 94105; (415) 495-4014.

*The U.S. Access Board:* provides helpful publications regarding accessible facilities. Especially helpful are *ADAG Accessibility Guidelines-# S-14,* and the *Recreation Advisory Committee Report-# S-26.*
*Contact:* 1 (800) USA-ABLE.

*U.S. Fish and Wildlife Service:* is the nation's principal conservation agency, responsible for most federally owned lands. It works toward protecting fish, wildlife, and their habitats, maintains the endangered species list, and has helped in the funding of nature centers.
*Contact:* U.S. Fish and Wildlife Service, Department of the Interior, 1849 C Street NW, Washington, DC 20240; (202) 208-5634.

*Western Regional Environmental Education Council:* environmental educational materials including *Project WILD Activity Guides.*
Contact: Western Regional Environmental Education Council, Salina Star Route, Boulder, CO 80302; (303) 444-2390.

Wildlife Information Center: dedicated to securing and disseminating wildlife conservation, recreation, and scientific research information. Programs include in-service teacher training, public education, conferences, wildlife tourism, and publication of the *Wildlife Activist.*
*Contact:* Wildlife Information Center, 629 Green Street, Allentown, PA 18102; (215) 434-1637.

*Wildlife Management Institute:* dedicated to the restoration, sound management, and wise use of natural resources in North America.
*Contact:* Wildlife Conservation Institute, 1101 14th St. NW, Washington, DC 20005; (212) 371-1808.

*Worldwatch Institute:* provides thorough, complete, and relevant information about the physical health of the planet. Publishes *World Watch,* a bimonthly magazine, *The State of the World,* an annual book, and periodic reports on specific topics.
*Contact:* Worldwatch Institute, 1776 Massachusetts Avenue NW, Washington, DC 20036.

*World Wide Outfitters and Guides Association:* providing information and help in obtaining liability insurance for nature adventures.
*Contact:* Worldwide Outfitters & Guides Assoc., PO Box 520400, Salt Lake City, UT 84152-0400; (800) 321-1493.

*YMCA of the USA:* Youth programs vary widely from area to area, possibly including programs like "Y Without Walls." Some of these programs also seek opportunities for outdoor recreation and community service.
*Contact:* YMCA of the USA, 101 N. Waacker Drive, Chicago, IL 60606; (312) 977-0031; (800) USA-YMCA.

*The Xerxes Society:* an international, nonprofit organization dedicated to invertebrates (particularly butterflies) and the preservation of critical biosystems worldwide. Publishes *Wings,* a biannual journal with articles on individual species, biosystems, and programs.
*Contact:* Xerxes Society, 4828 SE Hawthorne Blvd., Portland, OR 97215; (503) 232-6639.

# *Appendix* B **Publications**

*Acclimatization: A Sensory and Conceptual Approach to Ecological Involvement,* by Steve Van Matre. American Camping Association, 1972. This is the pioneering work of one of the most outspoken innovators in environmental education. Contains a clear philosophical approach to breaking down barriers between people and nature, including lesson plans and techniques. See other publications, such as *Earth Education.*

*Adopting a Stream,* by Steve Yates. University of Washington Press, 1988.

*Americans with Disabilities Act Handbook,* by the U.S. Employment Opportunity Commission and the U.S. Justice Dept.,1992.

*Audubon: Natural Priorities,* by Roger DiSilvestro. Turner Publishing Co., 1994. This beautiful publication describes the state of the environment, how we got to this point, and what we need to do.

*Beyond Banquets, Plaques and Pins: Creative Ways to Recognize Volunteers,* by Sue Vineyard. Volunteer Management Series. VMSystems/Heritage Arts Publishing, 1989.

*Brukner Nature Center Primer of Wildlife Care and Rehabilitation* (2d ed.), by Patti L. Raley. Brukner Nature Center, 5995 Horseshoe Bend Road, Troy, OH 45373; (513)

698-6493. Cost: paper, $24.95 plus $2.00 postage and handling.

*Chronicle of Philanthropy,* a biweekly newspaper covering wide range of topics of interest to nonprofits. Annual subscription: $60. *Chronicle of Philanthropy,* 1255 23rd St. N.W., Washington, DC 20037; (800) 728-2819.

*Community Garden Book,* by Larry Sommers. National Gardening Association, 1980. Most complete resource on starting and developing a community garden project.

*Community Greening Review,* journal of the American Community Gardening Association, 325 Walnut St., Philadelphia, PA 19106; (215) 922-1508.

*Connecting People and Nature: A Teacher's Guide,* by the Great Smoky Mountains Institute at Tremont, n.d. This is an excellent collection of environmental lesson plans. Route 1, Box 700, Townsend, TN 37882. (615) 448-6709.

*Creating Community Gardens: A Handbook for Planning and Creating Community Gardens to Beautify and Enhance Cities and Towns* (2d ed.), 1992. Minnesota State Horticultural Society, 1970 Folwell Avenue, #161, Saint Paul, MN 55108; (612) 624-

*Designing a Nature Center Discovery Room,* by Dianna E. Ullery.

Aullwood Audubon Center and Farm, 1987. To order, call (513) 890-7360.

*Development and Status of Science Centers and Museums for Children in the United States,* by Melville W. Fuller Jr. University of North Carolina at Chapel Hill, Ph.D. thesis, 1970. A survey of 128 children's museums, many of which had outdoor science programs, and a history of children's museums in the United States.

*Directory of Natural Science Centers.* Natural Science for Youth Foundation, 1990. See Natural Science for Youth Foundation entry in Appendix A for ordering information.

*Earth Child: Games, Stories, Activities, Experiments, and Ideas About Living Lightly on Planet Earth,* by Kathryn Sheehan and Mary Waidner, Council Oak Books, 1991. Filled with absorbing activities, exercises, and games to be shared by children and the adults who care for them. In addition it includes a trove of ecology-related resources for teachers, parents, and others, and celebrates the gift of the written word with annotated lists of hundreds of books that children will love.

*Earth Education: A New Beginning,* by Steven Van Matre. The Institute for Earth Education. 1990. Proposes a new direction for environmental educators, which is to teach students not only to understand relationships in ecosystems but also to craft lifestyles that will lessen their impact upon the earth. Critical of much of the mainstream approach to environmental education, Van Matre is one of the most prolific and successful pioneers in the field. Other books include *Acclimatization: A Sensory and Conceptual Approach to Ecological Involvement; Sunship Earth; and Earthkeepers,* which offer innovative curricula for upper-level elementary students.

*Earth Island Journal.* David Brower's Earth Island Institute conducts environmental projects around the world and reports on international environmental news. Earth Island Institute, 300 Broadway, Suite 28, San Francisco, CA 94133-3312.

*The Earth Manual: How to Work on Wild Land Without Taming It,* by Malcolm Margolin. Heyday Books. A good resource for land management.

*EcoLinking: Everyone's Guide to Online Environmental Information,* by Don Rittner. Peachpit Press, 1992. A thorough listing of environmental forums and data bases available on EcoNet, Fidonet, Bitnet, Usenet, Internet, America OnLine, CompuServe, GEnie, the WELL, and commercial on-line research data bases. Also explains basics of buying and installing a modem, and connecting with on-line services.

*Ecopsychology: Restoring the Earth, Healing the Mind,* edited by Theodore Roszak, Mary E. Gomes, and Allen D. Kanner. Sierra Club Books, 1995. This landmark book brings together leading-edge psychologists and ecologists to redefine sanity on a personal and planetary scale. This is the first in-depth exploration of the exciting new field of ecopsychology, presenting revolutionary concepts of mental health along with a vision of renewal for the environmental movement.

*Effect of Greenways on Property Values and Public Safety,* by Leslee T. Alexander. The Conservation Fund, Colorado State Parks and State Trails Program. To order, send $10 to Sasha Charney at Colorado State Trails Program, 1313 Sherman St., Room 618, Denver, CO 80203.

*Environmental Building News,* a bimonthly newsletter discussing a variety of issues about "Green Architecture." This is the newsletter for new construction and environmentally friendly materials and systems. Write: *Environmental Building News,* RR 1, Box 161, Brattleboro, VT 05301.

*Environmental Education Bibliography: Resources for the Elementary Teacher in the Outdoor Classroom,* by Gerald Nehman and Sally Hoelke. Environmental Institute for Technology Transfer, University of Texas at Arlington, 1992. Excellent coverage of wide range of environmental themes and major environmental education bibliography.

*Environmental Grantmaking Foundations: 1995 Directory,* Environmental Data Research Institute.

*Environmental Interpretation: A Practical Guide for People with Big Ideas and Small Budgets,* by Sam H. Ham. North American Press, 1992.

*Environmental Management Tools on the Internet: Accessing the World of Environmental Information,* by Michael Katz and Dorothy Thornton. St. Lucie Press, 1997.

*Environmental Restoration,* edited by John J. Berger. Island Press, 1990. A collection of technical papers on a diversity of woodland restoration projects.

*The Environmental Sourcebook,* by Edith Carol Stein, in cooperation with the Environmental Data Research Institute. Lyons & Burford, 1992. A comprehensive guide to the environmental movement, including environmental issues, organizations, periodicals, books, foundation grants, and more.

*Executive Leadership in Non Profit Organizations,* by Robert Herman and Richard Heirnovics. Jossey-Bass, 1991. Reviews the hierarchical model of board/CEO/ staff relationships, discusses typical problems, and presents an alternative model stressing CEO leadership.

*Foundation Directory,* published by the Foundation Center, 79 Fifth Avenue, Eighth Floor, New York, NY 10003.

*Full Circle: Restoring Your Habitat to Wilderness,* by Bayliss Prater and Kathleen McNeal. Last Resort Press, 1993. This is a good overview of restoring a wide range of habitats: wetlands, grasses and legumes habitats, old fields, cropfields, food plots, woodlands, shrub and tree areas, riparian zones, perches and cavities, urban landscapes, and backyard habitats.

*Fundraising for Nature Centers: A Collection of Fundraising Strategies,* Association of Nature Center Administrators (see Appendix A: Organizations).

*Golden Guides and Golden Field Guides,* by various authors. Golden Press. Golden has been publishing these little pocket guides for over thirty years; they include *Bird Life, Birds, Birds of North America, Butterflies and Moths, Dinosaurs, Exploring Space, Fishes, Fishing, Flowers, Fossils, Geology, Indian Arts, Insects, Mammals, Planets, Pond Life, Reptiles and Amphibians, Reptiles of North America, Rocks and Minerals, Seashells of North America, Seashells of the World, Seashores, Sky Observer's Guide, Spiders and Their Kin, Stars, Trees, Trees of North America, Tropical Fish, Venomous Animals, Weather, Weeds, Whales and Other Marine Mammals,* and *Wildflowers of North America.* Excellent general guides for beginners.

*Grass Roots Fundraising Book,* by Joan Flanagan. Contemporary Books, Inc., for the Youth Project, 1988.

*The Green Box,* Humbolt County Office of Education, Environmental Education Program. An open-access, humanistically oriented environmental curriculum for grades K–8, with activity cards for small groups. Price: $80; order from Humbolt County Office of Education, Environmental Education Program, 901 Myrtle Ave., Eureka, CA 95501; (707) 445-7082.

*Greening of America,* by Charles A. Reich. Random House, 1970. The milestone book that voiced the new conservation ethic of the seventies.

*Green Nature/Human Nature,* by Charles Lewis. Ingram Book Co., 1996. A Horticultural Therapy Manifesto.

*A Guide to Volunteer Trail Building on Public and Private Land in Texas,* by the Texas Parks and Wildlife Department, 1985. Clear principles can apply to volunteer trail building in any state; provides good advice on complicated issues like easements, leases, licenses, liability, as well as trail construction.

*Habitat Conservation Planning,* by Timothy Beatley. University of Texas Press, 1993. An informative and comprehensive summary of the status of wildlife habitat protection.

*Hands-On Nature: Information and Activities for Exploring the Environment with Children,* edited by Jenepher Lingelbach. Vermont Institute of Natural Science, 1986. Activities for teaching children to understand and appreciate the natural world, including science process skills, a multidisciplinary approach, and hands-on philosophy.

*Helping Nature Heal: An Introduction to Environmental Restoration,* by Richard Nilson. Whole Earth Catalog/Ten Speed Press, 1991.

*Home Power: The Hands-on Journal of Home-made Power.* Bimonthly. P.O. Box 520, Ashland, OR 97520. (800) 707-6585. hp@homepower.com.

*How to Form a Nonprofit Corporation,* by Anthony Mancuso, Nolo Press, 1990. A good resource for the beginner, with tear-out forms for all fifty states.

*How to Save a River: A Handbook for Citizen Action,* by the River Network and David M. Bolling. Island Press, 1994. A concise and readable summary of approaches to river protection, with numerous examples and references.

*Interpretation for Disabled Visitors in the National Park System,* by David Park, Wendy Ross, and W. Ellis. National Park Service, Washington DC, U.S. Government Printing Office, 1984.

Interpreter's Handbook Series. *Creating Environmental Publications: A Guide for Writing and Designing for Interpreters and Environmental Educators; The Interpretive Guide Book: Techniques for Programs and Presentations; Making the Right Connections: A Guidebook for Nature Writers; Signs, Trails, and Wayside Exhibits: Connecting People and Places.* Also see *The Interpretive Center Book: Guiding People to a Sense of Place,* to be available in 1998. This is an excellent series for helping your nature center develop interpretive programs. Order through the College of Natural Resources, University of Wisconsin; Stevens Point, WI 54481; (715) 346-2076. (Contact Michael Gross.)

*Issues in Wilderness Management,* by M. Frome. Westview Press, 1985. Studies the practicality of minimum-impact recreational practices.

*Keepers of the Earth: Native American Stories and Environmental Activities for Children and Keepers of Life: Discovering Plants Through Native American Stories and Earth Activities for Children,* by Michael J. Caduto and Joseph Bruchac. Fulcrum, 1988. Teachers' guides and other titles available.

*Kid Heroes of the Environment: Simple Things Real Kids Are Doing to Save the Earth,* by the Earthworks Group. Earthworks Press, 1991.

*Kids Camp! Activities for the Backyard or Wilderness,* by Laurie Carlson and Judith Dammel. Chicago Review Press, 1995. More than a hundred hands-on activities and games that teach kids the basics for safe, fun camping while showing them how to really explore the tiny things in nature.

*Kids' Guide to Social Action: How to Solve the Social Problems You Choose—And Turn Creative*

*Thinking to Positive Action,* by Barbara A. Lewis. Free Spirit, 1991.

*Lightly on the Land: The Student Conservation Association Trail-Building and Maintenance Manual,* by Robert C. Birkby, The Mountaineers Publishers, 1996. A comprehensive guide to trail building and maintenance, based on the award-winning "Work Skills Program" of the Student Conservation Association, which has more than forty-six years of experience providing skilled volunteers to the Forest Service, Park Service, and Bureau of Land Management.

*National Audubon Society Almanac of the Environment: The Ecology of Everyday Life,* by Valerie Harms et al. Putnam, 1994. A richly illustrated overview of the issues that affect the state of the Earth, and how to restore and protect it.

*National Park Service Trails Management Handbook,* by Lennon Hooper. U.S. Department of the Interior. Good source on all aspects of trail design and construction; bridge design.

*The Nature Catalog,* edited by Joel Makower. Vintage Books, Tilden Press, 1991. How to get started on everything from bird feeding to weather watching. In addition to basic information, it includes extensive listings of sites, organizations, publications, activities, computer software, and other resources.

*Nature as a Guide: Using Nature in Counseling, Therapy, and Education,* by Linda Lloyd Nebbe.

Educational Media Corporation, 1991.

*Nature as Teacher and Healer: How to Reawaken Your Connection with Nature,* by James A. Swan, Ph.D. Villard Books, 1992.

*1996 Conservation Directory* (41st ed.), edited by R. E. Gordon. National Wildlife Federation, 1996. An extensive list of organizations, agencies, and officials concerned with natural resource use and management.

*NonProfit Times,* a monthly newspaper dedicated to nonprofit news, marketing, and management. Sub: $49 per year, free to executives of large organizations that raise more than $500,000 annually. *NonProfit Times,* 190 Tamarack Circle, Skillman, NJ 08558-9972.

*Organizing Outdoor Volunteers* (2d ed.), by Roger L. Moore, Vicki LaFarge, and Charles L. Tracy. Appalachian Mountain Club, 1992.

*Outdoor Biological Instructional Strategies (OBIS),* a program for fifth and sixth graders in ecology, developed by the Lawrence Hall of Science, and available from Delta Education Inc., Box 915, Hudson, NH 03051; (800) 258-1302.

*Park Ranger Guide to Rivers and Lakes,* by Arthur P. Miller Jr. and Marjorie L. Miller. Park Ranger Guides. Stackpole Books, 1991. Explores the world of aquatic wildlife with the park rangers.

*Park Ranger Guide to Wildlife,* by Arthur P. Miller Jr. Park Ranger

Guides. Stackpole Books, 1990. Rangers across the United States share their personal secrets for discovering wildlife.

*People–Plant Relationships: Setting Research Priorities,* edited by Joel Flagler and Raymond P. Poincelot. Food Products Press, 1994. This is a groundbreaking compilation of discoveries, questions, and research propositions. The authors contribute to the investigation of how plants affect the quality of life of individuals, communities, and cultures.

*Permaculture International Journal,* a cutting-edge journal concerning agricultural sustainability, encouraging biodiversity, and working with nature.

*Points of Light 1996 Volunteer Community Service Catalog,* Points of Light Foundation, PO Box 66534, Washington, DC 20035. This large collection of products for the volunteer coordinator includes books on leadership and volunteer management, board development, marketing and fund management, customized gadgetry, and recognition gimmicks.

*Prairie Restoration for the Beginner,* by Robert Ahrenhoerster and Trelen Wilson. Wehr Nature Center, 1988. Wehr Nature Center, 9701 W. College Avenue, Franklin, WI 53132.

*Preserving Family Lands (Essential Tax Strategies for the Landowner),* by Stephen J. Small. Landowner Planning Center, 1992.

Landowner Planning Center, PO Box 2242, Boston MA 02101.

*Private Options: Tools and Concepts for Land Conservation,* edited by Barbara Rusmone. Island Press, 1982. Thirty authors writing on conserving private land, containing urban sprawl, conserving wetlands, and protecting wildlife. Also contains information on estate planning, tax incentives, marketing, and conservation options for buying and selling land, conservation easements, and management of conserved land areas.

*Proceedings of the National Education Association,* by Sarah L. Arnold. National Education Association, St. Paul, 1895.

*Project Learning Tree Publications,* by the American Forest Institute, 1977. An excellent set of environmental education materials for schoolchildren sponsored by the Western Regional Environmental Education Council and the American Forest Institute.

*Project WILD Activity Guides,* by the Western Regional Environmental Education Council, 1985. (See Appendix A: Organizations.)

*Public Relations in Natural Resources Management,* by Douglas L. Gilbert. Burgess Publishing Co., 1964. This is a classic (though dated) manual on the full range of public relations issues in natural resource management; it can be of significant help in providing a thorough look at various tactics, media, and formats.

*Real Goods Products Catalogue and Solar Living Center.* 555 Leslie Street, Ukiah, CA 95482-5576. (800) 762-7325. custserv@realgoods.com.

*Replenish the Earth,* by Lewis G. Regenstein. Crossroad Publishing Co., 1991. A history of organized religion's treatment of animals, nature, and conservation. Can be quite helpful when working with various religious groups.

*Restoration and Management Notes,* from University of Wisconsin Press. This semiannual newsletter describes projects in repairing damage to ecosystems, including topics of biodiversity, ecosystem restoration, endangered species, riparian lands, rivers/streams.

*Saving America's Countryside: A Guide to Rural Conservation,* by Samuel N. Stokes, with A. Elizabeth Watson and contributing authors. Johns Hopkins University Press, 1989. This is a comprehensive, step-by-step guide to protecting the entire spectrum of a rural community's resources– natural, historic, scenic, and agricultural. It shows how to organize a conservation effort, inventory available resources, pass effective new laws, set up land trusts, take advantage of federal programs, and change public attitudes.

*Saving the Best of Texas: A Partnership Approach to Conservation,* by Richard C. Bartlett. University of Texas Press, 1995. An excellent description of the Nature Conservancy's approach to protecting habitat, with numerous examples. Beautiful photographs by Leroy Williamson.

*Saving Our Ancient Forests,* by Seth Zuckerman. The Wilderness Society, Living Planet Press, 1991. A concise handbook inviting the reader to join forces with the growing national movement to save the redwoods and other giant trees, as well as their habitats.

*Seeds of Change: The Living Treasure,* by Kenny Ausubel. Harper San Francisco, 1994. The passionate story of a growing movement to restore biodiversity and revolutionize the way we thank about food. Describes a farm and seed bank in New Mexico that is a value-driven company whose primary goal is to reintroduce a biological diversity of crops into the food chain.

*Sharing Nature with Children* (1980), *Listening to Nature* (1987), *Sharing the Joy of Nature* (1989), all by Joseph Cornell. Dawn Publications.

*The Simple Act of Planting a Tree: Healing your Neighborhood, Your City, and Your World,* by Tree People, with Andy and Katie Lipkis. Jeremy P. Tarcher, 1990.

*Soft Paths: How to Enjoy the Wilderness Without Harming It,* by Bruce Hampton and David Cole of the National Outdoor Leadership School. Stackpole Books, 1988.

*Sources of Native Seeds and Plants,* by the Soil & Water Conservation Society of America.

A list of many of the native plant providers around the country. (See Appendix A: Organizations.)

*Stewart's Environmental Directory,* by Mary Lou Stewart, 1993. Claims to present the most comprehensive variety of environmental options available in the world, including products, publications, and organization lists. Write to 246 Centennial Parkway, Delta, BC, Canada V4L1K5.

*Successful Fundraising: A Complete Handbook for Volunteers and Professionals,* by Joan Flanagan. Contemporary Books, 1991.

*Sustain: A Journal of Environmental and Sustainability Issues,* published several times a year by the Kentucky Institute for the Environment and Sustainable Development, 203 Patterson Hall, University of Louisville, Louisville, KY 40292. internet: vlmalo01@ulkyvm.louisville.edu

*Take Action: An Environmental Book for Kids,* by Ann Love and Jane Drake. World Wildlife Fund, 1992.

*Talking to Fireflies, Shrinking the Moon: A Parent's Guide to Nature Activities,* by Edward Duensing. Penguin Books, 1990.

*Talking Leaves,* journal of the Deep Ecology Education Project, 1430 Willamette, Suite 367, Eugene, OR 97401.

*Teaching Kids to Love the Earth,* by Herman, Passineau, Schimpf, and Treuer. Pfeifer-Hamilton, 1991. A collection of 186 earth-

caring activities designed for use with children of all ages to help them experience and appreciate the earth.

*Thinking Like a Mountain: Towards a Council of All Beings,* by John Seed, Joanna Macy, Pat Fleming, and Arne Naess. New Society Publishers, 1988. A collection of readings, meditations, poems, guided fantasies, workshop notes (and exquisite drawings of the Tasmanian rainforest) designed by experienced workshop leaders, and activities to help us move beyond the sense of alienation from the living earth that most of us feel.

*Touch the Earth: A Self-Portrait of Indian Existence,* by T. C. McLuhan. Outerbridge & Dienstfry, 1971. A selection of statements and writings by Native North Americans.

*Trail Building and Maintenance,* (2d ed.), by Robert D. Proudman and Reuben Rajala. Appalachian Mountain Club and National Park Service Trails Program, 1981.

*Universal Access to Outdoor Recreation: A Design Guide,* by PLAE, Inc., 1993. Distributed by MIG Communications, 1802 Fifth Street, Berkeley, CA 94710; (510) 845-0953. Expanding on the requirements of the Americans with Disabilities Act (ADA), this design guide provides a framework for determining the appropriate level of accessibility in a range of outdoor recreation settings and presents detailed guidelines for designing the elements and spaces necessary for ensuring accessible paths, signs, restrooms, drinking fountains, picnic tables, tent pads, and much more.

*Vandalism Control Management for Parks and Recreation Areas,* by Monty L. Christiansen. Venture Publishing, 1982.

*The Voice of the Earth,* by Theodore Roszak. Simon & Schuster, 1992. A manifesto for ecopsychology, viewing the human psyche as embedded in the matrix of the earth.

*Ward's Earth Science Product Catalogue,* by Ward's Natural Science Establishment, 5100 West Henrietta Road, PO Box 92912, Rochester, NY 14692-9978. Catalogue includes products for earth science educators.

*Wetland Activity Guides and Curricula,* by the Lake Pontchartrain Basin Foundation, n.d. An extensive collection of well-produced books, videos, and newsletters. P.O. Box 6965, Metairie, LA 70009-6965. (504) 836-2215.

*Whole NonProfit Catalog,* a free quarterly compendium of resources for nonprofit organizations. The Grantsmanship Center, PO Box 17220, Los Angeles, CA 90017; (213) 482-9863.

*Wilderness,* by the Wilderness Society. This quarterly magazine covers conservation, ecological ethics, forests, protected lands, wilderness, and wildlife.

*Wilderness: The Way Ahead,* edited by Vance Martin and Mary Inglis. Findhorn Press, Lorian Press, 1984. Presents the edited proceedings of the Third World Wilderness Congress in Scotland in 1983, addressing the fundamental question: How can we balance the needs of individuals, society, and the earth itself in order to assure that wild places will remain a functioning and valuable part of our planet?

*Wildlife Planning for Tourism Workbook,* by Texas Parks and Wildlife Department, 4200 Smith School Road, Austin, TX 78744; (512) 389-4800. 1993. Excellent statistics on a national level for promoting wildlife watching on a local level.

*Willy Whitefeather's Outdoor Survival Handbook for Kids,* and *Willy Whitefeather's River Book for Kids,* by Willy Whitefeather. Harbinger House, 1994. This series gives children (and adults) the confidence and knowledge they need to survive outdoors and on the river, in hand-lettered, cartoon style.

*WOW! The Wonders of Wetlands: An Educator's Guide,* by Kesselheim, Slattery, Slattery, Higgins, and Schilling. Environmental Concern, Inc., and The Watercourse, 1995. User-friendly manual for educators, refuge managers, park service educators, nature center interpreters, and others for simulating activities and studies of wetlands.

The following publications by the National Audubon Society are dated and out of print, but quite helpful if they can be located:

*A Nature Center for Your Community,* 1962.

*Outdoor Conservation Education,* 1964.

*Trail Planning and Layout,* 1965.

*Wildlife Habitat Improvement,* 1966.

# *Appendix* C Nature Centers Surveyed

Anita Purves Nature Center
1505 N. Broadway
Urbana, IL 61801
(217) 384-4062

Ansonia Nature and Recreation
Center
10 Deerfield Road
Ansonia, CT 06401
(203) 736-9360

Armand Bayou Park and Nature
Center
8500 Bay Area Boulevard
PO Box 58828
Houston, TX 77258
(713) 474-2551

Asbury Woods Nature Center
4105 Asbury Road
Erie, PA 16506
(814) 835-5356
e-mail: woodsowl@aol.com

Ashland Nature Center—
Delaware Nature Society
PO Box 700
Hockersin, DE 19707
(302) 239-2334

Aullwood Audubon Center and
Farm
1000 Aullwood Road
Dayton, OH 45414-1129
(513) 890-7360
e-mail: CKrueger@Audubon.org

Austin Nature Center
301 Nature Center Drive
Austin, TX 78746
(512) 327-ANSA

Battle Creek Cypress Swamp
Nature Center
c/o Country Courthouse
Prince Frederick, MD 20678
(410) 535-5327
e-mail:
teriandy@mail.ameritel.net

Bay Beach Wildlife Sanctuary
1660 E. Shore Drive
Green Bay, WI 54302
(414) 391-3671

Bear Branch Nature Center
300 John Owings Road
Westminster, MD 21158
(410) 848-2517

Bear Creek Nature Center—
El Paso County Parks
245 Bear Creek Road
Colorado Springs, CO 80906
(719) 520-6387

Beaver Creek Reserve
Rt. 2, Box 94
Fall Creek, WI 54742
(715) 877-2212

Beaver Meadow Nature Center
1610 Welch Road
North Java, NY 14113-9712
(716) 457-3228

Bernheim Arboretum and
Research Forest
Highway 245
Clermont, KY 40110
(502) 955-8512

Birdsong Nature Center
2106 Meridian Road
Thomasville, GA 31792
(912) 377-4408

Blackacre State Nature Preserve
Blackacre Foundation, Inc.
304 W. Liberty Street
Louisville, KY 40202
(502) 581-0786

Blue Jay Center for Environmental Education
3200 Pleasant Union Church Road
Raleigh, NC 27614
(919) 870-4330

Brukner Nature Center
5995 Horseshoe Bend Road
Troy, OH 45373
(513) 698-6493

Buckley Wildlife Sanctuary
1305 Germany Road,
Frankfort, KY 40601
(606) 873-5711

Carpenter St. Croix Valley Nature
Center
12805 St. Croix Trail
South Hastings, MN 55033
(612) 437-4359

Cayuga Nature Center
1420 Taughannock Blvd.
Ithaca, NY 14850
(607) 273-6260

Children's Schoolhouse Nature
Park
9045 Baldwin Road
Kirtland Hills, OH 44060
(216) 256-3808

Chippewa Nature Center
400 S. Badour Road
Midland, MI 48640
(517) 631-0830

Cibolo Nature Center
PO Box 9
Boerne, TX 78006
(830) 249-4616
e-mail: cnc@Texas.net

Cincinnati Nature Center
4949 Tealtown Road
Milford, OH 45150-9752
(513) 831-1711

City of Chicago Department of
Environment, North Park Village
Nature Center
5801 North Pulaski
Chicago, IL 60646
(312) 744-5472

Connecticut Audubon's Ragged
Hill Woods 4-H Program
139 Wolf Den Road
Brooklyn, CT 06234
(860) 774-9600

Corkscrew Swamp Sanctuary
375 Sanctuary Road
Naples, FL 33964
(813) 657-3771
e-mail: amackie@audubon.org

Deep Portage Conservation
Reserve
Rt. 1, Box 129
Hackensack, MN 56452
(218) 682-2325
e-mail: HHN3327@HandsNet.org

Delaware Nature Society, includ-
ing Ashland Nature Center,
Abbott's Mill Nature Center,
Burrows Run  Preserve, Flint
Woods Preserve, Marvel Saltmarsh
Preserve, and Cedar Bog Preserve
PO Box 700
Hockessin, DE 19707
(302) 239-2334

Effie Yeaw Nature Center
PO Box 579
Carmichael, CA 95609
(916) 489-4918
e-mail: yeaw@promedia.net

Energy and Marine Center
PO Box 190
Port Richey, FL 34673
(813) 848-4870

Flat Rock Brook Nature Center
443 Van Nostrand Ave.
Englewood, NJ 07631
(201) 567-1265

Fontenelle Forest and Neale
Woods Nature Centers
1111 N. Bellevue Blvd.
Bellevue, NE 68005
(402) 731-3140

Ft. Worth Nature Center and
Refuge
9601 Fossil Ridge Road
Ft. Worth, TX 76135
(817) 237-1111

Francis Beidler Forest
336 Sanctuary Road
Harleyville, SC 29448
(803) 462-2150

Glen Helen Ecology Institute
405 Corry St.
Yellow Springs, OH 45387
(513) 767-7375
e-mail:
rflood@college.antioch.edu

Goodwin Conservation Center
23 Potter Road
North Windham, CT 06256
(860) 455-9534
e-mail: RHaley5@aol.com

Great Smoky Mountain Institute
of Tremont
9275 Tremont Road
Townsend, TN 37882
(423) 448-9040
e-mail: ken@smoky.igc.apc.org

Greenburgh Nature Center
99 Dromore Road
Scarsdale, NY 10583
(914) 723-3470

Greenway and Nature Center of
Pueblo
5200 Nature Center Road
Pueblo, CO 81003
(719) 549-2414

Hartman Reserve Nature Center
657 Reserve Drive
Cedar Falls, IA 50613
(319) 277-2187
e-mail:
hartman@www.cedarnet.org

Hunt Hill Nature Center and
Audubon Sanctuary
N2384 Hunt Hill Road
Sarona, WI 54870
(715) 635-6543

Ijams Nature Center
2915 Island Home Avenue
Knoxville, TN 37920
(615) 577-4717

Indian Creek Nature Center
6665 Otis Road SE
Cedar Rapids, IA 52403
(319) 362-0664

Irvine Natural Science Center
c/o St. Timothy's  School
Stevenson, MD 21153
(410) 484-2413
e-mail: ScatPatrol@aol.com

Jamestown Audubon Nature
Center
1600 Riverside Road
Jamestown, NY 14701
(716) 569-2345
e-mail: James Yaich @ aol.com

Joy Outdoor Education Center
Box 157
Clarksville, OH 45113
(513) 289-2031

Kalamazoo Nature Center
7000 North Westnedge Ave.
Kalamazoo, MI 49004
(616) 381-1574

Lake Erie Nature and Science
Center
28728 Wolf Road
Bay Village, OH 44140
(216) 871-2900

Laurel Ridge Conservation
Education Center, National
Wildlife Federation
8925 Leesburg Pike
Vienna, VA 22184
(703) 790-4439
e-mail: geiger@nwf.org

Lincoln Memorial Garden Nature
Center
2301 E. Lake Shore Dr.
Springfield, IL 62707
(217) 529-1111

Long Lake Conservation Center
Rt. 2, Box 2550
Palisade, MN 56469
(218) 768-4653
e-mail: HN3328@handsnet.org

Louisiana Nature Center/
Audubon Institute
PO Box 870610
New Orleans, LA 70187-0610
(504) 246-5672

Manitoga, Inc.
PO Box 249
Gamson, NY 10524
(914) 424-3812
e-mail: manitoga @
highlands.com
www.highlands.com/Attractions/
manitoga.html

Max McGraw Wildlife Foundation
PO Box 9
Dundee, IL 60118
(847) 741-8000
e-mail: mcgrawwild@aol.com

Merry Lea Environmental Learning Center
Box 263
Wolf Lake, IN 46796
(219) 799-5869
e-mail: larryry@goshen.edu

Morrison Knudsen Nature Center
600 S. Walnut
PO Box 25
Boise, ID 83707
(208) 334-2225

Mt. Pleasant (nature center and
farm)
10520 Old Frederick Road
Woodstock, MD 21163
(410) 465-8877

National Wildflower Research
Center
4801 La Crosse Ave.
Austin, TX 78739
(512) 292-4100

The Nature Discovery Center,
Friends of Bellaire Parks
PO Box 77
Bellaire, TX 77402-0777
(713) 667-6550

New Canaan Nature Center
144 Oenoke Ridge
New Canaan, CT 06840
(203) 966-9577

Norskedalen Nature and Heritage
Center, Inc.
PO Box 225
Coon Valley, WI 54623
(608) 452-3424

Oregon Ridge Nature Center
13555 Beaver Dam Road
Cockeysville, MD 21030
(410) 887-3815

Oxbow Nature Study Area
3100 Dickerson Road
Reno, NV 89503
(702) 334-3808

Pine Jog Environmental Education Center
Florida Atlantic University,
College of Education
6301 Summit Blvd.
West Palm Beach, FL 33415
(561) 686-6600

The Pratt Center
163 Paper Mill Road
New Milford, CT 06776
(860) 355-3137

Rio Grande Nature Center State
Park
2901 Candelaria NW
Albuquerque, NM 87107
(505) 344-7240

River Bend Nature Center
1000 Rustad Road, PO Box 186
Faribault, MN 55021
(507) 332-7151
e-mail: riverbnd@deskmedia.com

Riverside Nature Center
150 Francisco Lemos St.
Kerrville, TX 78028
(210) 25RIVER

Riverside Urban Environmental
Center
PO Box 11678
Milwaukee, WI 53211
(414) 964-8505

Roger Tory Peterson Institute of
Natural History
110 Marvin Parkway
Jamestown, NY 14701
(716) 665-2473

Runge Conservation Nature
Center
2901 W. Truman Blvd.
Jefferson City, MO 65102
(573) 526-5544

Rye Nature Center
873 Boston Post Road, PO Box 435
Rye, NY 10580
(914) 967-5150
e-mail: ryenatur@emi.com

Sabal Palm Grove Sanctuary
PO Box 5052
Brownsville, TX 78523
(210) 541-8034
e-mail: kchapman@audubon.org

Schlitz Audubon Center
1111 E. Brown Deer Road
Milwaukee, WI 53217-1999
(414) 351-4200
e-mail: mdibben@audubon.org

Shaker Lakes Regional Nature
Center
2600 S. Park Blvd.
Shaker Heights, OH 44120
(216) 321-5935

Sharon Audubon Center
325 Cornwall Bridge Road
Sharon, CT 06069
(860) 364-0520
e-mail: sheth@audubon.org

Silver Lake Nature Center
1306 Bath Road
Bristol, PA 19007
(215) 785-1177

Springfield Conservation Nature
Center
4600 S. Chrisman
Springfield, MO 65804
(417) 888-4237

Stevens Nature Center
2616 Kildaire Farm Road
Cary, NC 27512-8005
(919) 387-5980

Stoney Kill Farm Environmental
Education Center
Rt. 9D
Wappingers Falls, NY 12590
(914) 831-8780

Teatown Lake Reservation
Spring Valley Road
Ossining, NY 10562
(914) 762-2912

Theodore Roosevelt Sanctuary
134 Clove Road
Oyster Bay, NY 11771
(516) 922-3200

Thomas Irvine Dodge Nature
Center
1795 Charlton Street
West St. Paul, MN 55118
(612) 455-4531

Treehaven—University of Wisconsin—Stevens Point Field Station
W2540 Pickerel Creek Ave.
Tomahawk, WI 54487
(715) 453-4106

Vermont Institute of Natural
Science
RR 2, Box 532
Woodstock, VT 05091
(802) 457-2779

Lee and Rose Warner Nature
Center
15375 Norell Ave., N.
Marine, MN 55047
(612) 433-2427

Waterman Conservation Education Center
403 Hilton Road
PO Box 377
Apalachin, NY 13732
(607) 625-2221

Weinberg Nature Center
455 Mamaroneck Road
Scarsdale, NY 10583
(914) 722-1289

Wild Basin
805 N. Capital of Texas Hwy.
Austin, TX 78746
(512) 327-7622

The Wilderness Center, Inc.
PO Box 202
Wilmot, OH 44689
(330) 359-5235

Woodcock Nature Center
56 Deer Run Road
Wilton, CT 06897
(203) 762-7280

# About the Authors

Carolyn:

*I am the sixth generation to dwell on my family's Hill Country ranch. In the last twenty years I have been able to live in the woods and have horses, goats, cats, dogs, ducks, chickens, and more. We have raccoons and armadillos for neighbors. I was raised in the city so I have never lost appreciation for wild places.*

*My children have been able to have the childhood I always wanted. But creating this woodland home for our own children was not enough. I wanted all children to have the opportunity to play in the creek or see a great blue heron fly overhead. I am in love with our natural world and I want every generation to have the chance to experience it.*

CAROLYN CHIPMAN-EVANS is the founder and executive director of the Cibolo Wilderness Trail and Nature Center in Boerne, Texas. For ten years she and her husband, Brent Evans, have worked with the City of Boerne to protect and preserve this park. She created The Friends of the Cibolo Wilderness, a non-profit organization dedicated to the conservation of natural resources through education.

As Founding Director, Carolyn has worn all the hats involved in nature center development. She has been resident naturalist, volunteer coordinator, educator, public relations coordinator, programs developer, newsletter editor, artist, and director of nature center operations. She speaks regularly to various groups to inspire and promote trail development and conservation education. She has worked to build community by involving service organizations, businesses, universities, Boy Scouts and Girl Scouts, schools, clubs, and many more organizations and individuals in the creation of the nature center. She also enjoys writing and illustrating nature essays.

Brent:

*I was born and raised in the Sierras and have always been drawn to nature. In 1976 I took up residence in the Texas Hill Country, along with my dogs and horses. Before long I encountered Carolyn, a beautiful Texan living in a cabin in the woods. We married, moved an old house onto the land, and lived there for three years without electricity. It was wonderful. Our children have lived in the country their whole lives. Eventually we moved our lives into the twentieth century, with telephone, electricity, television, and word processors. I've developed a private counseling practice with children, and I love my work. But it is nature that has provided the beauty in our lives, our spiritual grounding, and our fun. The Cibolo Nature Center allows us to share what we've been given.*

**BRENT EVANS** is a licensed social worker who has practiced family counseling and community organization for twenty-five years. He maintains a private practice, with offices in San Antonio and at his Guadalupe River office near Boerne. For Earth Day and local environmental projects, Brent created the costumed characters of "Green Man" and "Garbage Man," and appeared at schools and public events to promote environmental awareness in children. He developed the SEED Program (Self-Esteem Through Ecological Dynamics) for the adolescent unit of a psychiatric hospital.

Brent has developed training programs for therapists in utilizing natural settings for therapy, and is a member of the American Horticultural Therapy Association. For the Cibolo Nature Center project, he provided community organization know-how, as well as carpentry, children's programs, and musical interludes. Most recently, Brent developed the SAGE (Senior Activity for the Good Earth) Program, a horticultural therapy program for nursing homes.

**CAROLYN AND BRENT** continue their interest in connecting people and nature through a variety of projects, including nature center program development, community gardening, work with special needs children and nursing homes, writing, and consulting. A program has been developed to inspire involvement in local nature centers; it can be presented in your community. Telephone (830) 249-4616 or (830) 537-4141, or write to the Cibolo Nature Center, Box 9, Boerne, TX 78006. The e-mail address is cnc@Texas.net.

# Index